SOMEWHERE OUT THERE, AMONG THE CORNFIELDS OF THE STATE, LIES
A HIDDEN SOMETHING... A DARKNESS IF YOU WILL, LIKE NOTHING YOU WILL FIND IN
ANY OTHER CORNER OF THE MIDWEST. WHETHER IT COMES FROM THE STATE'S PAST
OR THE BLOOD THAT'S BEEN SPILLED WITHIN ITS BORDERS, THERE IS NO DENYING THAT
ILLINOIS IS A VERY HAUNTED PLACE.
FROM THE HAUNTING OF AMERICA

BOOKS FROM ILLINOIS HAUNTINGS AUTHORS

TROY TAYLOR

DEAD MEN SO TELL TALES SERIES
Dead Men Do Tell Tales (2008)
Bloody Chicago (2006)
Bloody Illinois (2008)
Bloody Hollywood (2008)
Without a Trace (2009)
Blood, Guns & Valentines (2010)

HAUNTED ILLINOIS BOOKS
Haunted Illinois (1999 / 2001 / 2004)
Haunted Decatur (1995 / 2009)
More Haunted Decatur (1996)
Ghosts of Millikin (1996 / 2001)
Where the Dead Walk (1997 / 2002)
Dark Harvest (1997)
Haunted Decatur Revisited (2000)
Flickering Images (2001)
Haunted Decatur: 13th Anniversary (2006)
Haunted Alton (2000 / 2003 / 2008)
Haunted Chicago (2003)
The Haunted President (2005 / 2009)
Mysterious Illinois (2005)
Resurrection Mary (2007)
The Possessed (2007)
Weird Chicago (2008)

HAUNTED FIELD GUIDE BOOKS
The Ghost Hunters Guidebook
(1997/ 1999 / 2001/ 2004 / 2007 / 2010)
Confessions of a Ghost Hunter (2002)
Field Guide to Haunted Graveyards (2003)
Ghosts on Film (2005)
So, There I Was (with Len Adams) (2006)
Talking with the Dead (with Rob & Anne Wlodarski) (2009)

HISTORY & HAUNTINGS SERIES
The Haunting of America (2001 / 2010)
Into the Shadows (2002)
Down in the Darkness (2003)
Out Past the Campfire Light (2004)
Ghosts by Gaslight (2007)

OTHER GHOSTLY TITLES
Spirits of the Civil War (1999)
Season of the Witch (1999/ 2002)
Haunted New Orleans (2000)
Beyond the Grave (2001)
No Rest for the Wicked (2001)

Haunted St. Louis (2002)
The Devil Came to St. Louis (2006)
Houdini: Among the Spirits (2009)
And Hell Followed With It (with Rene Kruse) (2010)
Suicide & Spirits (2011)

WHITECHAPEL OCCULT LIBRARY
Sex & the Supernatural (2009)

STERLING PUBLICATIONS
Weird U.S. (Co-Author) (2004)
Weird Illinois (2005)
Weird Virginia (Co-Author) (2007)
Weird Indiana (Co-Author) (2008)

BARNES & NOBLE PRESS TITLES
Haunting of America (2006)
Spirits of the Civil War (2007)
Into the Shadows (2007)

HISTORY PRESS TITLES
Wicked Washington (2007)
Murder & Mayhem on Chicago's North Side (2009)
Murder & Mayhem on Chicago's South Side (2009)
Murder & Mayhem on Chicago's West Side (2009)
Murder & Mayhem in Downtown Chicago (2009)
Murder & Mayhem in the Vice Districts (2009)
Wicked New Orleans (2010)
Haunted New Orleans (2010)
Wicked Northern Illinois (2010)
Wicked Decatur (2011)

STACKPOLE BOOKS TITLES
Haunted Illinois (2008)
True Crime Illinois (2009)
Big Book of Illinois Ghost Stories (2009)
Illinois Monsters (2011)

LEN ADAMS
So, There I Was (with Troy Taylor) (2006)
Phantoms in the Looking Glass (2008)

LUKE NALIBORSKI
The Lighter Side of Darkness (2007)

KELLY DAVIS
The Paranormal Investigator's Logbook (2009)

MORE TALES FROM THE HAUNTED PRAIRIE!

ILLINOIS HAUNTINGS
BY TROY TAYLOR

LEN ADAMS – LUKE NALIBORSKI
JULIE RINGERING – JOHN WINTERBAUER
LOREN HAMILTON – KELLY DAVIS

- A WHITECHAPEL PRESS PUBLICATION FROM DARK HAVEN ENTERTAINMENT -

WHILE MY NAME MAY BE THE LARGEST ONE ON THE COVER, THIS WAS NOT A BOOK THAT WAS WRITTEN ALONE. EACH OF THEM WAS GIVEN CREDIT FOR THE STORIES THEY WROTE FOR THIS VOLUME, BUT I WANT TO THANK THEM AGAIN IN PRINT FOR ALL OF THE WORK THAT THEY DID.... SO THANKS TO LEN, LUKE, JULIE, JOHN, LOREN AND KELLY FOR MAKING THIS PROCESS AS PAINLESS AS POSSIBLE. THANKS ALSO FOR ALL OF YOUR HARD WORK AND DEDICATION AND I'LL BE LOOKING FORWARD TO THE ,MANY GREAT YEARS AHEAD!

Original Cover Artwork Designed by
©Copyright 2011 by Michael Schwab & Troy Taylor
Visit M & S Graphics at http://www.manyhorses.com/msgraphics.htm

This Book is Published By:
Whitechapel Press
A Division of Dark Haven Entertainment, Inc.
Chicago, Illinois / 1-888-GHOSTLY
Visit us on the internet at http://www.americanhauntings.org

First Printing -- June 2011
ISBN: 1-892523-74-4

Printed in the United States of America

INTRODUCTION

Every house has a history, there's no doubt about that. When seeking ghosts, there is no better way to discover the reason they might linger behind than to uncover the history of the house in question. Hauntings are created by the events of the past. Without understanding the history, we cannot begin to understand the reason why a place might be haunted. We can believe it to be haunted, but only history is able to tell us why. What occurred to make this place become haunted? And who is it that haunts it? Only history can provide these answers. Although many ghost hunters are loath to accept it, no amount of technology or sophisticated gadgets can provide the answers to these questions. Gadgets will never provide convincing evidence of the paranormal and unless a ghost is somehow captured and tested in a laboratory setting, technology is never going to prove that ghosts exist.

But history can. Find a house whose current occupants allege it to be haunted. Then contact past owners of the house. In a perfect situation, they will tell you the exact same things were happening during their tenure in the house that the current owners claim is happening in their own -- even though these people have never met, and have not compared stories. Such claims are not easy to dismiss.

But how do we find the history of a house? Every house has one if we know where to look. Even new houses might have a story to tell. You can ask the real-life family who bought a new home that was built on top of a cemetery. Had they checked into the history of the location, they might have discovered that the developer had failed to re-locate the graves as he promised. They would have spared themselves a lot of grief from the haunting that followed – but we would have missed out on an entertaining film when it was adapted by Hollywood into the movie *Poltergeist*!

Or you can ask the couple who moved into an old rundown house that once belonged to Chicago mobster Murray "The Camel" Humphreys, a top man in the Capone gang. The house contained secret rooms and human remains were later found on the grounds. I'm sure the couple wished they had checked out the past owners of the house before they moved in!

Actually, it's not hard to investigate a home's physical pedigree. An independent inspection will provide a lot about the house's current shape and a Comprehensive Loss Underwriting Exchange (CLUE) report will provide an inventory of any insurance claims that have been filed on the place.

But to check on the home's hidden history and whether the place is haunted or if some grisly event took place there, you have to become something of a detective, talking to people and searching for shreds of evidence that won't be easily found. You can't always count on real estate agents to tell you if the place is infested with spooks or that any previous owners committed suicide within its walls. While some states compel agents to disclose such information, others make it illegal to tell potential buyers what happened in what have been referred to as "stigmatized properties." What constitutes a "stigma" varies, as well. Some states don't consider a psychological stigma like a murder or haunting to be sinister enough to affect the value of the home since it does not affect its physical nature.

In most cases, you'll be on your own. You can start your investigation by talking to the neighbors and asking them what they know or what they might have heard. Then you can expand the search by contacting former owners and tenants and perhaps even their descendants. You can compile a chronological list of past owners from deeds on file at the county courthouse and from city directories and maps. If there are gaps in the deeds or listings, look for a mortgage or will that transferred the property from one person to another. Once you track down the names, start looking for newspaper articles and information at the local library. You just might uncover a death or scandal that could explain why strange things are happening in the house. Cemetery records, genealogy files and ancestry websites are good sources for death dates that will help to track down obituaries in the newspaper.

You never know what might turn up in your search. Whether you're searching for the "tainted" past of your house, or the reason it might be haunted, the history of the place will reveal everything that you could possibly want to know.

And houses are not the only places that become haunted. What about an entire state? There is no question that Illinois is a very haunted place and the events of the Prairie State's past have made it that way. Illinois was quite literally born in thunder, violence, fire and blood. From the days of the early French and British settlers to the Indian massacres of the War of 1812, it is a place that has been infamous for its crime and criminals, from the gangsters of the Prohibition era to some of the most deranged killers that have ever taken a life. The history of Illinois is often frightening and disturbing and filled with events that have left a bloodstained mark on its haunted landscape. Is it any wonder there are so many ghosts here?

This book is not my first foray into the ghostly tales of Illinois. Since my first book (actually *the* first book) about Illinois haunts, I have written more than a dozen volumes about various parts of the state and each area's resident ghosts, from Alton to Chicago, Decatur and beyond. But even after all of those books, I cannot make the claim to have tracked down every story the state has to tell. Every town in Illinois, no matter how small, has at least one or two ghost stories that are only told among those who make the place their home. Such tales may always remain unknown to outsiders, while others may someday see the light of day.

Like a homeowner who wants to discover what might be lurking in his house's history, I had to be a bit of a detective to find new stories of ghosts, hauntings and strangeness in Illinois. Over the years, I have pored through history books, strained my eyes reading yellowed newspapers, sneezed from the dust found in old archives and worn out shoe leather tracking down stories, looking for tales, knocking on doors and talking to people about their ghosts. Many trails ran cold, but other leads revealed new stories that I had never heard about before. And while some tales were merely snippets of a legend to be filed away for a possible book in the future, others turned out to be brand new stories and, in some cases, new information about old tales that managed to reveal something previously unknown about stories that I had written about in the past.

The tales that are contained in this book are stories that have emerged over time and which have not appeared in past *Haunted Illinois* series volumes. For one reason or another, they have revealed themselves over the last few years and are finally being put into print. In this book, you'll not only find accounts from my own files but also stories that were uncovered by members of the "Illinois Hauntings" staff, each of whom coordinates ghost tours and ghost hunts for the company in different parts of the state. Their hard work has made this new book a collaborative effort and each of them has presented tales that were never featured in my books (or, in most cases, anyone's books) before.

But keep this is mind... While this book contains stories that didn't appear in earlier volumes of the series, we can again make no claim that we have collected every story that "haunts" this state. We are well aware that there are tales of Illinois that have managed to elude us. There are haunted places here that have remained unknown since the first settlers came to our "seas of prairie grass." Even so, while we may not have uncovered every ghost story the state can offer, we will reveal tales from the history and hauntings of Illinois that you have likely never read before.

As with earlier books in the series, I hope you enjoy this new look at Illinois hauntings and I hope that at least some of these stories (and I suspect it will be many of them) will have you leaving the light on when you go to bed at night!

TROY TAYLOR
SPRING 2011

SOUTHERN ILLINOIS

BLOODSTAINED WALLS: THE AX MURDERS OF 1874 MILLSTADT, ILLINOIS

The small town of Millstadt is located a few miles from Belleville, a long-established and prosperous southwestern Illinois city, located across the river from St. Louis. Millstadt has always been known as a quiet community. It was settled long ago by German immigrants who came to America to work hard and live peacefully. It was a place where nothing bad could ever happen – or at least that's what the town's residents in the latter part of the 1800s believed. However, the murders that occurred just outside of town on Saxtown Road forever shattered that illusion. When a local family was brutally slaughtered in 1874, it created a dark, unsolved mystery – and a haunting that still lingers to this day.

On March 19, 1874, Carl Steltzenreide, age 66, his son, Frederick, 35, Frederick's wife, Anna, 28, and their children, Carl, 3, and Anna, 8 months, were found brutally murdered in their home on Saxton Road. The grisly crime was discovered by a neighbor, 28-year-old Benjamin Schneider, who had arrived at the sixty-acre farm early that morning to collect some potato seeds from Carl Steltzenreide. As Schneider approached the white farmhouse, he was unnerved by the quiet. The horses and cattle that were fenced in the front lot had not been watered or fed and no one was taking care of the morning chores. There was an eerie stillness about the place that left the visitor more than a little uneasy.

No one answered when Schneider knocked on the front door. He called out and looked in the window, but it was too dark inside for him to see anything. Finally, he turned the knob and pushed the door open. As he stepped in, he looked down and saw the body of Frederick Steltzenreide on the floor, lying in a pool of blood. The young man had been savagely beaten and his throat had been cut. Three of his fingers had been severed, perhaps while trying to defend himself from his attacker. Panicked, Schneider began looking for the other members of the family. He found Anna and her children lying on a bed in another room. They had been bludgeoned to death and Anna's throat had been cut. Her infant daughter was lying across her chest, her small arms wrapped around her mother's neck. The body of her son, Carl, lay next to her. His facial features were unrecognizable because of the brutal blows that had rained down on his head. All three had apparently been murdered as they slept.

In a separate bedroom, Schneider found Carl Steltzenreide sprawled on the bloodstained floor. He had been struck so many times, apparently with an ax, that he was nearly decapitated. It was later surmised that he had been roused from his bed by noises in the house and been struck down as he attempted to come to the aid of his family.

As Schneider looked frantically around, he realized that he was standing in an abattoir. The family's blood had sprayed wildly onto the walls, even staining the ceiling. He saw chips and indentions in the plaster that were later determined to have been made by the backswing of a maddox, a combination tool with the head of an ax and a large blade resembling that of a garden hoe. The killer had been swinging his weapon so wildly that he had torn deep gashes in the ceiling.

The only survivor of the carnage was the family's German shepherd dog, Monk. He was found lying on the floor next to Anna Stelzenreide's bed, keeping watch over the bodies of Anna and the children. Monk was known to be very protective of the family, and downright vicious toward strangers. This fact would lead investigators to believe that the killer was someone known to the Stelzenreides. Authorities also believed that the killer or killers entered the house through a rear door, killing Anna and the children first. Carl was attacked when he heard the struggles in the bedroom and Frederick was killed last. He had been sleeping on a lounge near the front of the house and had been murdered after a hand-to-hand struggle.

Schneider fled the house to summon help and several deputies and detectives from Belleville answered the call. Soon after arriving, Sheriff James W. Hughes discovered footsteps leading away from the house.
The prints were distinctive, having been made by boots that were cobbled with heavy nails. Hughes also found indentions in the ground that looked as though they had been made by someone dragging a heavy ax. He followed the tracks for about a mile, and at the end of the trail he found a blood-covered pouch of partially chewed tobacco. Hughes deduced that the killer had been wounded during the attack on the family and had attempted to stem the bleeding with chewing tobacco, a popular folk remedy that was believed to draw the infection from a cut.

The footprints, and the bloody tobacco pouch, led the police to the home of Frederick Boeltz, brother-in-law of Frederick Steltzenreide.

Boeltz was married to Anna Stelzenreide's sister and there was bad blood between Boeltz and Frederick Steltzenreide because of $200 that Boeltz had borrowed and never repaid. The two had quarreled over the debt several times. Boeltz was friends with an itinerant farm laborer named John Afken, who had once worked for the Steltzenreide family and who also harbored a grudge against Frederick. Afken was a large and powerful man who made his living as a "grubber," a backbreaking occupation that involved clearing trees and rocks from farm lots. He was considered an expert with an ax, as well as other hand tools, and was feared by many because of his quick temper. He also possessed another characteristic that was of interest to the investigators – he had a full head of light red hair.

Carl Steltzenreide had died clutching a handful of hair that was exactly the same color.

The bodies of the Steltzenreide family were prepared for burial by ladies from the Zion United Church of Christ in Millstadt. This gruesome task was carried out in the Steltzenreide barn, which still stands on the property today. The corpses were in such horrific condition that a number of the women became sick while washing them and had to be relieved. The killer had savaged the bodies so badly that the adults were nearly decapitated and the children were bloodied and pummeled beyond recognition. It was brutality unlike anything these small town folks had ever seen before.

The family was laid to rest on Sunday, March 22, at Frievogel Cemetery, located just a few miles from their home on Saxtown Road. The news of the horror spread across the region and even appeared on the front page of the *New York Times*. The terror and curiosity that gripped the area brought more than 1,000 people to the Stelzenreides' funeral service.

Immediately after the burial, Sheriff Hughes arrested Frederick Boeltz and John Afken on suspicion of murder. Boeltz initially resisted arrest and then demanded that he be provided with a Bible while at the Belleville City Jail. Afken, on the other hand, was said to have displayed an uncanny lack of emotion. He quietly allowed the officers to escort him to jail and remained silent while in custody. During the coroner's inquest that followed, Boeltz would not face the jury and refused to look at photographs of the victims' bodies. The two men were brought before a grand jury in April 1874 but they were not indicted due to the fact that there was insufficient evidence to connect them to the murders. Both suspects were released a week later.

Although the authorities had been unable to indict their main suspects in the case, the investigation into the two men's activities and possible motives did not come to an end. Investigators believed more strongly than ever that Boeltz was somehow involved in the murders, basing this on the fact that a small amount of cash and valuables inside the Steltzenreide house had been undisturbed. They believed there was a motive that was darker than mere robbery – and that Boeltz was definitely involved.

Just a few days before he was killed, on March 16, Frederick Steltzenreide confided to some friends and neighbors that he had just received a substantial inheritance from relatives in Germany. He was at an auction at the time and was seen carrying a large willow basket covered with a piece of oilcloth. Rumor had it that the basket contained the inheritance, which Frederick had collected at the bank just before attending the auction.

The Steltzenreide estate was reportedly worth several thousand dollars at the time of the murder. Investigators surmised that the wholesale slaughter of the family might have been an attempt to wipe out all of the immediate heirs. They believed that Frederick Boeltz, motivated by his dislike for Frederick Steltzenreide and his belief that he would inherit the money because of his marriage to Anna's sister, had hired John Afken to commit the murders. It was a viable theory but the police were never able to make it stick.

Boeltz later brought suit against the Steltzenreide estate in an effort to collect whatever money he could. He was eventually awarded $400 and soon after, he and his family moved away from the area and vanished into history.

John Afken remained in the Millstadt area and legend has it that he was often seen carrying a gold pocket watch. When asked where he had gotten such an impressive timepiece, Afken would only smile. Some whispered that the pocket watch looked exactly like one that Carl Steltzenreide had owned.

The Steltzenreide farmhouse was torn down in August of 1954. According to a report that appeared in the *Millstadt Enterprise* at the time, property owner Leslie Jines and his family were "glad to tuck the tale out of the way with whatever ghosts are there." The Jineses found it easy to get rid of the cursed, old house but the ghosts that lingered there were not so easily dismissed.

The current owner of the property is Randy Eckert. In 2004, he told a reporter from the *St. Louis Post-Dispatch* that he believed the land where the murders took place is haunted. His first experience occurred one morning when he and his wife were awakened by strange noises. They both heard the sounds of doors opening and closing in the house, although nothing was disturbed. The family dog, which had been sleeping at the foot of the bed, was also awakened by the mysterious sounds and was terrified and shaking. Eckert added that the sounds were repeated many times over the years, always around the anniversary of the murders.

Chris Nauman, who rented the house from Eckert in the early 1990s, reported his own chilling occurrences, "It was 6 o'clock in the morning, and there was a loud knock on the door. At the same time, my girlfriend heard someone walking up the steps in our basement." Nauman, startled by the sounds, quickly checked the front door and the basement stairs, but found no sign of visitors or intruders. The next day, he shared his story with Eckert, asking him on which date the Steltzenreide murders had taken place. Eckert confirmed it for him – the ghostly happenings had taken place on March 19, the anniversary of the murders.

Nauman still remembers the effect this had on him, recalling, "A cold shiver ran up my spine."

To this day, the slaughter of the Steltzenreide family remains unsolved. While many suspects have been suggested over the years, there is no clear answer to the mystery. The area where the farmhouse once stood along Saxtown Road has changed very little since 1874, and it's not hard to imagine the sheer terror of those who lived nearby after news of the murders began to spread. It's a lonely, isolated area and, if the stories are to be believed, a haunted one.

But what ghosts still walk in this place? Are they the tragic spirits of the Steltzenreides, still mourning the fact that their deaths have never been avenged? Or do the phantom footsteps and spectral knockings signal the presence of the killer's wicked wraith, perhaps forced to remain here as a penance for the crime for which he never answered while among the living?

We may never know, but for now, the haunting continues and the people of Millstadt still remember the day when horror visited their little town.

ANNA
MASCOUTAH, ILLINOIS
BY LUKE NALIBORSKI

It was a spring day in 1962 when tragedy struck the small town of Mascoutah in southern Illinois. It was early morning, and a woman named Anna was burning trash in her yard. It was an uneventful morning of chores until her dress accidentally caught on fire. Panicked, Anna ran into the basement of her home. About ten minutes later, the mail carrier heard screams as he walked onto the front porch. He ran around the back of the house and into the basement where he found Anna engulfed in flames. An ambulance was called and she was taken to a local hospital, where she died that night. It was mentioned in newspaper reports that her entire body, with the exception of her legs, was removed from the home. No one has ever known what happened to her legs, they were simply never mentioned again. It's been assumed that as the fire burned up her dress, most of the damage was done to her lower extremities; perhaps there were simply nothing left of them.

Whatever the case, Anna's spirit (and perhaps her legs) never left the place that she called home for most of her life.

Shortly after Anna's death, a new family – a mother, father and three children-- moved into the home. At first, they all shared the same bedroom. It didn't take long for Anna to welcome her new guests. One of the children, now grown, recalls that he had fallen asleep only to be awakened late at night. He sat up in bed and found that his parents were sitting up, as well. To protect the privacy of those involved, we'll call him "Jason." Jason said that he could see that his parents were troubled by something. He sat there rubbing the sleep from his eyes, trying to figure out what was going on. It was then that he heard footsteps walking across the floor above them.

The footsteps were moving back and forth, sounding like multiple people. They were sometimes quiet, sometimes loud. It was almost as if there were adults and children moving around up there. The sounds continued for a long time.

After his mother finally made it clear that she wasn't going to get out of bed to see what was making the noises, Jason's father decided to go investigate. He checked upstairs -- the closets, the windows, all the rooms, the nooks, crannies, everywhere. Not a living soul was to be found. The footsteps stopped as soon as he reached the second floor.

But that was not the last time they were heard. The footsteps continued nightly for weeks. Each night, Jason's father would get out of bed and check to see if anyone was there, but the second floor was always empty. Was the house haunted? Or were the sounds simply those of an aging building settling? The family didn't know for sure yet. It would take a bit more to help them decide.

On another occasion, Jason woke up and saw someone standing in the bedroom doorway. Initially, he thought it was either his mother or his sister. As he looked closer, he realized it wasn't a person at all, just a dress hovering in the doorway. He saw no face, no arms, no legs, just a dress hanging in midair. Jason kept blinking his eyes, hoping that whatever it was would go away, but it did nothing more than give him a headache. Finally, he pulled the sheets up over his head and began to talk to himself, wishing the thing would leave. Eventually, it did.

Jason thought of everything he could to explain what he had seen. The next morning, he asked his mother if his grandmother had stayed with them the night before, but the answer was no. That was the last logical explanation that Jason could conjure up, and it too was dismissed.

As Jason grew older, he and his brother, whom we will call "Thomas," moved into one of the upstairs bedrooms. They were accustomed to the things that were going bump in the night by this time and were no longer terrified. Instead, they accepted the fact that the place was haunted. Odd things were happening on a regular basis. There were sounds of someone walking throughout the house. Furniture was being moved around, and shadows and disembodied voices were commonplace. Jason and Thomas learned to ignore these occurrences.

Eventually, two more siblings were born and raised in the haunted house. Over time, the mysterious activity started to increase.

Their father started working swing shifts – rotating hours of mornings, afternoons, midnights. The work was tough, but when you had five kids, it was also a way to get away from things. One night, when the youngest son was two years old, the father came home from work around midnight. His wife waited up for him and then made her way to bed. The youngest son, who was still up, sat on the couch and watched some late-night television with his father.

As they sat engrossed in the TV show, a ghost decided to make itself known; it wasn't a woman this time, but a child. Both father and son saw a young boy cross through the middle of the room and exit through a wall. It appeared to pay no attention to the people on the couch. It could be that it was what is sometimes called a "place memory," an image without conscious thought that follows a route that it had used in life. Perhaps the wall that the child walked through had once contained a doorway.

At first, the father thought he was just tired and was seeing things that weren't there. Maybe it was an optical illusion caused by the room being dark with the exception of the television's glow. *I'm just tired*, he thought, *my eyes are playing tricks on me*. He had almost convinced himself when his son looked up at him and asked, "Who was that little boy?"

Weird things continued throughout the years. When Jason was twelve, he had another encounter with the disembodied dress. He was sleeping one evening when he woke up to once again see it standing at the foot of his bed. It was ghostly white, of a style that was from an older era. As he did the first time the dress appeared, Jason tried blinking to make it go away. It didn't work and eventually, he pulled the bed covers up over his head and he kept them there until morning.

A year after that event, Jason and Thomas were home alone one afternoon. They were upstairs in their room when they heard someone walking downstairs. Whoever it was, they were pacing slowly back and forth. Initially, the boys thought it was one of their parents or one of their siblings, but as they continued to listen, without warning, all hell broke loose. It sounded like someone was pounding on the walls as hard as they could. Doors began slamming and the boys heard what sounded like someone jumping up and down and breaking things. Jason and Thomas were terrified that an intruder had broken into the house. They crawled under the bed and decided to wait it out – until they recalled the horror films that they had watched over the years and realized that people who hid under beds usually suffered horrible deaths at the hands of assorted monsters, zombies, and crazed killers.

They scrambled out from under the bed and each of them grabbed a baseball bat. Thus armed, they carefully made their way to the staircase leading down to the first floor. Just as they were about to descend, they heard a knock at the door. Both boys jumped and started to run before they heard the voice of one of their friends outside. They told him to come in, coolly calculating that if an intruder were lurking inside the house, their friend could be used as bait to lure him out. The friend called out that the screen door was locked, so they told him to go to the back door. The boy went around back and shouted that that door was locked as well. Jason and Thomas checked and found that both screen doors were indeed locked with an eyehook latch from the inside. Whatever, had been making that awful racket couldn't have gotten in with the doors locked and couldn't have left and locked the doors behind it. So, maybe it had never left at all...

The last experience Jason recounted happened when his parents went away for the night and left the children home alone. The older boys decided to make the most of the opportunity and have a party. The next morning, their father came home and picked them up to take them to the cabin where he and their mother had stayed the previous night. Jason and Thomas assigned a friend to clean up the mess left behind by the party.

After he finished cleaning, the boy went to the front porch to relax. As he sat there he kept hearing noises coming from inside the house. It sounded as if children were running up and down the stairs. They were laughing, giggling, and seemingly having a great time. The boy got up and went back inside to see what was going on. To his surprise, he found no one there. The house was just the way he had left it moments before. He shrugged it off and went back to the porch. He wasn't out there very long when he heard voices coming through the bedroom window next to the porch. Unnerved, he gingerly reached his hand inside the front door, locked it, and left. He later told Jason and Thomas about the incident and it was quite some time before he returned to the house.

In 1977, the family moved out of Anna's house. There have been other owners since that time, but from what I've found, the hauntings have slowly faded away. The ghostly energy seems to have been used up over the years and no longer seems to exist. Families that have lived in the house over the past two decades have experienced no paranormal activity at all.

Was the house really haunted? There were ghosts seen there after Anna's death; was one of them hers? Did the footsteps belong to Anna as she roamed around her old home? Was the dress that Jason saw floating in his room the one that Anna was wearing when she had her tragic accident? Were the crashing sounds Jason and Thomas heard the sounds of Anna flailing in agony as she was being burned alive?

And if she haunted the house, was she alone? Who were the phantom children and why were they there? Since the hauntings have stopped, we may never know. Unfortunately, as with most paranormal cases, there may be more questions than answers about this strange tale from Illinois.

THE HOUSE ON STATE STREET
GRANITE CITY, ILLINOIS
BY JULIE RINGERING

The house at 2118 State Street in Granite City was built in 1905 by an undertaker named John G. Tate. Tate lived on the second floor with his wife, Leona, who gave piano lessons. They rented out the third floor as an apartment and utilized the basement and first floor for the funeral home business.

The funeral home was very successful and Tate became well known, eventually becoming deputy coroner for Madison County. Many autopsies were performed at 2118 State Street, including that of Elsie Barnhouse, whose murder was part of a scandal that rocked Madison County in 1926.

The story began on January 24, 1926, when William Ragen was beaten to death, allegedly by an off-duty police officer named Herman Gerking at the notorious Yociss' Hall, a bar and dance hall in East St. Louis. The only witness was Elsie Barnhouse, wife of the hall's owner, Theron Barnhouse. On Sunday May 27, just prior to Gerking going on trial for Ragen's murder, Elsie's bullet-riddled body was found in a clearing near Horseshoe Lake. The autopsy determined that she had been shot six times and had died at approximately 8:00 p.m. on Friday night. Gerking was determined to be the last person to have seen Barnhouse on the night she died. He was arrested

and subsequently sentenced to twenty years in prison for Elsie's murder.

John Tate lived in the house until his death in 1963. It was then sold and turned into an apartment building. Later, it housed various businesses. It was not used as a single family home again until a family by the name of Ross bought it in 1976. The nineteen-room house was in terrible shape by that time and required a lot of work to make it livable. The Rosses moved in and began an extensive renovation. It wasn't long before they began noticing strange smells that were suddenly there and then gone. They experienced frigid cold spots and saw fleeting shadows out of the corners of their eyes. At first, the family was able to find excuses for these things, but over time the activity in the house became much more direct and intense.

At the height of the activity, most of it seemed to be directed at the three teenage daughters of the family. Their hair was pulled, they heard strange sounds and decorative curtain chains were found removed from windows and coiled up next to their sleeping heads. The girls' beds were shaken, waking them up in the middle of the night, and they frequently complained of being poked and touched by unseen hands.

The whole family experienced hearing the recurrent sound of a body falling down the stairs. They also heard disembodied voices and footsteps and saw lights that would flicker and dim. Even more disturbing, family members would experience the sensation of being pushed down the stairs. They saw objects being moved and doors were yanked out of their grasp and slammed shut.

The most upsetting experience was a sense of menace in the basement. The sensation was so intense that family members would often venture down to the basement only to flee back upstairs when the feeling became overwhelming. The terrible evil feeling was occasionally felt by people outside of the family. On more than one occasion, visitors entered the house and then left within minutes, refusing to go back in again.

The Ross family lived in the house for eight years. They were never able to determine who or what was with them, why it remained in the house, or even how many entities actually haunted the house. They often speculated that the activity might have been related to the period when the building had been a funeral home.

Ironically, when the Rosses sold the house, the buyers asked if it was haunted. When it was confirmed that there had indeed been paranormal activity experienced there, the new owners were excited about the prospect of owning a haunted house.

The Ross family had no doubt the new occupants would get definitely get their money's worth.

A GHOST NAMED JENNIFER
ROSEWOOD HEIGHTS, ILLINOIS
BY JULIE RINGERING

In 1997, John and Cindi Dvorchak moved with their three young sons into their dream house at 105 South Circle in Rosewood Heights. As they began to settle into the home everything seemed normal, but it wasn't long before their boys began to suspect they might not be the only ones living there. Cindi recalled that within six months of moving in, her sons began talking about seeing a teenage girl in the house. Each of the three boys described seeing a young woman with long dark hair, wearing a white shirt tucked into blue jeans. Cindi asked the boys where they had seen the girl and they explained that they had seen her walking from the front door into the hall and toward the bedrooms, also coming down the stairs into the basement and going around the bar or into the laundry room. At that point, she would disappear.

Soon after, John and Cindi also began having experiences they couldn't explain, like glimpsing something moving out of the corner of their eyes. Then, one evening while sitting at the kitchen table, Cindi looked up to see a young woman standing in the living room looking back at her. As Cindi stood up in surprise, the girl turned and walked toward the bedrooms. Cindi followed but the girl had disappeared.

When she told her husband about what she had seen, he was supportive but also a little skeptical. But John would not have to wait long before he had his own odd experience. One evening, he had dozed off in the basement and awoke to see a girl with long dark hair and wearing a white shirt and jeans standing at the foot of the stairs. The girl appeared to be in her late teens or early twenties. Just as he was about to ask her what she was doing there, she became transparent and disappeared. Later, John told Cindi what he had seen. When Cindi asked him to describe what the girl looked like, he thought for a minute, then laughed and said she looked like " a Jennifer." It was then the apparition received a name.

As the years passed and the boys grew into teenagers, Jennifer's presence became more apparent. She tended to remain primarily around the boys and appeared to enjoy interacting with them. John and Cindi's daughter-in-law Heather remembered her first encounter with Jennifer as being a little intimidating. Heather said that she and her husband, Nick, had just started dating and had been watching movies in his room. She came out of the bedroom and was immediately blasted with a loud noise that she described as sounding like an audiotape that was being rewound. Heather said she was frightened by the incident and sensed that Jennifer was perhaps jealous of her relationship with Nick. Fortunately, such frightening incidents were few and far between; Jennifer was mostly a playful prankster. According to Nick, things would frequently disappear from one place, only to be found somewhere conspicuous later. He told the story of a time when Heather's hairbrush had gone missing while she was at the house. Everyone searched but the brush was nowhere to be found. On a whim, Heather asked Jennifer to return it and shortly after, the brush turned up in the center of Cindi's bed. Immediately after that, Cindi discovered her own hairbrush was missing.

Nick and Heather also recalled a time when they were getting ready to have a snack in the kitchen. Nick had taken a bite of a cookie, set it on the table, and then turned to get a plate. Heather was getting some milk and glasses when Nick asked her if she had taken his cookie. Heather denied touching the cookie; that's when they realized that Jennifer had decided to join them for a snack.

Jennifer seemed to especially enjoy it when the house was filled with teenagers. Cindi recalled one evening when several young people were at the house. As they sat around the kitchen table talking and laughing, one of the visiting teens asked Nick why the girl in the living room wasn't joining them in the kitchen. Nick asked what the girl looked like and was told she had dark hair and was wearing a white shirt and jeans. Nick recalled later that when he said that the girl was Jennifer, their ghost, the teen who had spied her immediately got up and left the house.

As the boys grew up and went away to college, sightings of Jennifer all but stopped. John and Cindi thought that she might have moved on but it was only recently that they discovered that this might not be the case.

Cindi, while watching her nine-month-old granddaughter, Zoe, noticed on more than one occasion that Zoe would suddenly stop playing. Cindi said the baby would look intently toward the hall and then start laughing and babbling as if she were talking to someone. Then, just as suddenly, she would turn around and resume playing. Could Zoe have seen a young woman with long dark hair?

The Dvorchaks have often speculated about who Jennifer might have been and why she was in their home but there is no clear answer.

One thing they do know, though, is what whoever she is, Jennifer is always welcome.

GHOSTS OF HARRISON WOODS
HERRIN, ILLINOIS

One of the most shameful events to ever occur in American history happened in the small southern Illinois town of Herrin in the summer of 1922. It would be a horrific massacre that would garner national outrage and would forever stain the area with blood. It would also leave behind a fearful haunting that would linger in a place outside of town called Harrison Woods for more than three decades after the carnage occurred.

The small town of Herrin was located in the heart of what was once considered coal country. In the surrounding area, rich veins of coal were discovered in the late 1800s. For a time, coal became the chief source of wealth and industry in the region, overshadowing the farms that once dominated the economy.

Despite the prosperity that coal brought, conditions for the miners were less than adequate. The lives and health of their employees were of little concern to the mine owners. Men worked in water up to their knees, in gas-filled rooms, and in unventilated mines, where the air was filthy and filled with toxins. There was no compensation for the accidents that frequently occurred, and the average daily wage was usually less than $2. Then, around 1900, the mineworkers began to organize and form unions to combat the low pay and horrible working conditions. New laws were implemented and wages doubled, tripled, and then rose as high as $15. The standard of living finally began to rise and small towns like Herrin began to prosper.

HERRIN IN THE 1920S

None of these changes came easy. There were many struggles between the unions and the mine owners, frequently leading to strikes and violence. The workers wanted fair treatment and good pay and the mine owners were interested solely in profits. The two sides often clashed in bloody incidents that sometimes led to murder. But nothing could compare to what happened in Herrin in 1922.

By the early 1920s, the mineworkers' unions were secure in southern Illinois. Around this same time, strip mining came into practice. In this method, large

18

shovels and draglines were used to strip the earth above coal deposits that were close to the surface. In September 1921, William Lester of the Southern Illinois Coal Company opened a new strip mine about halfway between Herrin and Marion. The mine employed fifty workers, all members of the United Mine Workers of America.

On April 1, 1922, the United Mine Workers went on a strike across the country, ceasing all coal-mining operations. Lester, who was deeply in debt with his new operation, was in fear of losing his company, so he negotiated with the local union and they agreed to let him continue taking coal from the ground, as long as he did not try to ship it out. With this stockpile in place, Lester would be able to ship the coal as soon as the strike ended.

By June, the union workers had dredged almost 60,000 tons of coal. The price for the product had risen considerably, thanks to the strike, and the chance for making a big profit was a temptation too great for Lester to resist. He fired all of his union miners and hired fifty strikebreakers and mine guards from Chicago. On June 16, he shipped out sixteen railroad cars of coal, effectively breaking the agreement he had made at the start of the strike.

Word soon got out about what Lester was doing and officials from the United Mine Workers, the state of Illinois, and the Illinois National Guard tried to convince him to stop

STRIP MINING EQUIPMENT AT THE SOUTHERN ILLINOIS COAL COMPANY MINE

shipping the coal and honor the arrangement that he had made with the union. Local miners were outraged and began to rally. They knew that if Lester got away with what he was attempting to do, other mine owners would follow suit. If this happened, everything the union had fought for would be lost.

In the days that followed, many people tried to reason with Lester, but he refused to listen. He was contacted repeatedly by Colonel Samuel Hunter of the Illinois National Guard, who warned him that the situation he was causing could be very dangerous. Lester ignored him, as he did the local sheriff, Melvin Thaxton, who also urged him to stop shipping out the coal. Instead of heeding the warning, Hunter advised the sheriff to deputize additional men in case of problems.

Rumbling continued among the local miners. On June 21, a truck carrying eleven armed guards and strikebreakers was ambushed east of Carbondale, at a bridge over the Big Muddy River. A contingent of union workers sprayed the truck with gunfire. Three men were wounded and six others escaped by jumping into the water below the bridge. Newspapers later reported that none of the six men were accounted for.

Later that same day, several hundred miners gathered at the Herrin Cemetery and then marched into town. They looted the local hardware store and gathered up all of the firearms and ammunition they could find. With no law enforcement officers in sight, the mob moved on to the mine. The union men began shooting and gunfire was exchanged with the frightened strikebreakers who were huddling inside the mine complex. Three of the union men were fatally shot.

Throughout the rest of the day, a number of attempts were made to try and defuse the situation. The union men were noncommittal and continued to carry out their siege of the mine. Late in the day, Colonel Hunter received a telephone call from C.K. McDowell, the mine's superintendent. He explained that the mine had been surrounded and shots were being fired. He had been unable to locate Sheriff Thaxton and he begged Hunter to send National Guard troops as soon as possible. Orders were sent down from Hunter's officer and National Guardsmen were initially dispatched to stop the attack and disperse the miners. Before they could leave Carbondale, the troops were recalled when Colonel Hunter received word that the mine operators and workers had worked out a truce. The promise of a truce turned out to be premature.

By evening, more union supporters had arrived at the mine. Colonel Hunter, concerned over the situation and worried about the truce, tried to telephone the mine office, but found that the lines had been cut. Strangely, in spite of the fact that he still could not reach the sheriff, he did not dispatch any soldiers.

The terms of the possible truce had called for the strikebreakers to be safely escorted out of the county. The men inside the mine complex were ready to surrender and somehow, Sheriff Thaxton was finally reached. He reluctantly agreed to check with the mineworkers and see if they would still honor the truce. Then, he decided that the hour was too late. He was tired, and he decided that the situation could wait until morning. He agreed that he would meet with Colonel Hunter and officials from the Carbondale National Guard unit the following morning.

Meanwhile, Hugh Willis, a spokesman for the United Mine Workers of America, arrived in Herrin to take stock of the situation. He addressed the local men and, if anything, made matters even worse. He told them, "God damn them, they ought to have known better than to come down here; but now that they're here, let them take what's coming to them." As far as he was concerned, the strikebreakers deserved whatever they got.

All through the night, mine guards and workmen huddled inside the complex, cowering under empty coal cars and behind piles of railroad ties. Gunshots rang out of the darkness and union miners who slipped into the complex used dynamite to blow up buildings, machinery, and the mine's water plant. Bullets bounced off the steel sides of the rail cars and splintered the wooden ties. The men inside were safe for the time being, but they were trapped with no way out.

At dawn, John E. Shoemaker, the assistant superintendent, and Robert Officer, the mine's timekeeper, ran from the barricade to the office to telephone for help. The line was dead. While they were working on the telephone, bullets ripped into the side of the building where they were hiding. The heavily armed miners had created large piles of dirt in a circle around the mine complex and opened fire from this protected position. The men huddling inside the complex were terrified and begged the superintendent to surrender. McDowell finally agreed.

Bernard Jones, a mine guard, tied a cook's apron to a pole and cautiously came out from behind the barricade where he had been hiding. He asked to speak to the mineworkers' leader, stating that the men inside would surrender with a promise that they could come out of the mine unmolested.

He received a curt reply, "Come on out and we'll get you out of the county."

The guards and workmen behind the barricade threw down their weapons and walked out with their hands raised above their heads. They walked along the railroad tracks and emerged where the spur line entered the mine. The besiegers, consisting of some 500 striking miners and their sympathizers, surged toward them. They searched the prisoners and lined them up two abreast. One of the captives near the end of the line went back to the bunk car and grabbed his satchel. A striker took it from him, telling him that he wouldn't need it where he was going.

The procession started along the railroad line toward Herrin, five miles to the northwest. After a short distance, the prisoners were ordered to lower their hands and take off their hats. The mob began to grow ugly. Some of the strikers fired their guns into the air and swore at the strikebreakers.

At Crenshaw Crossing, a scattering of houses about a half-mile from the mine, they were approached by an armed group of men who threatened to kill the strike-breakers. Cooler heads apparently prevailed and the procession continued on – but things were getting more heated by the minute. Some of the strikers began beatng the prisoners with pistol butts. The union men were angry and were determined not to let the strikebreakers and hated guards get off without some sort of punishment. The workers particularly despised mine superintendent C.K. McDowell, who had previously treated the union men with arrogance and bragged that the mine would stay open whether there was a strike or not. On his forced march, McDowell was repeatedly struck and badly bloodied. His wooden leg made it difficult for him to keep pace, further infuriating his captors. When he reached Moake Crossing, he collapsed and declared that he couldn't go any farther. Two men grabbed McDowell by the arms and pulled him off to one side of the rail line. A few moments later, the captives heard two shots fired. It was later learned that McDowell was shot twice in the chest. One newspaper also reported that he had been beaten with rocks after being shot.

When the procession reached a powerhouse for the Coal Belt Electric Railroad, which connected Herrin, Marion, and Carterville, it came to a halt. The leader of the column announced that the prisoners were going to be systematically executed in groups of four. However, at that moment, an automobile drove up and a man got out. Several of the prisoners would later remember that he was referred to as "Hugh Willis" and "the president." According to these survivors' accounts, he told the miners not to kill the strikebreakers on the public road. He was reported to have said, "There are too many women and children around to do that. Take them over in the woods and give it to them. Kill all you can." After that, he got back into his car and drove away.

The prisoners were then marched to a cluster of trees known as Harrison Woods, located across the tracks and to the north of the powerhouse. Less than 300 yards into the trees, they came to a fence strung with four strands of barbed wire. A big bearded man in overalls called out, "Here's where you run the gauntlet! Now, damn you, let's see how fast you run between here and Chicago, you damned gutter-bums!"

He fired his gun and an instant later, the woods rang with the sound of rifle and pistol cracks. Several of the terrified strikebreakers fell on the spot. The others began to run. Many of them never even made it to the fence. Others scrambled up and over it or became trapped in the wire, then blasted apart with bullets. The strikebreakers, unfamiliar with the area, plunged into Harrison Woods or ran towards Herrin. The miners tracked them through the trees and continued to slay them, one by one.

Sherman Holman, a guard at the mine, fell during the first volley of gunfire. As he dropped, he fell across the arm of assistant superintendent Shoemaker, who was wounded and unconscious. One of the miners came over and kicked Shoemaker's body. When he realized the man was still breathing, he leaned over and fired his revolver at Shoemaker's head.

William Cairns, another guard, managed to almost make it through the fence before his shirt caught in the barbed wire. He was shot twice as he struggled to free himself. He fell but was still alive and was able to see what was happening around him. Not far away, a strikebreaker, covered in blood, was leaning against a tree, screaming. Each time he screamed, someone shot him. Finally, one of the miners placed a pistol to his head and blew out the back of his skull.

Another guard, Edward Rose, made it through the fence, but fell down on the other side. With the

attackers close behind, he tried to lie still and pretend to be dead. One of the union men was not fooled and shot Rose in the back. The wounded man stayed conscious and saw boots stomping on bodies nearby and heard the sound of gunshots, both close and far away, as the mob continued to fire on the fleeing captives. Screams could be heard for a time and then, eventually, they died away.

About 8:30 a.m., a local farmer named Harrison, for whom the woods were named, and his son were working in their barn when they heard a barrage of gunfire to the southeast. As they looked in that direction, they saw a man running toward them, with fifteen or twenty men in pursuit. Several of the pursuers stopped and fired and the first man tumbled to the ground. The Harrisons watched as several of his pursuers dragged the man into the nearby timber. A few minutes later, another group arrived with two prisoners at gunpoint. They walked into the trees and the sound of gunshots followed. After a safe amount of time had passed, the Harrisons walked to the spot where the men had entered the woods. There, they found a body hanging from a tree. Three other bodies were splayed out beneath the dead man's feet.

One of the men who managed to make it over the fence was a mine guard, Patrick O'Rourke, from Chicago. In the woods, he was shot twice, but was still able to move. He hid in the underbrush for a time and his pursuers missed him. When they were gone, he started up the road towards Herrin, when, coming around a bend, a car caught him by surprise. He ran to a nearby farmhouse and hid in the cellar, but his pursuers found him. O'Rourke was pulled from his hiding place and clubbed over the head with a pistol butt. He was dragged to a car and by this time, other cars had stopped. A small crowd gathered and they argued about whether to shoot O'Rourke or hang him. During the argument, one of the new arrivals reported that five other captives had been taken and were being held prisoner at the schoolhouse in Herrin. O'Rourke's captors decided to take him there.

In the schoolyard, the six prisoners were forced to take off their shoes. One of the union men forced a captive who was a World War I veteran to remove his Army shirt. The prisoners were then ordered to crawl on their hands and knees for fifty or sixty feet, and then they were allowed to walk again, but without their shoes. About 200 people had gathered by this time, including many women and children. The prisoners were then marched to the Herrin Cemetery. The crowd was vicious as the men stumbled along the road. They were kicked and beaten as children screamed curses and called them "scabs."

At the cemetery, the march stopped. As the prisoners stood along the road bordering the burial ground, several members of the mob came up with a rope and tied them together. Once more, they were forced to march, but had only gone a short distance when word spread through the mob that the sheriff was on his way. An angry taunt came from the crowd, "God damn you, if you've never prayed before, you'd better do it now!"

Several shots were fired. O'Rourke was hit again and he fell, pulling the other five men to the ground with him. Shots continued to ring out and bullets pounded into the bodies of the fallen men. After they had fallen quiet, one of the union men filled the magazine of his pistol and methodically fired into each man. When a few of the men moved about and showed signs of life, one of the bystanders took a large knife from his pocket and slashed the throats of those who still lived. It was a scene of unbelievable horror.

A little while later, Don Ewing, a Chicago newspaper reporter, arrived at the cemetery. O'Rourke and a man named Hoffman, both partially conscious, were calling for water. Ewing found a small pail, filled it from a nearby hose, and started to give Hoffman a drink. A bystander appeared, pointed a rifle at the reporter, and forced him away. A young woman holding a baby taunted the dying man, telling him that she would see him in hell before he got any water. As she spoke, she casually pressed her foot down on the man's body. Blood bubbled out of his wounds and he moaned in agony.

Another man emerged from the crowd, offering to give the men a drink. He opened his pants and began to urinate into the faces of the victims.

During all of this, Sheriff Thaxton was noticeably absent. When he failed to meet Colonel Hunter and Major Davis, they went looking for him. The three men soon arrived at the mine to find the operation in flames. They were able to follow the footsteps of the mob and found a trail of bodies left behind. Those who had not died were taken to Herrin Hospital. The dead (eighteen of them on the first day and one more who was found on the next) were taken to a vacant storeroom downtown. They were stripped, washed, laid on pine boxes and covered with sheets. Then the doors were opened and, for hours, men and women, some carrying babies in their arms, filed past; many of them spit on the dead men. The dead were buried in a common grave in the Herrin Cemetery. Their identities remain unknown to this day.

HERRIN CEMETERY, WHERE MANY OF THE BRUTAL AND BLOODY ACTS OCCURRED DURING THE MASSACRE

Word quickly spread across the country about the terrible events. Newspapers and officials cried for justice. Editorials railed against the viciousness of the attack, congressman took the opportunity to attack the unions and President Warren G. Harding denounced it as "butchery ... wrought in madness."

Area miners remained stoic and remorseless. When a newspaper reporter asked a miner how many men had been killed, he replied, "No one was killed at all. We didn't kill them. They just dropped dead of fright when we surrounded the mine." A woman from the area told the same reporter, "One of these days, people will realize that it doesn't pay to break a strike in Williamson County."

The coroner's reports on the massacre ruled that the strikebreakers were killed by "unknown individuals" and declared that the deaths had been caused by the actions of the Southern Illinois Coal Company and not the striking miners. These findings further outraged some factions of the public and several months later, pressure forced a grand jury to indict six men for the murder of one of the strikebreakers. The prosecutor used eyewitness testimony from surviving workers to present his case, but the defense managed to justify the mob's actions. A jury acquitted all six of the defendants.

The press and public officials outside of the area were again infuriated and called for a new trial, which took place in 1923. By this time, public interest in the case had waned, but the prosecutor again tried the same six defendants, although this time for the murder of another strikebreaker. Reliable testimony was once again presented, but once more, the defense attorney justified the mob's actions. The jury was convinced and the defendants were again set free.

Still not satisfied, the Illinois House of Representatives launched its own investigation of the incident on April 11, 1923. The committee drilled the military, police officers, and former sheriff Melvin Thaxton, who was now the county treasurer. All of them claimed that they could do nothing to stop the massacre and were unable to find out who was responsible. Jake Jones, a Herrin policeman admitted knowing about the massacre but claimed that he was unable to stop it. Committee members remarked that he ought to have been indicted for complicity in the murders of the slain men.

The members of the committee soon ran out of patience with the witnesses. Chairman Frank A. McCarthy put into record the statement that he had been practicing law for eighteen years and had never seen more reluctant witnesses. All told, some sixty witnesses appeared before the investigating committee. Mine owner William Lester refused to testify, Hugh Willis left the state and could not be called, and one deputy sheriff and two Herrin policemen moved out of the area after appearing. But what testimony they did obtain was enough for the committee to be able to reach some conclusions about the incident.

After the hearings, the committee drew up a report that became a comprehensive account of what occurred on June 22 and the days surrounding the massacre. It assigned blame to a number of people and entities. The Illinois Adjutant General, Carlos E. Black, was blamed for not taking personal charge before the massacre and ordering out troops. He had been on vacation at the time and had left matters in the hands of Colonel Hunter, who was heavily blamed by the committee. In the words of the committee, Hunter was "absolutely incompetent, unreliable, and unworthy to perform the duties assigned to him." Sheriff Thaxton and his deputies were "criminally negligent" and all of the local police officers were "absolutely derelict in their duty." Hugh Willis, they believed, should have been convicted of murder. If he, and other union officials, "had been prompted by high and lofty motives," the disaster could have easily been prevented. Lester, on the other hand, was not absolved from blame. His greed and foolhardiness were sharply condemned.

The report was filed, but nothing was ever done about it. Union sympathizers in the Illinois House and Senate managed to torpedo the investigation, which infuriated the committee. They had only one last bitter comment to make, stating that they hoped the lawmakers who sabotaged their work would "be replaced by men of high moral stamina and courage, who will think more of the protection of the fair name of the state of Illinois than their own selfish political ambitions."

And the Herrin Massacre simply became another blood-soaked page in the history of Illinois.

Perhaps because no one was ever brought to justice for their role in the massacre, legend states that many of the victims of the day's events have refused to rest in peace. The horrific violence of their deaths, combined with the fact that many were never identified and were buried in unmarked, common graves, apparently left unsettled spirits behind for many years.

For more than thirty years after the massacre, travelers and nearby residents who passed by Harrison Woods at night claimed to see the shadowy figures of the murder victims moving among the dark trees. Their screams, cries and moans, often accompanied by mysterious gunshots were also heard on occasion. During this time, locals avoided the woods, likely both because of their fear of the angry spirits and their own guilt about the events that had occurred.

The stories continued until the 1950s, when they began to die out. Stories of ghosts were replaced with a macabre ritual that occurred every Halloween night, when local boys would hoist dummies into the trees in a sort of twisted homage to the massacre. Today, Harrison Woods has been replaced by a subdivision and homes now stand where men once bled and died.

And the spirits of the past seem to have finally crossed over to another time and place.

GHOSTS OF THE LOOKING GLASS PRAIRIE
TALES FROM LEBANON, ILLINOIS
BY LEN ADAMS

Since the summer of 2003, I have been actively investigating paranormal activity in the little community of Lebanon. For years, I kept saying that I believed that the ghosts of Lebanon could match those of just about any community in Illinois for their sheer number. Thanks to my claims, the Haunted Lebanon Tours became a part of the Illinois Hauntings family and my book, *Phantoms in the Looking Glass*, was born.

THE MERMAID HOUSE

After years of conducting tours, you tend to have your favorite stops along the way. My favorite location in Lebanon is The Mermaid House. This is also popular with patrons because they get to go inside. People can experience an inn built in 1830 that was visited by none other than Charles Dickens, one of the greatest writers of all time.

Having hosted the Lebanon tours for over three years now, I've started to amass quite a collection of side incidents that aren't normally part of the tours. I've done live theater for many years and have done some movie work as an extra. I've always told anyone who would listen that the best parts of these productions are the things that the audiences never see. The backstage jokes, rehearsal bloopers, costume malfunctions, and lighting and sound disasters are just a small part of a production that never make it

THE MERMAID HOUSE

onstage during a real show. Well, a haunted history tour is very much the same way. Doing tours throughout the Midwest, I've had my share of slamming doors, moving furniture, and shrieks and howling of all varieties. Many of these occurrences have scared the heck out of me, while others just seem to be a normal part of the show. Most of my encounters at the Mermaid House, though frightening to many tour patrons, are just normal occurrences to me these days.

I joined the Lebanon Historical Society to help preserve the history of the little town I love so much. This would also be of great value in researching the stories of the locations I believed to be haunted. Even though I had been told about ghostly encounters in the Mermaid House, all the society members at the monthly meetings were a bit skeptical, both towards the stories and my research in trying to verify them.

I've always believed that, as adults, we tend to put up a brick wall that obscures our view of things happening around us that don't seem to be part of our normal world. I tell folks that if they can just knock down a few rows of those bricks, they might be more aware of their surroundings and the otherworldly things that are happening around them. It took a bit of time, but ever so slowly, others in the society are admitting to strange goings on at the Mermaid House. Everyone is there at least once a month for society meetings. Others, such as myself, who are officers, are there much more often. The Mermaid House is our headquarters, as well as the first stop on my tour of Lebanon. Besides gathering there for meetings, or conducting tours, we are there, individually or in small groups, to help keep the old building going.

The house was built in 1830 and became a private residence in 1845, staying that way when it was sold again in 1904. The Historical Society acquired it in the 1960s. The building has seen an assembly line of folks over the years. I've always believed that there's nothing stronger than human emotion. Whether we believe it or not, I think if we're in a location long enough, we leave a little bit of ourselves behind. I believe there are energies, some just imprints, some actual intelligences, that occupy the Mermaid House to this day. Because of my position, I am at the house several times a week and at different hours of the day and night. I've always felt that you can develop a rapport with an intelligent entity (I don't like to use the word "haunting" here) if you're at a location often enough and if you have something in common with the entity.

The Mermaid House is a strange bird. The current house is only about one-third of its original size. The second owners only wanted whatever was on the single lot that they had purchased, so two thirds of the house was demolished. About one-third of the structure that was torn down was a barn or stable area.

None of the furniture or paintings in the place today are from the original house. They are all period pieces that have been donated over the years. But the original structure on the current lot is almost completely intact as is ninety percent of the flooring. Most of the doors and windows are from the 1830s. That's quite an achievement and it demonstrates the love and commitment Lebanon has for its past as it moves into the future.

My question has always been, is it the house that is haunted or could a ghost have tagged along with something that was brought in for display? I never believed that an entity could attach itself to a piece of furniture or an article of clothing until I inherited a ghost in the middle 1990s. My wife's grandmother had passed away. Kim (that's my wife) inherited a mystery box along with other treasures. The box was a cylindrical container that when opened revealed an old 1800s-style lamp. It had been crudely wired for a single light bulb and the top globe was missing. Other than that, it was a fantastic piece to have acquired. We put it back in the container until we could find a top for it and a proper spot in the house to display our new treasure. As it turned out, the lamp sat in a downstairs closet for five years. It took a flooded basement to get us to clean out that closet and rediscover our prized possession. The cardboard container had been ruined by the water but the lamp was unscathed. I placed it in a corner of an unused upstairs bedroom until we could get a top made for it.

As time passed, other items started to pile up around the lamp; that's when the fun started. Ghostly footsteps throughout the house would soon be followed by large shadows moving along the walls. It would become icy cold around the lamp as more and more junk piled up around it. Our Scottish terriers, Mollie and Maggie, refused to go into that bedroom. Then one day, as I came home from work, Kim met me at the door excitedly yelling that she knew who was haunting our house and why they were doing it. Our inherited lamp belonged to her great-grandmothers' second husband, August. Kim had seen him earlier in the day standing in the room next to the lamp. We just happened to have a photo of August and Kim's great-grandmother hanging on a wall with other antique photos of her family and Kim recognized him right away. After a few phone inquiries, Kim found out the lamp belonged to August and that he had to be the one causing all the commotion. We didn't blame him since we obviously weren't showing his beloved lamp the proper respect. We moved the lamp to the dining room table and in a loud voice, I told August that we were sorry and that we would fix the lamp immediately. We scoured many antique shops and finally found one that made replaceable parts that looked old fashioned. After racing home, we put the new top on the lamp. It was perfect. We then moved the lamp into our bedroom. After about a week, when August saw that we were taking proper care of his lamp, the hauntings ceased. He moved on and the lamp is still a prized possession in our home.

So, we return to my problem with the Mermaid House. Is it the house that's haunted, a piece of furniture, or maybe a little bit of both? During countless investigations I've proven the place to be haunted, but by whom? I'm running into that brick wall that I mentioned earlier. Whoever is there, though, seems to have taken a shine to me. About eight out of every ten times I'm at the house, I have some kind of paranormal experience.

Because this location is on the National Registry of Historic Places, it had to be fitted for the public to safely visit. A small bathroom was installed containing a toilet and a small vanity. The toilet is equipped with handrails for our handicapped patrons. I recently found out that small repairs can sometimes lead to big stories. The toilet seat had become old and cracked and needed to be replaced. A new seat was donated and I volunteered to install it one afternoon. It was a lovely warm summer day when I decided to tackle the job. With the outside conditions being so comfortable, I left the back doors open to let in the fresh air. To my dismay, I found out that I would have to dismantle the handrails before I could replace the toilet seat. The metal plate that was holding the railing was very rusty, with most of the enamel paint peeling off. I decided to repaint it while I had everything apart. I managed to find a wire brush and some old enamel paint in a closet under the staircase. I left my backpack in the room next to the small kitchen where the bathroom is located. You have to walk into this first room before you can get to the kitchen area.

After a little while, I had taken everything apart, cleaned the toilet, and replaced the seat. This just left the rusty old handrail plate to be cleaned, painted and replaced. Even on warm days, the arthritic demons that inhabit my body were letting me know it was past the time for a break. I decided to stop for a snack and a cold soda. As I was sitting on the bench by the back door I heard a tremendous crash, as if a chair had been smashed on the floor behind me. I limped into the building to find not a thing out of place. Nothing, that is, except for my backpack, which was no longer on the table where I had placed it but was now in the middle of the floor, a good seven to eight feet from where it had been. It just didn't fall off the table; it appeared as if someone had just picked it up and placed it on the floor. But what caused the crashing sound?

The paint was now dry on the plate that I had to reinstall to lock in the handicap rails. I wanted to finish the project as I was getting tired and a bit wary of what might happen next. I placed my pack just outside the open door and re-entered the building. I then went into the bathroom with the newly painted metal plate. After installing the plate, I exited the bathroom and fell over a small wooden chair that had been in the next room only moments before. I assumed whoever was with me decided that I needed a break. I thanked whoever brought the chair in but told them I needed to get the project done.

I put the chair back in the other room, then I finished reinstalling the handicap railings and returned all the tools to their place under the staircase. As I turned around, I stumbled over the same chair that had plagued me before. This time, it not only followed me to the next room, but it brought my backpack with it! I assured my unseen partner that I would indeed take a break now that I was finished with my project. I moved the chair to a better spot and finished my earlier snack and soda. The whole time I was talking aloud to whoever was helping me. When I was finished, I returned the chair to its proper place, grabbed my things, and out the door I went.

I really get excited when things happen during a tour because it reinforces my point that there is more out there than what we see or hear. The Mermaid House has been fantastic for helping me prove that physical death isn't the end of the road for us. Many of the frights at the Mermaid House are paranormal in nature. I have also had things happen that were scary, but completely human. Though unnerving at the time, some of the human stories have been the best ones to pass on during a tour.

I'm often asked what scares me the most doing the tours. I always reply that after the patrons leave a location, I have to go back in alone and turn out the lights and lock the doors. Many spots are so eerie that I would rather stay with the patrons, but as the tour leader, I go back in and do what I must.

During a tour in May 2010, I had a group of about fifteen people in the Mermaid House. We were upstairs in the area that consists of two bedrooms. The east room is rather large, taking up about two-thirds of the available space. The west bedroom is a tiny little thing. The larger bedroom is one of the most active areas in the house for paranormal activity. We spend quite a while there telling stories of past tours and investigations, with history and ghosts dominating the tales.

We move through the small bedroom fairly quickly because not much of a paranormal nature has happened there. After our tales in the small bedroom are finished, we go down the back staircase to the kitchen area on the main level. This back staircase is original to the building. Charles Dickens used those stairs! When electricity was installed in the house, a small light was placed in the ceiling above the back steps. Unlike the front staircase, the rear steps didn't get a double switch. Its on/off switch is at the top of the stairs, just inside the small bedroom. Because of this, I let the tour patrons go down the steps and into the kitchen before I turn off the light in the stairway and make my way down with the assistance of my flashlight.

During one of our tours, I was a bit weary, as it had been a long day. After the guests had descended the back stairway at the Mermaid House, I too, made my way down. At the bottom of the stairs I realized that I had not turned out the light. Back up the stairs I plodded to remedy my error. Rather than walk into the small bedroom to turn off the light, I just reached around the doorway from the second step. As I located the switch and turned off the light, a hand, or I should say, the fingers of a hand, brushed across and down the back of my hand. Knowing that all the living members of the group were downstairs, I made my way in a rapid fashion back down the stairs. To this day, I don't know if I ran or fell down the steps. Either way, it was quicker than how I normally descended!

Some of the guests could see that I was a bit shaken, so they asked me what had happened. After telling them of my experience, *they* decided it was time to leave. Who was I to argue?

The more I thought about it, the more I felt that this would be a great story to tell on the next tour. Two weeks later, I had a group of folks in the small bedroom of the Mermaid House. I decided to demonstrate how I got into a position where a ghostly hand could touch me without me seeing it coming. I informed the group that I was about to relay a frightening experience that happened only two weeks ago. I told them how I normally worked the lights, but forgot this last time. I then went down a couple of steps to show where I was standing when I reached for the light switch. There was a teenage girl who must not have been paying attention to this part. After walking down a few steps, she moved to the open doorway to see what I was doing. It was at this moment that I reached around the door to show the group how I reached for the light switch. I grabbed, and it wasn't the light switch that I located! I had no idea that the old building had such a tremendous echo until this young lady tested it out. With my hands in my pockets, and a multitude of apologies, I somehow managed to get through the rest of the tour unscathed.

Since that time, I have combined the ghostly hand touch and me accidentally grabbing a young girl into one of the best (and most remembered) stories on the Haunted Lebanon Tours. I'm just glad I didn't end up in jail!

Nothing gives me greater joy than to have someone who belittled me because of my belief in the paranormal have an experience of their own. When that happens, they usually tend to berate me; as if it was my fault they had a ghostly encounter. Two perfect examples of this happened at the Mermaid House.

On a beautiful July afternoon in 2010, I came upon a friend of mine, Joe Vastine, at the house. For an eighty-five-year-old guy, he gets around. Joe, at that time, was the House Committee Chairman for the Mermaid House. I inherited the mantle from him just before Christmas. If somebody needed a tour of the house, Joe got the call. I was his backup. I was rarely needed unless the groups were really large. I was mostly just doing my Haunted Lebanon Tours through the house.

As Joe approached me this fine day, he seemed a bit upset. He stopped, looked me square in the eye, and called me a foul name referring to my maternal parentage. He indignantly informed me that he had never had any trouble in the Mermaid House until I showed up. Now that he had my attention, I needed to know more.

Joe said he had opened up the Mermaid House about two hours earlier. He was sitting in the front room at a large table with the door open waiting for a bus tour from out of town. Being built in 1830, the old house tends to smell a bit musty when shut up for long periods of time. On nice days it helps to air out the place a bit. There is air conditioning on the lower level but we try not to use it if at all possible. We are a non-profit, historical organization that runs on volunteer labor and the generous donations of many patrons. In other words we're poor and we only spend money when we absolutely have to.

Joe was sitting and scribbling in the small leather notebook he takes with him wherever he goes. Suddenly, he heard the back door open and slam shut. Then multiple footsteps ran up the back steps to the second floor. Thinking that vandals had broken in, Joe raced to the back door but found it still secured with the trusty deadbolt. He then climbed the back steps to the upper floor. If intruders were in the house, Joe could handle them. Only two years before, he overpowered a much younger man who had broken into his house. Joe Vastine is a World War II veteran. On top of that, he was an Army Ranger. He"s old but he can kill you in more ways than you can count. I'm just glad he's on our side. He held the intruder while his wife calmly called the local police.

On his search of the upper floors of the Mermaid House he came up empty. Assuming that the sounds he had heard were just the joists and floorboards settling, Joe went back to his notebook in the front room of the house. After about two minutes, he said it sounded like someone was holding a parade upstairs. Joe marched back upstairs only to find the rooms empty. As he walked back to the front room, Joe thought to himself about what a beautiful morning it was; he could think of no reason why he shouldn't wait for his bus group outside. There was even a bench where he could sit and wait in comfort.

The tour group eventually arrived and was given the grand tour by Joe. An hour later, when the guests left, Joe slowly and methodically went through the house locking doors and turning out lights. From that point forward he never had the feeling of being alone at the Mermaid House. Joe has since forgiven me for stirring up all the weird happenings at the house. And now that he's retired from the post, it's my headache to deal with.

One of my favorite incidents happened during the first weekend of December 2010. Lebanon was having its local Christmas Open House Tour, which included the Mermaid House Being a member of the Historical Society, I was at the house to give guided tours. These were strictly historical, no ghosts. Later in the afternoon, during a lull in the action, one of the girls who were helping us came up to me and asked, "Aren't you that ghost guy everybody's talking about?" I replied that it sure sounded like me. She informed me that she didn't believe in that stuff and that it was all nonsense. I told her that was okay. Everyone's entitled to his own opinion. She then let me know that she would take the large upstairs bedroom for her section of the tour.

After about twenty minutes, my new friend who didn't believe in ghosts ran down the back steps and informed me that I could take over the large upstairs bedroom. She was done for the day and off she went! I don't know what happened up there. I just know the Mermaid House had just made someone else into a believer.

I don't get many pregnant women on my tours due to the excessive walking. But one young woman who was with child came on one of my Haunted Lebanon Tours. I didn't see any problems because the Haunted Lebanon Tours are flat, no hills (unlike the Alton Hauntings Tours). The Haunted Lebanon Tours also have more bathroom opportunities, so I figured that we'd have no problems with a gal who was in the family way.

The tour proceeded as every one of our fall tours had started in the past. I had the three or four people who saw ghosts everywhere. I had history buffs who didn't care about ghosts. I had ghost enthusiasts who didn't care about history. And last, but certainly not least, I had one or two guys who were dragged onto the tour by their girlfriends or wives and didn't appear to be happy about it.

Everything was going just fine until we reached the Mermaid House. Because of the large group, and the small house, I would have to break the group in half and do two inside tours. Often, under these circumstances, things seem to happen while the second group is touring the location. I think it has something to do with the first group's energy stirring up the pot. Things were fine as the second group toured the two bedrooms upstairs. As I was cramming the group into the smaller west side bedroom, the pregnant young woman let out a blood-curdling scream. I'm thinking, "Oh sweet Jesus, she's dropped the baby! I'm not equipped for this!" As fast as she could waddle into the smaller bedroom, she got right in my face. Evidently, a large rocking chair had started to rock all by itself. Her husband and several others that were with them couldn't figure out how this could be happening and they all were quite excited and scared. As the future mother screamed her story at me, she became more and more upset. It wasn't because the chair started moving on its own; it was because I didn't get as excited as she was. I assumed she wanted me to jump up and down and scream as loudly as she had done. She just didn't realize that I experience these things on a regular basis. Though a bit unnerving the first time, you do get used to it.

To satisfy her, I took her husband and two of their friends back into the large bedroom. Try as we might, the heavy rocker stood there like a stone. Nevertheless, I believed her; there were multiple witnesses.

Though we never promise that anything paranormal will happen on a tour, the Mermaid House in Lebanon, Illinois, has quite a track record for entertaining our tour guests.

THE ST. LOUIS STREET CAFE

One of the most active locations on the Haunted Lebanon Tour is the St. Louis Street Café. As those who have read my book or have already been on the tour know, the place is home to a male entity that is often seen in a brownish, sepia color. It's like looking at an old tintype photo. This specter has delivered frights time and time again on our tours. Several patrons, all of them women, have gotten glimpses of our brownish gentleman wandering the hallways of the restaurant. He usually appears only to women so what happened on a past tour was really out of character for him.

Our fall tours are usually filled way past our normal capacity because as we all know, ghosts only come out around Halloween. That being the case, we take the maximum amount of people we believe we can handle because we don't want them to miss out. While conducting a large tour I just make sure I stop in areas where everyone can hear. If our indoor

THE ST. LOUIS STREET CAFE

locations are too small to handle the entire group, my assistants tell stories about the paranormal to the part of the group that's left outside, while I handle the inside group. Then we switch groups. That way everybody gets to see everything.

As I mentioned earlier, the second group almost always seems to experience more ghostly action. I feel it's because the first group's energy helps stir things up. Not that long ago during a fall tour, I had to split the group in half when we reached the St. Louis Street Cafe. Even though it is a large building, it contains a series of small areas where it's too difficult to bring in fifty patrons all at once. Because half of the group appeared to be chain smokers, I figured that I would take them through first. They could hear the stories, maybe experience something ghostly, then go back outside and smoke to their hearts' delight.

With the first group out of the building, I now had group two, the non-smokers, safely locked inside with me. The two upstairs locations went well and we then proceeded to the basement. At that time, all the paranormal energy seemed to radiate from the basement. It was so bad at times that the restaurant workers would draw lots to see who would go downstairs to get whatever supplies were needed.

I now had all of group two lined down one side of the large basement. Halfway through my downstairs story I noticed something odd. If you turn around after descending the concrete steps into the basement, you can see the top step and a small area of the room that you just exited. As I was telling my story, I noticed someone standing at the top of the stairway. All I could see were two legs from the knees down to the shoes. There is almost always someone on every tour who can't seem to follow directions and it makes my job that much harder. Rather than cause a big scene, I decided to keep telling my story and just amble slowly over to the steps to see which knucklehead from group one was still in the building. As I got within ten feet of the bottom step the legs slowly turned. I bent down quickly to see who it was and received quite a shock. The legs and feet that turned to walk away were just that -- legs and feet! There was no body attached to them. And you guessed it, they were brown in color. Not wanting to panic the group, I turned around to continue my story. Evidently, because I had stopped talking and my eyes were now the size of saucers, the people nearest to me assumed something strange had just happened. I tried to assure them that nothing had happened. They assured me that I was lying. After telling them what I saw, a near riot ensued. The problem was they didn't know where to run. They were in the basement; the only way out was up the stairs where the ghostly legs were. But, that was also where the door was and out they ran. They had a slight problem, though. The front door was locked and I, still in the basement, had the key. I eventually made my way upstairs and let everyone out.

What always amazes me about nights like this is that half the people come on the tours hoping to encounter an entity and the other half are afraid that they will. Then, when we are lucky enough to have something happen, all of them want to run away and hide!

In 2003, when I was first contacted to do an investigation of the St. Louis Street Cafe, the owners were Walt and Jo Turk. Their daughter, Kathi, was the manager. They sold the place because it had become unmanageable, from a ghostly standpoint. Because the business was for sale, time was of the essence. I documented quite a lot of activity and spoke with enough witnesses to believe the location was without any doubt, haunted. Then it was sold.

I was very fortunate that the new owners, Greg and Kathy Heberts, had heard of me and had no problems with allowing me to continue my investigations at the restaurant. They both told me they didn't believe in ghosts, but they heard I was harmless and at times, good for business. They even let me include the restaurant on the tour that was just coming together.

Over the next several years, Greg, a non-believer in the paranormal, would let me know from time to time that the building was just messed up. Things would move by themselves, voices would come from unoccupied spots, and mechanical items would seem to have a life of their own.

Kathy never believed in ghosts either, but for a non-believer she was very skittish. She would open up in the morning but wait at the front counter until Jessica, the cook, showed up. Also, poor Jess was the one who had to go downstairs for supplies because Kathy wouldn't go down there alone.

Tragedy struck the St. Louis Street Cafe about two years ago but it had nothing to do with the entities that inhabited the location. Kathy started acting strangely, with sudden outbursts one minute, followed by tears the next. For the ray of sunshine that Kathy always was, something was definitely wrong. After a multitude of tests she was diagnosed with a brain tumor. Though quite extensive, it was removed and we all felt that she would make a full recovery.

Life can be cruel sometimes and it seemed to take particular joy in tormenting poor Kathy. Every time she went back to the doctor, the cancer seemed to reappear out of nowhere and relocate in a different part of her body. Kathy was a beautiful, petite blonde in her late thirties. To me, she looked like she was about twenty-three. The cancer just ravaged her poor body. Her friends stood by helplessly wondering how something so horrible could happen to someone so sweet. Kathy, though sick, was still the worker bee she had always been. She came to the restaurant every day she could. When the chemotherapy took her hair, she donned a wig and kept on working. Finally it became too much and death claimed this wonderful person in early summer.

After Kathy's death, I didn't know what would happen with the cafe. I assumed that Greg would probably sell it and it would no longer be a stop on the Lebanon tour. I didn't care. I didn't want to go in there anymore because the memories just broke my heart.

To my amazement, Greg brought a lifelong friend of his named Darla in to help keep the place open. I stopped in one day to see how Greg was doing and that's when I met Darla. She was friendly, energetic and would talk your ears off if you gave her half a chance. Rather than tiptoe around the subject of Kathy, Darla brought her up right away. It would seem that Kathy, who never believed in ghosts, might have come back to watch over things at the cafe.

This time around, the items that were moving were personal items that would disappear and then reappear days later. Items from the St. Louis Street Café's past would appear from nowhere, such as an old menu, a utensil, or an old photo. But the real kicker to Greg and Darla was when they would be encircled by Kathy's perfume. It was her scent, only magnified. It would surround them and then vanish as quickly as it appeared.

I wasn't sure if I believed them or not. I was just glad they were keeping the place open and to my delight, they wanted me to continue bringing the Haunted Lebanon Tours into the place.

The first several tours were hard for me as I recounted the ownership history of the location. When I got to Kathy, it was all I could do to keep myself together and not start crying for my lost friend. But time heals all wounds and the tours became easier for me to do. This is about the time that different people on the tours would ask me where the perfume scent was coming from. It would only happen to a couple of people at a time, and then suddenly vanish. It even happened to one of my helpers, Sandy Guire, on a tour in October 2010. We searched everywhere and could find no source for the scent.

Two weeks after it happened to Sandy, I finally got my turn. As I was recounting the history of the building, I was enveloped in Kathy's perfume. It stayed with me throughout the building. The strangest part was that no one else could smell it.

As if to reinforce that the new entity in the restaurant was Kathy, I had one more ghostly episode that would mean something only to me. I was conducting an overnight investigation at the restaurant. That's when a few people are allowed to spend the night and I try to show them how to do a proper investigation of a haunted location.

About two hours into the investigation, a couple of the guys who were in the front section of the cafe called for me. When I arrived they said that they had captured some great EVPs, or electronic voice phenomena. There were replies to three or four of the questions with what seemed to be a one-word answer in a feminine voice. It wasn't crystal clear, though. The investigators then asked if the entity knew me. A crystal clear woman's voice answered, "Certainly!" After hearing this I felt it would be too much of a coincidence for it to be Kathy. I stood by the front counter and said aloud, "Kathy, if you're here with us now, give me a sign." Just then the Diet Coke started shooting out of its dispenser. The others in the room were more amazed at my reaction than anything else. I stood there laughing and crying at the same time. I went over to turn off the dispenser, but the lever was back in the off position; it had never moved. I explained to the group that the Diet Coke was a private joke between Kathy and I. It ran so slowly, with only foam coming out, that I swore you would have to call an hour ahead of time to get a soda. Kathy would have to fill up a pitcher of foam and let it slowly turn into soda. Was it just a coincidence or did Kathy really mess with the soda fountain? I can't say for sure. The timing, though, was spot on!

If this was Kathy, and I believe it was, how ironic that a confirmed non-believer in ghosts would come back as one. Even Harry Houdini couldn't pull that one off! Her appearances have become fewer. I have a feeling that she only came back to check on the place that she put her heart and soul into. Perhaps she is satisfied now and has moved on. I just hope she's happy and pain free, and that I get to see her again when my time comes.

TAPESTRY ROOM RESTAURANT

It seems like around fifty percent of the locations that I investigate turn out to be restaurants, or other places that serve food. So it shouldn't come as a surprise that three of my stops on the Haunted Lebanon Tours are places to eat. The last one I'll mention here is the Tapestry Room. I was haunting this eatery long before I found out it was indeed haunted. The food is fantastic and the desserts are spectacular! When I found out that the restaurant was supposed to have its own ghosts, my life was perfect.

As in most of the locations that I have investigated in Lebanon, the owners contacted me hoping to get an explanation for the weird happenings they were experiencing.

Over the years, I heard stories about many of the Main Street businesses being haunted. I eventually gained the trust of the property owners and they came to realize that I was a legitimate paranormal investigator and that I wouldn't belittle them or make fun of their distressing situations. After some time passed, these business owners became very good friends. Such was the case with Pat Peterson, the owner of the Tapestry Room Restaurant.

The Tapestry Room has an entity that inhabits the cellar regions. Once, when an electrician was doing a minor job down there, a misty form started to come together. It eventually grew to about three feet by five feet in size. It then floated to the bottom of an old stairway that had long ago been boarded off from the upstairs. As the electrician stood there, frozen in fear, two legs with feet attached came out of the bottom of the misty cloud. That's when the ghostly show was over for the electrician. With a shriek that half of Lebanon could have heard, out of the cellar he ran. He didn't stop running until he was about three blocks away, a distance he judged to be far enough from the ghostly legs to prevent them from pursuing him.

When I investigated the restaurant, I immediately went to the cellar. While it's true that I've encountered similar misty forms in the past, I've never come across one with legs sprouting from it. But the cellar of The Tapestry Room Restaurant has held many other surprises for me. This is probably a good place to mention that you are never supposed to go ghost hunting alone, mostly for safety reasons. If you fall or injure yourself, there is no one to go for help or to assist you in any way. And it's never a guarantee that your cell phone will work. Despite all that, I've been known to break this rule.

One afternoon, during lunch, I stopped in The Tapestry Room to investigate an opening to a tunnel that was located under the steps where the misty form appeared. Even though it was bricked shut, I wanted to take a few snaps of it with my disposable camera. Because I'm always falling down or dropping things, I use a disposable camera; if I break it, I'm not out a lot of cash. The other members of my team have all the expensive gadgets but they don't trip and fall like I do. With a restaurant full of people above me, I felt assured that it would be safe for me to venture downstairs on my own.

The place I wanted to photograph was in the very back section of the cellar. A series of small light bulbs along the east side of the

TAPESTRY ROOM RESTAURANT

ceiling gave me plenty of light. With all the noise from the busy restaurant above me, I felt perfectly safe.

After snapping a few photos of the tunnel entrance, I turned to make my way out into the main area of the cellar. The tunnel entrance was in a small room in the rear, under the kitchen. Just as I reached the main area all the lights went out downstairs. I was in complete and total darkness. Because I thought that I just run in and then run back out, my flashlight was resting comfortably in my car. I checked my cell phone and watch and found the batteries were drained on both. Time to panic, or was it? It dawned on me that my disposable camera probably didn't have a battery; if it did, I wasn't aware of it. I'm a people person. I never was, nor will I ever be, good with gadgets. I paused to compose myself and determine my next move. I wondered if maybe my cheap camera could save me. After priming the flash button, I aimed the camera in front of me and pushed the button. It worked! The flash allowed me to see about ten to fifteen feet in front of me. So that's how I made my way out of the cellar. Take a photo, run ten feet. Take a photo, run up ten feet. After what seemed like an eternity I made my way upstairs. The only light switch for all the lights downstairs is next to the door at the top of the stairs; it was in the ON position but the cellar was still cold and dark.

I, of course, was a bit unnerved. I told Pat about what had just occurred downstairs. He asked me why I didn't yell for help. I told him I did! Maybe because the restaurant was full of customers or maybe because no one was listening for screams, but either way, no one heard me.

Pat and I went back to the top of the stairs that lead into the cellar. The switch was still in the ON position. But something had changed. All the lights were on! I kept flicking the switch and the lights worked perfectly every time. The circuit breakers, on inspection, were in perfect working order. The lights going out could not be explained. It has happened to me several times, once on a tour. Now I carry plenty of handy glow sticks. Not too long ago, Pat had an electrician doing some work in the restaurant. He had him check out the cellar lighting and all was as it should be.

So who, or what, is in the basement? And why does he, she, or it, have an aversion to lights? Now when I, with or without my helpers, go into the cellar on a tour, I am like an Old West gunslinger. But instead of guns, I'm armed to the teeth with batteries, flashlights and glow sticks.

The cellar of The Tapestry Room Restaurant is becoming known for more than lights turning out unexpectedly. During the tours, people have reported being touched, voices have been heard, and on two separate occasions, an unauthorized someone joined the tour.

In the spring of 2010, I was leading a small tour of intrepid ghost hunters. There were twelve of us in total. Bringing up the rear was my trusted fellow investigator and no-nonsense caboose, Julie Ringering. In ghost tour lingo, a caboose goes last in line to make sure there are no stragglers. I really enjoy having Julie on the tours. Over the last couple of years, she has become a well-trained investigator and a good friend. Best of all, she's also a nurse. I consider this a bonus because with everything that's physically wrong with me, it pays to have a nurse handy, just in case.

But, getting back to the story, it was a beautiful spring evening and the tour was flowing right along. Before I knew it, we were in the cellar of the Tapestry Room. The stories were told and the pictures were taken. I started to lead the group out in single file when Julie screamed from the rear of the line. As I mentioned previously, the lights in the ceiling run along one side of the main part of the cellar. When we make our way to the steps that lead us up and out of the cellar, the ceiling lights cast our shadows up the opposite wall. What alarmed Julie was that as we were leaving, she felt something not quite right behind her. We had my shadow, followed by those of the ten patrons, followed by Julie's shadow -- followed by a thirteenth shadow about six feet behind her. It was as if whoever was casting the last shadow was right in line with us. More disturbingly, besides there being no body to cast that shadow, it was twice the size of ours!

As Julie screamed, the entire group (Julie and I included) decided to run instead of walk out of the cellar. I valiantly made sure every tour guest made it up the stairs, followed by Julie. Before racing up the stairs myself, I took one last glance at the area we had just vacated. The shadow was still there, motionless, and twice as dark as it was before. Thank goodness everyone else was already upstairs because I would have plowed right through them if I had to. As of this date, that has been the only time our unwanted guest has joined us on the tour.

Upstairs in the restaurant, things are pretty normal during dining hours. At night, though, when the tours come through, if you are looking for an encounter with the paranormal, you can head right for the cellar. Or you can sit, nice and safe at one of the dining tables and wait. As you're waiting for the folks downstairs to come back up, don't be bothered by the moving furniture, mysterious shadows, rapping on the walls, or disembodied voices. They've never really terrified anyone – not yet anyway!

THE LEGEND OF "PURPLEHEAD"
ST. FRANCISVILLE, ILLINOIS

Nestled against the Wabash River, and just a stone's throw away from the Indiana border, is the tiny Lawrence County town of St. Francisville. It is a place that is haunted by history and steeped in lore and is home to a menacing face that has simply been known as "Purplehead" to generations of people who were born and raised in the area. The terrifying legend is linked to the unsettling Stangle Bridge spanning the Wabash River outside of town. No one can say for sure just how the strange story began but there are many versions of it and at some point over the years, it's taken on a life of its own.

The bridge around which the Purplehead legend revolves is an old Wabash Railroad bridge. Often referred to as the "Wabash Cannonball Bridge," this nickname comes from a fictional train in a folk song that first appeared in sheet music form in the early 1880s. The Wabash Railroad, however, was very real and served most of the Midwest from the 1860s into the middle of the twentieth century, when it was swallowed up by other rail companies. The railroad took its name from the river that runs along the Indiana border and the iron bridge at St. Francisville was constructed in the 1890s to run twice-daily passenger and freight trains between St. Francisville and Vincennes, Indiana.

As time went by and the heyday of the railroads passed, the Wabash Railroad Company abandoned the bridge and it was purchased by Maurice Stangle, after whom the current bridge is named. The rails were removed and the bridge was laid with wooden planks, making it usable by wagons and automobiles, but only with a single lane of traffic at a time. The Stangle family later turned it into a toll bridge in the early 1970s after ferry service across the river was closed down. It became St. Francisville's only direct link with Indiana but as years passed, and the condition of the old bridge deteriorated, people became wary of using it.

However, some still braved the treacherous crossing – and the story of Purplehead was born.

Over the years, there have been dozens, perhaps even hundreds, of people who have claimed to have experienced weird and unsettling things on the bridge. There have been varying accounts of how

A VINTAGE VIEW OF THE WABASH CANNONBALL BRIDGE

STANGLE BRIDGE TODAY

the spirit that haunts the bridge is supposed to be experienced. Some say that if you drive your car out onto the bridge in the middle of the night and honk the horn three times, the ghost will appear. Others say that the ghost emerges from the river and chases your car to the other side. Others claim that you have to drive onto the bridge for anything to happen, while others swear that just being in its vicinity will cause strange things to occur.

But every version of the story has one thing in common – a disembodied mottled purple head that comes out of the river to menace visitors, whether by chasing them, lurking in their rearview mirrors or simply appearing between the wooden planks that make it possible to drive across the rusting iron span.

There are nearly as many different types of reported encounters with Purplehead as they are stories about why this eerie vision haunts the bridge.

According to some legends, the spirit of Purplehead is only seen during storms. Supposedly, a man once decided to commit suicide by hanging himself from the bridge during a heavy rain. As he was tying the noose, he slipped and fell on the wet girders and the plunge snapped his head from his body. Since then, the story goes, his head has been seen floating along the bridge, frightening passersby.

There are also stories that claim the bridge was often used for lynchings by the Ku Klux Klan in the 1920s. The Klan was active in Illinois and Indiana at the time but no evidence exists to say that anyone was ever lynched on the Stangle Bridge. Regardless, rumors persist that the spirit is that of one of the infamous organization's unfortunate victims.

Another popular story involves a Native American medicine man. During the bloody years of the War of 1812, many skirmishes were fought between the local Indian populace and the white settlers along the banks of the Wabash River. One of these encounters took place near where the Stangle Bridge now crosses the river. It was said that a shaman from one of the local tribes was killed and because his body was never properly buried his spirit has never rested in peace. Because of this, he is now said to haunt the bridge. The stories say that if you venture out into the middle of the bridge, you might see the pale hands of the shaman reaching up out of the water, as if pleading for help. Soon after, his bloated purple head will rise from the water as well, perhaps searching for his body.

Some say that the ghost is that of James Johnston, seeking revenge on anyone who crosses Stangle Bridge at night and disturbs his rest. Johnston was one of the original settlers of the region, a Revolutionary War officer who was given land along the Wabash as repayment for his bravery during the fight for independence. Johnston died and was buried on his family farm in 1826. Since that time, it is said that his slumber has been interrupted by the passing of freight trains and the clatter of automobiles on the wooden planks of the bridge. His rotting purple head is said to appear on the bridge, sometimes peering up through the wooden planks and other times glaring at drivers in their rearview mirrors. Johnston's spirit is supposed to stay with motorists even after they leave the bridge, but luckily, he always vanishes when the driver reaches the old soldier's grave. After crossing the bridge into Illinois, travelers pass through a mile or so of swampy forested area before reaching St. Francisville. Just before coming into town, the road makes a curve to the left. On the right hand side of the road is a single headstone that is said to mark the grave of James Johnston. This is where the frightening journey of Purplehead comes to an end – at least in this variation of the story.

Or perhaps the disembodied head belongs to someone else altogether.

On a December night in 1906, a Catholic priest named J.B. Hatter fell from a train as it passed over the bridge. Father Hatter was on his way to St. Francisville for the first time, to take over the local parish. Local gossip claims that the priest had been drinking heavily in Vincennes and was quite drunk when he boarded the train. As it crossed over the bridge, legend has it that it blew its horn three times and Father Hatter, believing he had reached his destination, stepped off the train. (This is why some believe you must honk your horn three times to summon the ghost!) Stories say that the priest fell beneath the wheels of the train and was decapitated, but this was not the case. He actually fell and struck his head, then lay on the bridge all night, moaning for help. Workmen on the morning train spotted him the next day and he was taken to the home of friends, where he later died. Since that time, his ghost is said to have haunted Stangle Bridge.

So, who is the menacing spirit, given the name "Purplehead," who haunts the bridge over the Wabash River at St. Francisville? Is this merely a legend, a folk story, told by imaginative small town teenagers looking for something to do on a dark night? Or is there something to this story after all? No one can say for sure but it seems obvious that something strange happened on this bridge many years ago – something that caused a very unusual story to take root in the hearts and minds of those who grew up in the area.

GHOSTS, SPOOK LIGHTS & HAUNTED HOUSES
ODDITIES OF ROCK CREEK, ILLINOIS

Located near famous Cave-in-Rock on the Ohio River is the small community of Rock Creek. This is not the first time that I have written about strange happenings in Hardin County, where Rock Creek is located, and perhaps it will not be the last. It is a place that has long been known for weird activity. Since the arrival of the first settlers, the area along the creek has become infamous for ghosts, haunted houses, spook lights, mysterious figures and more.

Rock Creek is one of the strangest areas of Hardin County, itself a very haunted part of southern Illinois.

As chronicled in earlier books, the rough and unsettled lands of the western territories of Illinois became home to outlaws and pirates in the early 1800s, all of them preying on the travelers who journeyed down the Ohio River. Many of them established hideouts and settlements along the riverbanks. Perhaps the most famous of these locations was Cave-in-Rock, located in Hardin County in the southeastern corner of the state. The cave became the stronghold of pirates who plundered flatboats on the river and who murdered and robbed travelers.

The pirates operated for many years, later in conjunction with an outwardly respectable businessman named James Ford who operated a ferry a few miles upriver. Ford was a wealthy man with extensive land holdings in both Kentucky and Illinois. He was appointed as a justice of the peace by Kentucky's governor James Girard, and was generous to his neighbors in Illinois. He believed in education and saw to it that his daughter Cassandra was well schooled, something unusual for a young woman at the time. His family was well taken care of and he had a genuine love for his children. He provided for them during his life and after his death but his generosity did not apply to his second wife, to whom he left nothing in his will. Ford was a huge man in both stature and reputation and when in a rage, he was a man to be feared.

Ford's first wife was Susan Miles, daughter of a prosperous early settler. Together they had three children, Phillip, William and Cassandra. His daughter was later married to Dr. Charles Webb of Princeton, Illinois, and was respected and admired by all who knew her. Dr. Webb repeatedly said in later years that his wife never knew Ford as anything other than a kind and loving father.

In a short period of time, from 1797 to 1818, James Ford went from poverty as a land surveyor to great wealth as a ferry operator and landowner. He owned vast holdings in his own name and in the names of his children. By 1818, he had acquired over 850 acres of land in Kentucky and Illinois, along with slaves, horses, timber land and salt works. Some wondered about the source of his wealth, but they remained silent, fearing his anger and his political clout.

The early 1800s were a boom time for the river pirates but it wasn't long before warnings began to be issued and soon flatboat captains began refusing to stop for pirates posing as stranded passengers. They also began ignoring distress calls and armed guards began accompanying the boats, making piracy hazardous. James Ford was smart enough to realize that he had to change his methods of operation to keep up with the times. This led him to start his river ferry, creating a whole new arm of operation for his criminal enterprise.

He opened the ferry in 1823 and the river pirates became land robbers and murderers. They seized wagons and raided the homes of settlers who crossed over on Ford's Ferry from Kentucky. In time, Ford would own and operate a number of ferries but the only one connected to his illegal operations was in Hardin County. Wagons belonging to prosperous travelers were stripped and burned and the occupants killed and buried in the woods. No one was ever left alive to identify the outlaws. Ford ran the entire operation from the background and if any of his men were caught or suspected, he would use his legal connections to get them out of the territory before they could come to trial.

After Ford's first wife died in the early 1820s, he married a widow named Elizabeth Armstead Frazer. She had come downriver with her husband, James, and three daughters. Having known Ford in the past, they visited with him. While they were Ford's houseguests, Frazer became stricken with a mysterious illness and died. Alone and destitute, Elizabeth married Ford in 1829 but they did not live happily ever after. Frequent disagreements arose because she was not the quiet, mild woman that the first Mrs. Ford had been. She probably suspected that Ford had something to do with her former husband's death. Reports have it that Ford often abused his wife and treated her horribly. Given the type of men that he did business with, she likely never knew how lucky she was that her fate was not a more heinous one.

As Ford's wealth grew, more and more suspicion began to fall on him and more people began to wonder about the source of his money. During this time period, a number of citizens formed vigilante Regulator groups throughout southern Illinois when local residents began to feel that organized law had failed them. The Regulators were almost as violent as the criminals they pursued, shooting and lynching the lawbreakers who defied them.

A group of Regulators eventually brought an end to James Ford's operations. An argument between two of Ford's own men set things into motion. Henry Shouse quarreled bitterly with Vincent Simpson, a henchman of Ford's whom Shouse accused of treachery. Ford himself had previously sued Simpson over a slave named Hiram that Ford maintained had been misrepresented to him at the time of purchase. The trial was thought to be a ruse to discredit Simpson, who it was suspected of planning trouble for the outlaws. It was thought that if his reputation could be besmirched, no one would take seriously any accusations that he might make against Ford. One day after a court hearing, Shouse and Simpson began fighting. Later that day, Simpson was on his way to Shouse's home with a loaded gun but Shouse shot him first without warning. Simpson was taken to his home, where he lingered for several days and then died.

Shouse and two of his cronies, James Mulligan and William H. J. Stevenson, rode out for Arkansas but were soon captured and returned to Illinois. Shouse was indicted for murder while in jail in Equality and his friends were named as accomplices. Mulligan later died in jail and Stevenson escaped. Shouse was hanged in Golconda in 1834.

Meanwhile, the Regulators decided that although Ford had managed to stay ahead of the law with his money and power, he was as guilty as his men in the murder. He might not be stopped by one or two men, but the Regulators acting as a group might be able to take him down. One evening, a group of nightriders followed him to the home of the widow Simpson, where he went to have dinner and to provide comfort to the widowed woman. Mrs. Simpson, though, had little use for Ford's comfort – she wanted revenge. After making him supper, Mrs. Simpson brought a candle over to the table and asked Ford to read a letter aloud for her. The Regulators were waiting outside for this signal and opened fire on the house, aiming for the candle. Ford died on the floor with seventeen bullets in his body.

For years after his death, his slaves told stories about how James Ford had died and "landed in Hell head first." At his funeral, attended only by his widow, a few family members, neighbors, and some slaves, a terrible thunderstorm came up. Just as Ford's coffin was being lowered into the ground, lightning flashed and a deafening clap of thunder filled the air, causing one of the slaves to lose his grip on the rope holding the coffin. The box dropped into the grave head first and wedged there at a strange angle. The heavy rain that began to fall made it impossible to move the casket, so it was covered over the way that it had fallen – leaving Ford to spend eternity standing on his head.

James Ford was not alone in his sinister operations. One nearby place of murder and robbery was located near a spring that ran from the side of Potts Hill in eastern Hardin County, near Rock Creek. This site marked the end of Ford's Ferry Road and the beginning of the trails that led farther into Illinois.

Close to the spring was Potts Tavern, a disreputable establishment that worked in conjunction with Ford and his band of killers. The tavern was run by Isaiah L. Potts and his equally unscrupulous wife, Polly. The couple's only son, Billy, threw in with the local outlaws and even as a young man, was known as an accomplished thief and merciless killer. With his parents' assistance, he preyed on the unsuspecting travelers who came to the family's inn. He often lured them out to the nearby spring and robbed them after cutting them open with his knife. His mother helped to dismember the murder victims and his father dumped the pieces in an abandoned well or buried them in shallow graves on the property.

Billy later ran afoul of the law when one of his prospective murder victims escaped and was able to identify his attacker. He quickly fled from Hardin County and was gone for several years. While away, he gained weight and grew a beard. When he felt that it was safe to come home and visit his parents, he

POTT'S TAVERN AS IT LOOKED IN THE EARLY 1900S

traveled back to Illinois. On his way to his family's tavern, he almost became a crime victim himself when he was targeted by some of his former confederates who took him for a wealthy man traveling alone. Surrounded on Ford's Ferry Road by some of his old friends, he only escaped with his life when he identified himself and proved his identity by recalling some of their former crimes. Billy was welcomed back into the gang by his friends but he swore them to secrecy about his identity because he wanted to surprise his parents with his return.

He rode on alone to Potts Tavern and ordered dinner and a room. He had changed so much that his mother did not recognize him but his parents noticed the heavy bag of loot that he had with him. After eating, he went outside to have a drink from the spring when his father sprang out of the shadows and stabbed him. He also failed to recognize his son and merely saw him as another traveler to rob. The body was hastily buried in a shallow grave in the woods.

The next day, several members of Billy's old gang showed up looking for their friend. One of them asked Polly how she liked having her son home again and she nearly collapsed in shock. She and Isaiah quickly exhumed the body they had buried the night before, unable to believe they had robbed and murdered their own child. It is said that Mrs. Potts collapsed when she recognized his body from a birthmark – a red stain in the shape of a four-leaf clover that was supposed to bring him luck.

The Pottses abandoned their life of crime and never really recovered from what had happened. Polly painted an image of her son's face on the rock that overlooked the spring on their property

THE OLD POTT'S SPRING, WHERE MANY TRAVELERS MET THEIR END DURING THE HEYDAY OF THE TAVERN. I VISITED THE SPRING IN 2002 TO SEE WHAT REMNANTS REMAIN OF THIS SPOOKY SPOT.

and it remains there to this day.

The area around the spring became the scene of a number of reports of ghosts during the 1800s. Many believed that the lingering spirits were those of the travelers who lost their lives at the point of the Pottses' blades as they drank from the spring outside of the tavern. Many others claimed that the spirits of Billy Potts – and his heartbroken mother – lingered here, as well.

The spring is now located on private property a couple of miles north of the town of Cave-in-Rock. A trickle of water still flows from beneath the outcropping of rock that marks the site. If one looks closely, a visitor can see the faded image of a dead man's face. It remains here as a tragic reminder of a woman's grief and a wasted life that ended in murder.

THE ROCK CREEK GHOST

Every ghost story has a history behind it – or does it? The mysterious entity known as the "Rock Creek Ghost" by generations of residents in the area has no historical antecedent. It just seemed to show up one day and stayed for many years. It was witnessed by hundreds of people and took on many forms – although usually that of a dog – and always appeared near the Rock Creek Church.

When the ghost took the form of a dog, it was always an ordinary-looking creature. There was nothing strange about its appearance and yet it seemed to give off a feeling that made people unnerved or uncomfortable to be around the animal. It was never anything that could be adequately explained; it just gave people a bad feeling. Many tried to outrun the creature (with no luck) or to chase it away. One man tried to drive off the dog by kicking it, but was startled when his foot passed right through it with no effect at all. The dog just kept following him, apparently oblivious to the failed attack.

The ghost also made its presence known as the sound of footsteps walking along the road. Travelers passing by would suddenly hear the sound of someone walking next to them, trudging through the leaves on the side of the road. Of course, when they looked over to see who was there, no one was visible. The footsteps remained a mystery but were always encountered near the church, by both individuals and groups.

One of the bizarre incidents involving the Rock Creek Ghost involved a sheriff and his deputy who happened to be passing near the church during the early evening hours. They witnessed an object that they described as looking like a carpet bag (an old-fashioned carryall, covered in a piece of carpet) rolling down the road in their direction. Both men drew their weapons and opened fire at the weird object. When the smoke from their guns cleared, the entity had vanished into the dusk, with no sign that it had ever been there at all.

In most cases, though, when the ghost did not appear as a dog, it remained invisible. One night, a group of boys who were intent on hunting down the spirit heard footsteps traveling along with them. In an attempt to get to the bottom of the mystery, they lit a match in hopes of catching a glimpse of their odd fellow traveler. As soon as the match flared up, it was immediately extinguished – just as if unseen lips had blown it out! Terrified, the boys fled the scene.

THE ILLINOIS IRON FURNACE

The last fires were put out and the last of the equipment was hauled away from the Illinois Iron Furnace back in 1883 but even today, this lonely site in the woods still bears scars from the time when iron ore mining was a thriving industry in Hardin County. The reconstructed ruins stand close to the side of a steep hill and not so many years ago, curiosity-seekers who came to this place were able to carry away

A VINTAGE PHOTO OF THE OLD IRON FURNACE

weathered pieces of iron ore, broken chunks of limestone and bits of waste slag from the furnace. As time has passed, these souvenirs have vanished, along with the community that once surrounded the furnace.

The Illinois Furnace was once one of the most important industries in Southern Illinois. Located at Hog Thief Creek, about four miles north of Rosiclare, the furnace was constructed in 1837. During its first 37 years of operation, it was in continuous use but by 1874, the fires burned only sporadically. In 1883, it was closed for good, bringing an end to an era in the region.

The furnace was operated by Chalon Gard & Co. of Indiana for many years. Then in 1872, it was sold to the Illinois Furnace Company, a corporation chartered in Indiana on April 6 of that year. The ore used in the furnace came from the nearby hills, where the pits still remain to this day. The ore was made up from limonite, which was about fifty percent metallic iron. The ore was mined by workmen and then hauled by wagon to the hilltop just above the furnace. Other men from the vicinity provided the charcoal for fuel. It was burned at places convenient to the wood supply and also hauled to the furnace by wagon. When the furnace was in operation, it required about 1,800 bushels of charcoal daily.

When it was being run at full capacity, the Illinois Furnace produced an average of about nine tons of pig iron every day. During the Civil War, it was the principal source of iron for the United States Navy yards that were located down the Ohio River at Mound City. The iron was hauled each day by wagon to the river and then shipped downstream. According to local tradition, pig iron bars can still be found on old farms and along forgotten roads in the area where they were dumped off by teamsters who needed to lighten their loads.

While the furnace provided work for many who already lived in the region, thanks to the need for ore and charcoal, few of the natives possessed the skills necessary to operate the furnace itself. Because of this, most of the workers had to be brought in from places where an iron industry had already been developed, including a number of European countries. Thanks to the influx of workers, a small village sprang up across the road from the furnace.

The community grew to the point that a post office was established at Illinois Furnace on October 2, 1846. The village also boasted several small stores, a tavern and boarding house, blacksmith shop, carpenter shop, saloon and more. The town thrived thanks to the fact that the men were paid well and the saloon and eating places did a brisk business. Eventually, the village had a population of over 1,000 souls. The town lasted as long as the furnace did but when the industry here died, the village died with it.

After the company was closed down, the stone furnace fell into ruin. It slowly crumbled apart and collapsed and was eventually overtaken by the forest. In 1933, the structure was badly damaged when workmen blasted some of it away for use in building local roads. However, in 1967, the huge oven was rebuilt and six years later, it earned a spot on the National Register of Historic Places. Historians and volunteers carefully reconstructed the furnace to its original condition, consisting of a large chimney that stands about fifty feet high. The round core of the furnace was about eight feet in diameter and it was enclosed and strengthened by the chimney that was made from limestone bricks. Power for operating the furnace machinery was supplied by steam engines.

Today, nothing of the town remains, save for a well that provides water for a small picnic area that was built at the site. There is a small historic marker that reads, in part: "Here is the site of the first iron furnace in Illinois. Rebuilt in 1967, the furnace stands as a memorial to the community of 100 families who lived and worked in this pleasant valley. Only the ghosts remain but imagination can rekindle the hot fires of the furnace, rebuild the company store and echo the laughter of children from the surrounding hills."

Some claim that it's not only imagination that conjures up sounds from the past. Many believe the surrounding hills and woods still echo with the voices of the workers from the furnace and of the people who lived in the nearby village. Many claim to have heard laughter, shouts and eerie voices that cannot be explained. Occasionally, the clang of metal or the slam of a wooden door is heard, even though no structures are anywhere close to the site. Have the events of long ago left an impression behind on this historic spot?

The bridge near the furnace has also been the scene of several strange occurrences, each involving an older woman who vanishes shortly after being spotted. The first reported sighting took place in 1966 when a man traveling past in a pickup truck saw the woman standing in the center of the bridge. He slowed down to give her time to move out of the way and as she walked slowly along, she faded away and vanished. He was so unnerved by the event that he told several of his friends about it and learned that he was not the only one to see the old woman. Other encounters took place in subsequent years and she is believed to still make appearances on the bridge today. Who she might have been in life remains a mystery – likely some long-ago resident of the village – but today she remains as the last, albeit intangible, link to a part of Illinois history that few still remember.

ANNA BIXBY'S SPOOK LIGHT

One of the greatest mysteries of southern Illinois involves a woman named Anna Bixby (or Bigsby, according to some accounts). There are so many stories and legends, and various versions of the legends, about this woman that it is impossible to know what to believe. According to the census records of Hardin County, Anna was a real person and it has been generally accepted that she discovered a cure for what was once called "milk sickness." Amazingly, she did so more than sixty years before the medical establishment acknowledged that the source of the sickness was the plant that Anna had identified long before.

Anna Bixby was a talented midwife and healer who visited the sick, tended the wounded and traveled around what was then a wild and untamed region to help those who were ill. She likely had no formal medical education, nor was it likely she could read or write. Anna came to Illinois from Tennessee with her husband, Isaac Hobbs. Her medical training came from the study of herbs and folk healing techniques. When a strange disease began to break out in the region, killing both people and cattle, Anna was baffled. She watched, treated the sufferers as best she could, observed the illness and studied the habits of those who were stricken. As hard as she worked, though, she was unable to stop the scourge.

The number of deaths increased alarmingly and entire herds of cattle were wiped out. The superstitious came to believe that the illness was caused by a poison that was being scattered by a witch. There was even talk of retaliation against various persons who were suspected of witchcraft. Anna did not believe the illness was caused by magic. She felt that the cause of the sickness was likely a plant that the cattle were eating and then passing on to people through their milk. Anna spread the word to the surrounding communities that they should refrain from drinking milk until after the frost. Her warning saved many human lives but it did not save the young cattle that the settlers depended on. Greater tragedy had been avoided for the time being, but the sickness was sure to return in the spring. Anna would do anything to solve the mystery of the disease and she became even more determined after her husband fell ill and died from the milk sickness.

Anna puzzled over the problem through the winter and when spring came, she set off into the woods and fields to look for the plant that had caused so much misery. The solution finally came from an elderly Native American woman called "Aunt Shawnee." She was also a herbalist and healer and showed Anna a plant that we now call "milkweed." The older woman told Anna that the plant had caused the same symptoms as the milk sickness did in her own tribe. The plant had killed many of the Shawnee cattle and she told Anna that it was probably what she was looking for.

Anna again spread the word and according to tradition, troops of men and boys prowled the woods, destroying milkweed for many years afterward. The plague was finally wiped out and in 1928, more than sixty years later, medical scholars acknowledged Anna's find as the cause of the ailment. For this reason, she has long been considered something of a legend in Southern Illinois as a healer and medical worker. In fact, the Anna Bixby Women's Center in Harrisburg, Illinois, is named in her honor --- but this was not the end of her story.

There is no question that Anna became a legend after her discovery of the source of the milk sickness and perhaps because of this, mystery surrounds the next great incident in her life, which took place during her second marriage to Eason Bixby. Legend holds that Bixby was involved in a number of criminal enterprises and while are some elements of truth to the story, much of it turned out to more fancy than fact. The legend originated in the book *The Ballads of the Bluff* by Judge W.M. Hall, who allegedly had a diary that belonged to Anna Bixby. Historians have since disputed much of the story, although it was believed that Hall was simply passing along stories that he had heard. Here is the basic version:

Legend holds that John Murrell and his gang, along with James Ford and other disreputable characters, distilled whiskey and made counterfeit money in a headquarters in Hardin County that has since become known as Bixby's Cave. Enos [sic] Bixby, Anna's husband, took over after these men were driven out or killed and continued their operations, along with committing robberies and stealing timber. Bixby married Anna when she was an old woman because he hoped to steal her money from her. Finally, he attempted to kill her by tying her up with ropes and heavy chain and pushing her off a bluff. As it happened, though, she fell into a tree and managed to escape. Not long after, Anna died suddenly and she was buried with the rope and chain that her husband tried to kill her with. Her ghost has haunted her burial site ever since, often appearing as a shimmering light.

Despite the popularity of the tale, it contains only a few elements of the truth. The time period when all of this allegedly occurred seems to be the biggest problem with the story. Bixby's Cave did (and does still) exist, however, after 1811 it is unlikely that it would have been big enough to house a moonshine distillery and certainly not a counterfeiting operation. The cave was heavily damaged in the earthquake that rocked the New Madrid Fault in 1811 and afterward it was much less accessible than it had been before. Several of the men who were involved in the criminal aspects of the story were dead long before Anna married Eason Bixby and others were children during the time of some of the other criminals' careers. If the story had involved these men, then it would have had to take place in the 1820s. This wasn't possible since Anna's first husband did not die until 1845 and Anna lived into the 1870s.

However, historians do believe that there may have been a grain of truth to the story but it became muddled when it was told and re-told using well-known outlaws as the key players in the tale, when the real culprits may have been much lesser known. There were counterfeiters operating in Hardin County at the time and it has been learned that Anna's second husband was involved with criminals.

In 1935, a Hardin County newspaper published what was likely a more accurate account of Anna's escape from her murderous husband. The writer of the account, Charles L. Foster, had left Hardin

THE OLD COUNTERFEITER'S CAVE AT ROCK CREEK THAT HAS COME TO BE KNOWN AS ANNA BIXBY'S CAVE OVER THE YEARS.

County in the 1880s but had grown up in the Rock Creek area, and had been a neighbor of Anna Bixby. He had been born in 1863 and vaguely remembered Eason Bixby, which seems to date the escape to the late 1860s, in the years following the Civil War.

According to the account, a rider came to the Bixby household late one night during a terrible thunderstorm. He called out to the house that someone needed Anna's medical skills. She mounted the rider's second horse and they rode off into the woods. The trail was shrouded in darkness, thanks to the heavy storm clouds overhead, and Anna soon became disoriented and unsure of the route. However, at one point during the ride and saw a flash of lightning illuminate the face of the mysterious rider-- it was her husband Eason.

When he realized that she had discovered his identity, Bixby brought the horses to a halt and quickly bound and gagged Anna. When she heard the jingle of chains being removed from the saddlebags, Anna became so frightened that she began to ran into the dark woods. As she plunged into the forest, her fear became even stronger as she realized that she had no idea where she was. The storm continued to rage, sending rain lashing down on her and causing the wind to whip through the trees in a wild fury. Anna ran for some distance and then suddenly, the ground beneath her vanished as she tumbled over a large bluff and crashed to the ground far below. The fall broke the ropes that bound her hands but it also broke some of her bones, seriously injuring her. Nevertheless, Anna managed to crawl a short distance to a fallen tree and slithered behind it.

A few moments later, a light appeared in the darkness at the top of the bluff and Eason Bixby came into view carrying a burning torch. He climbed down from the top of the rocks and searched in vain for Anna. After a few minutes, he returned to his horse and rode away.

Once he was gone, Anna began crawling and stumbling out of the forest. It took her until sunrise to find a nearby farmhouse but when she reached it, she found herself at the doorstep of friends -- only a few houses away from her own. They quickly took her in and she told them the story of what had happened.

Bixby was arrested and taken to the jail in Elizabethtown, from which he escaped. He was later captured again in Missouri, but once again, he escaped. This time, he disappeared for good and was never seen again.

Anna lived on in the Rock Creek community until the 1870s and when she died, she was buried next to her first husband with only a simple "A" inscribed on her tombstone.

But the legend of Anna Bixby lives on...

The legend states that her husband wanted to do away with her because of a fortune that she had managed to collect over the years. What her nest egg may have amounted to is unknown but it was doubtlessly not what we would think of as a fortune today. The legend further states that when Anna learned of Eason's greed, she hid the money away somewhere, just before he attempted to kill her. It is believed that the hiding place was the cave beside Rock Creek in Hooven Hollow, which was also said to have been the hideout of the outlaw gang.

The cave is still known as Anna Bixby Cave and it is along the bluff, in the vicinity of the cave, where people have reported seeing a strange light appear over the years. The large, glowing light moves in and out of the trees and among the rocks, vanishing and then re-appearing without explanation. Some believe that the light is the ghost of Anna Bixby, still watching over the treasure that she hid away many years ago.

One of the most detailed accounts of the Bixby ghost light was collected by folklorist Charles Neely in 1938. The story of the spook light was told to him by Reverend E.N. Hall, who once served the Rock Creek Church and who had a number of brushes with the uncanny in this part of Hardin County. One evening in his younger days, Hall and a friend of his named Hobbs, walked over to a nearby farm to escort two of the girls who lived there to church. When they got to the house it was dark and unoccupied. It appeared that the girls left without them. The two young men stood around for a few moments, wondering what to do.

As they stood talking at the edge of the yard, they glanced toward the darkened house, which stood on a small knoll with a hollow that ran away from the gate to the left for about one hundred yards and then joined with another hollow that came back to the right side of the gate. Hobbs was looking eastward along the bluff when he saw what he described as a "ball of fire about the size of a washtub" going very fast along the east hollow.

At first, the young men thought that it might be someone on a horse carrying a lantern, but then they realized it was moving much too fast for that. The light followed the hollow to the left of the gate and along a small curve where one hollow met the other. Then it followed the opposite hollow and came right up the bank where the two men were standing. It paused, motionless, about thirty feet away from them and began to burn down smaller and smaller, turning red before it simply vanished.

The two young men decided not to go to church. Instead they went directly to the farm where they had been working and went to bed. The next morning, at the breakfast table, they told the farmer, a man named Patten, what they had seen the night before. He laughed at them and said that it had just been a "mineral light" carried by the wind. However, he had no explanation for how fast the light had moved or for the fact that there had been no wind the previous evening. He also couldn't explain why the light seemed to follow the two hollows and then stop in place and wink out.

Later, Hall had the chance to speak with a woman named Mrs. Walton, who owned the farm where the light had appeared. She told him the story of Anna Bixby, who had once owned the property and who had hidden her fortune in a cave. Mrs. Walton always believed that the spook light was Anna's ghost, checking to see that her money was still safely hidden away. She said she had seen the light on many occasions and it always disappeared into the cave.

Hall asked her why, if she knew where the money was hidden, she had never bothered to go and get it. "I would," Mrs. Walton answered, "if I thought that Granny Bixby wanted me to have it."

LINGERING SPIRIT OF FORT MASSAC
METROPOLIS, ILLINOIS

Located along the Ohio River at one of the southernmost points of Illinois is the reconstructed remains of Fort Massac, an outpost that dates back to the early days of the region's history. The land where the current fort stands has seen more than its share of tumultuous events over the centuries, including war, exploration, treachery, death and at least one murder that have left a haunting presence behind.

The first fort was erected at the site in 1757. In order to protect their communication lines and supply routes leading to forts on the upper Ohio River, French commanders in North America scouted the area adjacent to the mouth of the Tennessee River and built a suitable outpost there. Under the command of Captain Charles Phillipe Aubry, the French named it Fort Ascension. It was strengthened two years later and renamed Fort Massiac in honor of French Admiral Claude Louis d'Espinchal, marquis de Massiac. The French held the fort until 1765, when it was surrendered to the British under the terms of the treaty in 1763 that ended the French and Indian War in North America.

The British had plans to occupy the fort, but no garrison was ever moved into the area, leaving it empty for nearly thirty years. The fort was only used once for military purposes on June 28, 1778, when George Rogers Clark invaded the Northwest Territory for the state of Virginia during the Revolutionary War. Clark, with 160 men under his command, landed north of Massac, a short distance from the fort, on their way to successfully capture the British troops stationed at Vincennes.

In 1794, President George Washington ordered General "Mad Anthony" Wayne to rebuild and fortify the post. A detail of men under Captain Thomas Doyle arrived there in June 1794 and spent the next several months on various

A RECONSTRUCTED FORT MASSAC AS IT LOOKS TODAY

construction projects. In October, they renamed it Fort Massac, an Anglicized version of Massiac. Over the course of the next few years, the fort became a major point of entry for settlers coming down the Ohio River. Fort Massac was placed under the direct command of Alexander Hamilton in 1799. Plans to garrison as many as 1,000 men at the fort in response to a French threat were abandoned in favor of a new fort downriver at Grand Chain, but a smaller garrison was established under the command of Captain Daniel Bissell in 1802.

In 1803, Fort Massac became one of the many recruiting points used by Meriwether Lewis and William Clark as they prepared for their western exploration of the country. On November 11, 1803, Lewis and Clark arrived at Fort Massac where they expected to meet eight soldiers who had volunteered for the Corps of Discovery while the expedition had been in Tennessee. The soldiers never appeared but Lewis did hire a local woodsman named George Drouillard, the son of a French settler and a Shawnee Indian mother. Drouillard was assigned to find the soldiers and report with them to a fort near present-day Wood River, Illinois, where the expedition planned to winter before heading west. Only two volunteers from Fort Massac met Lewis' standards and on November 13, the Corps of Discovery left the fort on its way west.

In 1805, one of the most volatile figures in American history, Aaron Burr, came to Fort Massac, allegedly in hopes of enlisting a conspirator in his scheme to create his own nation west of the Allegheny Mountains. Burr was a former U.S. Vice President and according to the accusations again him, planned to create an independent nation in the center of North America or in the southwest regions near Mexico. His plan was to take possession of nearly 40,000 acres in the Texas Territory that had been leased to him by the Spanish. When the expected war with Spain broke out, his army would seize the land and keep it for themselves, which was illegal by rules of warfare. Thomas Jefferson had Burr arrested and indicted for treason, even though no real evidence of any conspiracy existed. Most of the claims against him were made by those who distrusted Burr but had no real proof that he had plans to create an empire in the West over which he would rule.

AARON BURR

General James Wilkinson was one of Burr's most important co-conspirators. Though it was eventually discovered that his involvement was most likely an attempt to further his own personal and political goals, he worked closely with Burr to develop a plan for secession. The commanding general of the Army at the time, Wilkinson was known for his corrupt practices, including his attempt to separate Kentucky and Tennessee from the union during the 1780s. Burr persuaded President Thomas Jefferson to appoint Wilkinson to the position of governor of the Territory of Louisiana. It was with Wilkinson that Burr met at Fort Massac, although exactly what the two men discussed remains unknown. Wilkinson would later come to betray Burr by revealing his plot to Jefferson and denying all involvement in the conspiracy.

Burr was brought to trial but was released after his accusers failed to prove their conspiracy claims. With his career in shambles, he fled to Europe but later returned to America and lived under assumed names until his death in September 1836. After his connection with Burr was exposed, James Wilkinson was twice investigated by Congress. Following an unsuccessful court-martial, ordered by President James Madison in 1811, he returned to his military command in New Orleans. During the War of 1812, he was posted to Canada where his only major offensive, a campaign against Montreal, was unsuccessful. He was discharged from active service and died in Mexico in December 1825.

The next great events in Fort Massac's history were the devastating New Madrid earthquakes in the winter of 1811-1812. During that season, a series of massive quakes shook the nation from southeastern Missouri to Boston, New Orleans, and Washington. Centered in the Mississippi Valley region, they were the strongest known seismic events in North America east of the Rocky Mountains. They caused destruction like nothing that had been seen before or since.

The earthquakes began at about 2:00 a.m. on the morning of December 16, 1811. The ground shook and heaved like waves on the ocean and the violent shock was accompanied by a loud sound like distant thunder, but more hoarse and vibrating, witnesses said. The violent trembling caused roofs to collapse, chimneys to fall, items in homes to be thrown about and numerous injuries. Rocks and dirt collapsed along the bluffs of the Mississippi and in some places, sand and water were forced to the surface in frightening eruptions. In the darkness before dawn, no one had any idea just how much damage was being done. Between the time of the initial earthquake and sunrise, a number of lighter shocks occurred. Another violent shaking occurred just as the sun was coming up. The local populace was thrown into a state of terror. People began to flee in every direction, perhaps believing that there was less danger if they could get away from the rivers. Many were injured, not only from the shock of the earthquakes, but in their haste in trying to escape.

Thousands of minor shocks and occasional stronger earthquakes were experienced during the following days and weeks. On January 23, 1812, at about 9:00 a.m., an earthquake comparable to the one in December took place. It was reportedly felt as far away as Boston. According to many accounts, the earth remained in continual agitation until February 4, when another strong quake occurred. Four additional events took place over the course of the next few days and then on February 7, around 4:00 a.m., another violent concussion shook the region. One witness, Eliza Bryan wrote: "The awful darkness of the atmosphere, and the violence of the tempestuous thundering noise that accompanied it, together with all of the other phenomena mentioned as attending the former ones, formed a scene, the description of which would require the most sublimely fanciful imagination."

It was as if the gates of hell had opened in southeastern Missouri and southern Illinois.

The earthquake caused severe damage at Fort Massac that took months to repair. For a short time afterwards, the fort became the headquarters for the 24th Infantry. In 1814, Fort Massac was evacuated and its garrison was moved to St. Louis. After falling into a state of ruin, local settlers stripped the fort of its wood and bricks.

For nearly a century, only a few scattered remnants of the fort remained. In 1903, the Daughters of the American Revolution purchased 24 acres around the site and five years later, it was officially dedicated as Illinois' first state park. The site was excavated by a team of archaeologists in 1939 and the first replica of Fort Massac was built in the early 1970s. It was replaced with what was considered to be a more accurate reconstruction of the 1757 fort in 2003 and remains a fascinating spot for history buffs today.

And Fort Massac is definitely of interest to ghost enthusiasts, too.

The ghost story connected to the fort dates to 1808 when the body of a man named Dillworth was discovered on the Ohio riverbank near the fort with its throat cut. The murder was investigated but officers at the fort ruled that the death was a suicide, despite the fact that no bloody knife was discovered at the scene. Many wondered if the true story of Dillworth's death was being covered up for some reason.

ONE OF THE REBUILT STRUCTURES AT FORT MASSAC

If he was murdered, and his killer never brought to justice, this might explain why he has been haunting Fort Massac ever since.

The old visitor's center at the park was rumored to be haunted for many years. Staff members and visitors reported hearing the sound of footsteps, whispers, and doors that opened and closed by themselves. After the old building was torn down and replaced by a new one, the haunting has reportedly moved into the replica of the 1757 fort that was completed in 2003. Even though the structure is new and has no connection to the past, Dillworth's ghost doesn't seem to know the difference. The sounds of his heavy boots are still being heard stomping up and down in the rooms of the fort, banging doors and making a general nuisance.

If the spirit still lingers here because a killer was never brought to justice, then it's possible that this haunting may continue indefinitely since the murderer – and his victim – have both been lost to the pages of history.

"AGED COUPLE IS SLAIN IN HOME" GHOSTS OF THE HUNDLEY MURDERS CARBONDALE, ILLINOIS

Although more than eighty years have passed since two murders were committed in a historic home in Carbondale, those who have lived and worked there have come to believe that the spirits of the dead still linger within its walls. The legend of the house claims that "you can bury the bodies in Oakland Cemetery, but you can't make them rest there." Such stories are spread about a myriad of allegedly haunted houses in the state of Illinois, but few of them have seen the kind of carnage and violence that occurred in the Hundley House in December 1928.

John Charles Hundley was a prominent wealthy citizen of Carbondale at the time of his death. He had been the city's mayor in 1907 and 1908 and enjoyed many friendships and business acquaintances throughout the area. But Hundley's life had not always been perfect. In fact, in 1893, he had committed murder. At that time, Hundley had killed a music teacher in town, but was acquitted by a jury after pleading the "unwritten law," meaning that he had murdered the man who had been sleeping with his wife. The incident led to him divorcing his wife, which caused bitter feelings between him and his son, Victor. Although the problems between them had supposedly been settled years before the elder Hundley's death, some witnesses would later claim that the quarrel continued. This led to Victor becoming the chief suspect in his father's murder.

Hundley remarried a few years later and in 1915, he and his new wife, Luella, purchased a lot at the

52

DOUBLE MURDER HERE

CAIRO SHERIFF PLEADS GUILTY TO LIQUOR PLOT

Leslie Roche Surprises Both Sides by Sudden Plea

Vengeance Leads Boy to Hammer Killing

C'DALE SPENT $2000 STAGING HALLOWE'EN FETE

However, Surplus of More than $500 Exists, Report Shows

J. C. HUNDLEY AND WIFE SLAIN BY MYSTERIOUS ASSAILANT AT PRETENTIOUS HOME LAST NIGHT

corner of Maple and Main streets and constructed what became a sprawling and luxurious home.

Luella Hundley was the daughter of Ruffin Harrison, one of the founders of the city of Herrin and the owner of numerous coalmines in the region. She was the sister of George Harrison, president of Herrin's First National Bank. She was said to have been an accomplished musician and very involved in local charity work. Perhaps for these reasons, she was regarded as having no enemies, which made her murder all the more puzzling.

The lives of the Hundleys were destroyed just before midnight on Wednesday, December 12, 1928. Investigators believed that John Hundley was murdered first. His body was found in an upstairs bedroom, dressed only in a nightshirt and socks. He had been shot six times from behind by a .45-caliber revolver. His face had been ripped apart as the bullets exited his head. Mrs. Hundley was killed downstairs. She had been shot twice in the back of the head and once in the heart. She was killed in a rear stairway as she was apparently going to the aid of her husband. Her body had rolled into the kitchen and a pencil was resting next to her left hand. An unfinished letter on the table in an adjoining room was mute evidence of what she was doing when she was alarmed by the sound

VICTIMS AND SCENE OF MURDER

The diagram at the left shows how J. C. Hundley, former mayor of Carbondale, Ill., and Mrs. Hundley were slain in their home there. The broken line marks the course the murderer took from the bedroom where he killed Hundley to the first floor where he shot Mrs. Hundley. He escaped out the back door. Mr. and Mrs. Hundley are shown at the right. Below, the Hundley home.

of gunshots.

According to newspaper reports, police officers, called by neighbors across the street who heard the shots being fired, arrived at the scene within minutes. Police Chief Joe Montgomery told the press the following morning that robbery seemed to be the most likely motive for the murders, even though there was no sign of a break-in. The only evidence that pointed to a robbery in the house, which contained valuable artwork, expensive furnishings, and a large amount of cash, was the discovery of an empty pocketbook on the floor near Luella Hundley's body. Neighbors told police that they believed the purse was usually kept in a writing desk downstairs. For this reason, and others still to be discovered, the police soon began to believe that there were other, darker motives for the crime.

On the morning of December 13, police investigators thoroughly searched the Hundley house. Tracking dogs were brought in and placed on the trail of the killer. Four times the dogs led their handlers straight to the home of John Charles Hundley's son, Victor, a prominent coal dealer in the city. Investigators believed that the killer might have been known to Mrs. Hundley because it appeared that she had opened the door and let him into the house, as she would have done, even at that late hour, for her step-son.

LUELLA HUNDLEY'S BODY WAS FOUND AT THE BOTTOM OF THESE STEPS. SHE HAD BEEN SHOT IN THE HEAD AND HEART.

Victor also seemed to have a motive for the murders. At an inquest that was held that afternoon, Joab Goodall, a friend of the Hundleys and the last person to see them alive, testified that the elder Hundley had recently told him that he planned to make a new will and disinherit Victor "because he was no good." A bitter feud had long existed between father and son and, while allegedly patched up, it had possibly flared into existence again. If this was the case, then Victor Hundley stood to lose a great deal of money if his father changed his will. With an estate worth more than $350,000, Victor would be left with only his trust fund, which amounted to less than $15,000.

Goodall also told the coroner's jury that the Hundleys had been in excellent spirits when he visited with them on the night of their murders. They were planning a motor trip on Sunday to their winter home in Florida. Goodall left the Hundley home around 8:00 p.m. on Wednesday evening and stated that Mrs. Hundley had locked the rear door behind him. Officers who arrived at the house four hours later found this door unlocked.

Another neighbor, Olga Kasper, who lived next door to the Hundleys, testified at the inquest that she had heard the fatal shots fired and had seen the lights in the house turned off immediately after. She said she heard someone running past her home, coming from the direction of the Hundley house and toward Victor's house, a short time later. The person was so close to the house, she said, that they stumbled against a radio ground wire.

Investigators from the Jackson County sheriff's office searched the route described by Mrs. Kasper and followed it to Victor Hundley's home, which was just 200 yards away. Along the path, officers found several slips of paper that were presumed to have been lost in flight. One paper, dated December 5, was a notice of the termination of a partnership between Mr. and Mrs. J.C. Hundley with Victor Hundley in his coal business. Another paper was a bank deposit slip, the back of which bore notes that figured out the interest on a loan that amounted to $532. The note was in Luella's handwriting and at the top of the paper was written "Vic."

Victor Hundley was brought in for questioning and subjected to seven hours of interrogation by Sheriff William Flanigan and his investigators. His house was also searched and a bloodstained khaki shirt was discovered. Hundley claimed that he had been wearing the shirt when he was told about the crime. Police officers awakened him and told him that his father and stepmother had been murdered and asked him to come to the house. While he was wearing the shirt, Hundley said, he had picked up the body of his stepmother. According to investigators, Hundley had never touched the body, so the blood had to have come from somewhere else. Suddenly, Victor recalled that he had been wearing the shirt while quail hunting and that was where the blood had come from.

Victor denied that there was any trouble between him and his father. They had gone through some problems in the past, he admitted, but that was all over. He told investigators that on Wednesday night, he had been home all evening, reading and playing with his son. He had gone to bed early and was awakened by the police. Hundley also admitted that he owned a .45-caliber revolver, but he claimed that he had recently loaned it to his father. A search of both of the Hundley houses failed to turn up the gun. To this day, it has never been discovered.

After hours of exhaustive questioning, Victor broke into tears and cried out, "Oh my God! This is terrible!" He again swore that had had nothing to do with the murders. He was taken home, but was placed under house arrest as the investigation continued.

On December 15, immediately following the funeral of the Hundleys, Victor was arrested for their murders. While the coroner's jury was unable to name the killer, Fletcher Lewis, the state's attorney, believed that he could prove that Victor was guilty in a court of law. Unfortunately, it wouldn't work out that way and on December 31, Lewis was forced to let Victor go. He filed a motion during Hundley's preliminary hearing to dismiss the case due to insufficient evidence. The judge sustained the disappointed prosecutor's motion.

Lewis made a statement to reporters after the hearing. "While the facts and circumstances learned from the investigation amply justified the holding of Victor Hundley and the filing of a complaint charging him with murder... I have decided to prosecute this particular case no further," he said.

Then, he added, "I feel quite sure that the atrociousness of this crime will compel the conscience of the person who committed it to someday make public his guilt."

But Lewis was wrong. No one ever came forward and the killer of J.C. and Luella Hundley was never found. The case languished in limbo for a time and then was relegated to the "unsolved" section of the city's law enforcement files. There were many who believed that Victor Hundley had gotten away with murder, but they couldn"t prove it. Victor never spoke of the crimes again and he continued to live on in the Carbondale area for the rest of his life. Eight decades later, the murders of Carbondale's former mayor and his wife remain unsolved.

And perhaps, for this very reason, many have come to believe that their spirits do not rest in peace.

THE HUNDLEY HOUSE TODAY

The Hundley mansion at the corner of Maple and Main streets remained empty for two years after the murders. The only physical reminder of the horrific crimes that occurred there was a bullet hole in a wall near where Luella's body had been found, but the memories of that night remained in the minds of people in town.

The house remained vacant until 1930, when it was purchased by Edwin William Vogler, Sr., who bought the house and all of its contents from the Hundley estate. It remained in the Vogler family until 1972, when it was sold to a family named Simonds, who converted the huge residence into a gift shop with apartments upstairs. In 2000, it was sold to Victoria Sprehe, who ran the gift shop for five years before selling it to make more time for her young son.

Rumors dating back many years claim that the Hundleys still haunt this house. A number of past owners and tenants in the building have had strange encounters that they are unable to explain. One former resident told of loud knocking sounds that reverberated in her room at night and the faint sound of the downstairs piano as the keys tinkled by themselves. Her family also recalled hearing footsteps going up and down the stairs, as if the killer was doomed to repeat his walk to J.C. Hundley's bedroom again and again.

Former owner Victoria Sprehe said that whenever she was alone in the house, lights would turn on by themselves, as if someone were watching over her. She said that she believed that Luella's ghost followed her home from work on at least one occasion. Walking into the empty house, she heard pots and pans clanging and noticed that lights were on in the kitchen. However, she noted, "It's not like a scary presence. It's a very peaceful vibe."

Perhaps it was not a scary presence, but it could be unnerving. Sprehe was sometimes bothered by a door that opened by itself and by footsteps that she heard walking on the stairs – the same stairs where a previous family also reported hearing disembodied steps. Tenants who lived in apartments on the upper floor also told stories of the creaking stairs and what seemed to be the sound of boots, or heavy shoes, clomping on the wooden risers. One tenant laughed and stated that this was only the sound of the old house settling and then lost his grin when he admitted that he had never heard of a house that settled in just that way.

Victoria Sprehe's daughter, Nina Bucciarelli, also recounted odd incidents in the house, like the front porch swing that would move by itself, even when there was no wind. Sprehe's husband had also noticed this odd occurrence. Nina had her own explanation for the swing's strange movement. "As night, if you drive by the porch swing, it's just swinging away. I think Mr. and Mrs. Hundley still like to swing at night," she said.

And perhaps she's right, because if the stories of the past decades are to be believed, the Hundleys have not yet departed from the house they called their own – and the place where their lives were taken away too soon.

CENTRAL ILLINOIS

GHOSTS OF THE HAUNTED OPRY
WINCHESTER, ILLINOIS
BY LOREN HAMILTON

It's strange at times how you can stumble into a haunted location; that's what I did in Rural Scott County. In my day job, as one of my duties as law enforcement coordinator for Crimestoppers of Morgan/Scott counties, I was approached a few years ago to see if I would be interested in The Great River Road Opry holding a benefit fundraiser show for our Crimestoppers program. I quickly agreed, hoping to get a stronger foothold for the program in Scott County. I had my doubts about whether we would draw a crowd in such a rural location so I was pleasantly surprised when I pulled into a jammed parking lot on the night of the event. The old building on the Hillview blacktop was said to hold 400 people and I think we were bursting at the seams that evening.

The Opry was originally constructed as an airplane hangar at Scott Air Force base near Belleville, Illinois, in 1945. In later years, it was moved to its present location and was home to two different seed corn companies. Hard times closed the last company in the late 1980s, but not before one of the employees committed suicide inside the old hanger.

The building was empty for over a decade before my new friend Charles Craver and his wife decided to turn it into a country music venue. It was a huge task to take out the corn conveyor belt that ran the entire length of the building, add a stage and install a dressing room behind it, but with the help of friends and band members, the work was completed and the Great River Road Opry was born.

58

THE GREAT RIVER ROAD OPRY

It was common for a loud burst of music and happiness to fill the river valley every weekend. On the night that I was there for the Crimestoppers benefit, I not only had the pleasure of meeting my hosts, the Cravers, but also singer Connie Bugg, and her husband and his band as well. At the conclusion of their show, they asked me about my interest in ghosts, which had gotten around in this small area. They began telling me tales of the hauntings at the Opry. They said they had heard noises and seen things that led them to believe at least one of the spirits of the building was that of a former guitar player named Jim. Jim was one of the most enthusiastic members of the band and led much of the work to convert the old hangar into a music venue. But sadly, he didn't live long enough to enjoy playing to the packed audiences. The Buggs and my friend, Del Dawdy, who had helped me on many ghost hunts, had heard some EVP recordings made in the building and believed the voice on the tape was Jim's.

After hearing their stories, I asked to do an investigation of my own. I contacted my friend, Kelly Davis, and members of her team to join Del, Connie, Charles Craver and myself. I can't say we saw much activity that first night but it was enough to convince us to come back another time. Each time we returned, things became more active and later, I put the Opry on a list of public locations we began visiting with small groups through the Illinois Hauntings tours.

During one visit, on a rainy night in the spring of 2010, two reporters from a local newspaper, the *Journal-Courier*, asked to come along. I was happy to oblige since the staff has been very kind to me over the years and offered plenty of coverage for many things I have done. As it turned out, the reporters had to leave early that evening so that they could make their deadline for the next day's edition. Of course, they left just before things started getting interesting.

During a late night EVP session, the entire group was on the stage asking questions and using K-2 meters (small devices that measure changes in electromagnetic fields, which may be manipulated by ghosts) while I sat in the audience on the floor. I'm not sure what question was asked but I, along with everyone else, heard footsteps near the front door. There was a wooden wheelchair ramp nearby and we all heard the sound of heavy, hard soled shoes on the ramp. It was so loud and vibrant that I dismissed it at first; I thought it must be one of the reporters coming back to join us.... but why didn't I hear their car pull back in the lot?

It was then that we all heard a loud crash come from the kitchen area where concessions were sold at the Opry. That crash caused a couple of investigators to flee the building. They had heard enough from Jim, or whoever it was, for that night! Del joined me in checking the area by the door, the kitchen area, and finally the parking lot but there was no one there and nothing out of the ordinary. Nothing had been upset in the kitchen and there was no sign that anyone had been there. We definitely heard the strange sounds, though, and I later posted the audio clip from that night on my website.

I returned to the Opry in the fall of 2010. On this night, the group was made up of two young novices, a couple from nearby Springfield, and a local doctor. They joined Del, Connie and myself for the night. During another EVP session in the old dressing room behind the stage, the group had a long "interview" with the resident spirits. In all the years that I have been investigating the paranormal, I have never experienced such constant responses to our direct line of questioning. We were led to believe that we were communicating with the gentleman who took his life in the building many decades before. He was trying the best way he could to explain the reasons behind his dark decision.

After more than an hour, it was time to take a much-needed break. When we returned to the same area afterwards to see if the activity was still going on we weren't disappointed. Although we didn't have as strong or direct answers to our questions, we did witness the door behind the stage open three times on command – each time in the opposite direction that the wind could have moved it. We also recorded an odd sound at the opposite end of the building, a sound that resembled a needle running on the outside track of an old LP record. Was it perhaps the same noise a conveyor belt would make? The old conveyor belt from the seed corn companies was located in that exact spot more than three decades before.

Sadly, the rough economic times of recent years took their toll on the Opry and it has since closed its doors. The building now sits quiet and still – but is it empty? Weather and time is wreaking havoc on the old building and I hope to go back before the place is gone for good. If given the chance, I invite you to not pass up the opportunity to come along and see what the spirits are trying to tell us before their voices are silenced forever.

HAUNTED BY HISTORY
THE JAMES ELDRED HOUSE
ELDRED, ILLINOIS
BY KELLY DAVIS

There hasn't been a place that I've investigated more compelling to me than the James J. Eldred House, located outside of Eldred, Illinois. The first time that I visited the Eldred House it provided me with two

THE JAMES ELDRED HOUSE

wonderful friends, Loren and Rosanne Hamilton, and an organization that I hold close to my heart, the Illinois Valley Cultural Heritage Association. My husband and I are currently working to restore the grand old house that so many have investigated through the Illinois and American Hauntings Tours. The other thing I will say about this house is that it has a magical quality about it. I would never attempt to explain it because I don't think my words would give it justice. Anyone who has been in the grand James J. Eldred House knows what I'm attempting to say.

I've said it before but this house proves that Hollywood's perception in regard to the paranormal is way off base. Every time I set foot into my favorite haunted home, I feel welcomed. I'm sure that there have been some investigators who have run into the nasty ghost that the majority of the population feels is out there but I would invite anyone to walk into the Eldred House and I'd show them the softer side of the paranormal. Day or night, you won't be disappointed.

In 1818, Ward and Swift Eldred traveled on foot from New York to scout out the Illinois property that they wanted to purchase for their cheese business. The deciding factor for the Eldreds to make the move from New York to Illinois was to ensure that the soon-to-be state would not support slavery. Upon their return to New York, they awaited confirmation of the state's anti-slavery views. During their visit Swift made acquaintances with George Churchill, a local politician. In a letter that he sent in late 1818, Churchill stated that at the state constitutional convention they had signed the Illinois Constitution of 1818. He stated they decided that "neither slavery nor involuntary servitude shall be hereafter introduced into this state." However, the people who already owned slaves were not affected by this new law.

Soon after the letter was received, the Eldreds began gathering their family to make the trip out West. The plan was for brothers Ward and Elon Eldred to head west first and the rest of the family would follow soon after. They would bring with them their father, Jehosophat, and twelve other family members. Before leaving his family in New York to head west, Ward married the first of four wives. A few weeks later, in January 1919, Elon and Ward started toward Illinois driving a herd of sheep. The wealthy family soon began purchasing land in the new state. Ward bought eighty one-acre tracts in Sections 17, 20 and 21, initially putting his home in section 21, where James J. Eldred was born in 1828. The section on which the Eldred House currently sits, known as Section 16, was purchased in 1840.

Ward's first two wives died before 1840, and he would marry two more times in the coming decade while raising cattle and growing crops on his expanding land. All four of his wives died giving birth. Then, at the age of 54, Ward Eldred passed away after contracting erysipelas, a bacterial skin disease which he caught while working with cattle in the flooded Illinois bottoms.

After his father's death, James John Eldred purchased his older brother's interest in Section 16 and married the sister of his father's fourth wife, Emaline Smead, in February 1851. While living in the old Eldred House, James finished the four-story limestone barn that his father had started to handle the growing family business. At the time of Ward's death they owned 194 heads of cattle, 70 cows, 58 calves, 30 horses, and five oxen and goats. James inherited all of this or purchased what he didn't inherit from his older brother, who did not want anything to do with the family business. James and his young family took over the cheese operation, traveling to nearby St. Louis to market their wares.

By 1860, James and Emaline had four children: Alice, Eva, Ward, and Alma. James's seventeen-year-old sister, Evaline, lived with the family, along with two domestic servants. In 1861, construction of the James J. Eldred House was completed and a new life began for the young family. James and Emaline raised their children, managed the farm, and regularly hosted lavish parties.

James was enjoying great success, believing that he had shaken off the bad luck that haunted his father but it was not to be. Soon, his life began to spiral out of control. In 1861, the family was shattered by the death of their daughter, Alma, who was four years old at the time. In 1870, they lost their oldest daughter, Alice, at the age of seventeen, and then tragedy hit once again, taking their last surviving daughter, Eva, also at age seventeen in 1876. Alice and Eva both died of tuberculosis, the disease that was raging across the county and claiming many lives. Some believe that Alma died from the same disease that claimed her sisters, but nothing was listed as a cause of death on her death certificate. The deaths of the three girls stunned James and Emaline and they never truly recovered.

Bad luck continued for the broken family. Due to the unpredictability of agricultural life, James' finances began to be strained. In 1870, a private tutor for the Eldred children sued James for non-payment for her services. James faced another lawsuit in 1900, involving a lease on the Eldred property. The suit was settled out of court. Even as the family's financial problems worsened, they continued to host their parties up until the day that they sold the house to a cousin named Albon E. Wilson in 1901. He allowed

James and Emaline to live in the house until 1910, when they moved to nearby Carrollton, Illinois. Both of them died later that same year. Their son, Ward, was left to carry on the family name with two sons of his own.

Over the course of the next century, the property changed hands from owner to owner, but the house remained the same. The architecture is one of the best surviving examples of Greek revival architecture in the area, combining the stylistic values of fashionable neoclassicism with traditional local material. They used limestone from the property to build the home, hand-chiseling every cornerstone and window sill. Over the years, the only modern accommodations added were two fifteen-amp fuses, which are no longer operable. To this day, there is no running water, no heating or air conditioning, or even an indoor bathroom. Thankfully, my friend Mark Brown built a wonderful outhouse that is a blessing during a long visit to the home.

But what of the ghosts?

One of the oldest spirits said to haunt the property dates back to before the Eldred family purchased the land. A number of years ago, the Center for American Archaeology discovered prehistoric deposits at the base of the bluffs where the house sits. These deposits resemble the nearby Koster Site, the subject of excavations over several decades. Archaeological teams have discovered mixed late-middle Woodland/late Woodland/ Jersey Bluff ceramics on the site. Later, the remains of a Native American Indian were discovered on the property of the Eldred House when local workers were digging a trench for a new water line to service some nearby houses. The bones were uncovered and tossed to the side. The following day, members of the Illinois Valley Cultural Heritage Association found the remains lying in the front yard of the Eldred House. Not knowing if the bones were human or not, they called local law enforcement officers and later the Center for American Archaeology, which determined that the bones came from a Native American burial site. Every effort was made to ensure that the spirit of this Native American was at rest when they placed him back into the ground – but the efforts apparently failed. Several years have passed since the body was laid to rest in a formal Indian ceremony but there are reports that the spirit is still roaming the grounds.

Another resident spirit is that of a traveling salesman, one who came calling and apparently never left. During the 1800s, it was very common for peddlers to travel from town to town to sell their merchandise. This was great advantage to farmers who lived in the outlying areas away from town and gave them the chance to obtain both the essentials they needed for daily life and luxuries they might not regularly purchase as well. According to legend, a salesman called on the Eldred family late one evening and when they saw that he was tired and ill, they invited him to stay for the night. When the family woke the next day, they found the salesman had died in the front parlor. To this day, the cause of his death remains a mystery – as does the reason why he chose to stay behind at the house. Witnesses say that from time to time, a solid knock is heard at the front door. When the door is opened, there is never anyone there. We have always wondered if the salesman is reliving his last night over and over again.

Over the past few years, we've had a few psychics in the home who have disputed the story of the salesman. A few have said that they believed the salesman died of natural causes in the front parlor, while others claim that the peddler was pushy and made threats toward the Eldreds to get them to buy his merchandise. Some said that they had visions of Emaline or James striking him in defense of someone in the family. In my opinion, though, the original story is likely the most accurate one. I believe he died from natural causes, but I suppose the other versions make for a good campfire story. In spite of this, when a knock comes at the door at 3:00 a.m., even I am a little leery about checking to see who it is. The ghost is harmless but we only hear the knock when the door is closed. If we left it open, the ghost just might join the party without asking – which is a little more unnerving than hearing a phantom knock.

Like many other investigators, I found this wonderful location on Troy Taylor's American Hauntings Tours website in 2007. I dragged my husband along to the house, calling it a "date night." Our tour guide, Loren Hamilton, gave us the history of the house and told stories about the hauntings that were known at the time. Then he cut us loose to find the hotspots in the house. Two hours into the investigation, three other women and I went into James and Emaline's bedroom for an EVP session. Once we began directing questions to James, we all began to feel a discomfort in our chests. I started to feel nauseated, making the discomfort even worse, so I excused myself and stepped out of the room. The moment I crossed the threshold into the hallway, I felt instantly better. The discomfort and illness left as quickly as it came. The only explanation I can come up with is that James was letting us know he was there. Since then, I have experienced this sensation multiple times at the house, both during the day and at night. When this happens, I just respond with a "Hello, James!" and it goes away. The night was active for the tour and I was simply amazed. Other investigators experienced strange readings with their equipment and temperature drops that couldn't be explained. It was exciting – but I wanted more.

I contacted Loren about going back into the house with my team, the Macoupin County Ghost Hunters, after the winter was over. We arranged for an April investigation. Loren invited our friend Bill Alsing from the History & Hauntings Bookstore in Alton to come along with the team, which consisted of my daughter, Amanda Davis; my son, Dylan Davis; team leader Kevin Beers, and two team members of 3M Paranormal from Staunton, Illinois, Daniel Mathis and Debbie Evans.

Shortly after arriving, we set up our equipment and began the night's investigation. Kevin and I were setting up the command station when our DVD burner shut off by itself. We turned it back on, blaming the malfunction on the generator we were using to power the system. This happened four more times and after a lot of troubleshooting, we knew it wasn't our equipment; it wasn't anything we were doing wrong. Laughing, I asked the spirits to please stop pushing the red button. They could touch anything else, I said, but not that button. After this little discussion, the DVD burner worked properly.

After conducting a few rounds of the house, we decided to do an EVP session in the attic. By this time, I was getting frustrated since I was the only one in the group that was not experiencing some sort of activity. I started to do anything I could think of to try and entice the interest of the spirits. I placed playing cards on the floor to entice James, who was reputed to have been a gambling man. I had a handful of marbles for the children of the Eldred family to play with and move around, but nothing happened. I tried to provoke one of the entities of the house by speaking directly to James Eldred, daring him to do something and telling him that a child could do the simple task I was asking of him, which was to wave his hand in front of my EMF meter or drop the temperature around me. Once I voiced this dare, the temperature began to drop around me to a low of 28 degrees. Shaking from the cold, I kept going and soon I began to feel the strong pressure on my chest that I felt the last time I visited. At that point, I thanked James for showing me that he was there and the temperature returned to normal and the pressure went away. Of course, this was just a personal experience and offered no real proof that a spirit was present, but it was fascinating enough to keep me going. My daughter repeated my experiment in the attic in James and Emaline's bedroom with the same response. We found out that night that the spirits in the James J. Eldred House almost always react to females.

The night continued with Amanda and her partner going back up to James and Emaline's bedroom while the remaining team members watched on the cameras in the downstairs command post. After a few minutes, we all heard the sound of footsteps that began at the top of the stairs and came stomping down.

Rushing to investigate, we ended up scaring each other more than we were scared by the phantom footsteps.

That evening was the beginning of our team's fascination with the Eldred House, the beginning of a great friendship with Loren and Bill, and the inspiration for my efforts in helping to restore the James J. Eldred House.

I have since returned to the Eldred House many times. Alma, one of the daughters of James and Emaline, is my favorite entity to play with and what I mean by that is playing "hide and seek." She's very good at it. Now I know what the reader might be thinking, "playing hide and seek with a ghost? Come on!" But I play this game hoping that she will show herself to me. I usually walk around the house saying, "Alma, I'm going to find you!" You have to remember she is a little girl and if she's in the mood and if you play it often enough, you'll hear her soft, sweet, innocent laughter coming from somewhere around you. That laugh is infectious and I giggle every time I hear it. Several times during our investigations/tours at the Eldred House, Alma has made herself known to our guests. She has been seen peeking out of windows, has answered questions during EVP sessions and has walked in front of an infrared camera. While we were conducting an investigation, a white mass moved past a doorway in the line of one of our cameras. The entity was no taller than a young child; we can only assume that it was our friend Alma.

Sometimes, things don't always go well at the Eldred House. Before one of the American Hauntings nights there, Loren called me at home with a big problem. He told me that part of the wall had collapsed into the nursery. Afraid for the safety of our guests, the Illinois Valley Cultural Heritage Association decided it was not safe for people to walk around the house. Loren and I put our heads together and arranged for the investigators to conduct their investigation around the property and the basement. We were just hoping it wouldn't rain. While conducting the tour, MCGH team member Kevin Beers was using an EMF meter and I had dowsing rods while we conducted an EVP session in a remote location. I had never used dowsing rods before, so I was surprised when they reacted to the questions that I was asking. At the same time, lights were flashing on the meter in Kevin's hand. I was flabbergasted and amazed at the activity that was going on around me. At about the same time, a young man snapped a picture of us using both devices. At the end of the session, we proceeded back to the house. I was a little shaken up from the rods moving in my hands, not to mention my hands feeling tired from using all my strength to stop them from moving. That's when amateur photographer Julian Makas came up to me and showed me a strange photograph (which unfortunately was too dark to be reprinted here).

When you look at the picture you can see a little face that resembles a child just to Kevin's left side while the meter in his hand was reacting. Interestingly, the spirit that we believed we were talking to at the time was that of Alma Eldred. That night wouldn't be the last time that she would show up film or be seen in the house. Since this is the first time that this picture has been published, the descriptions that eyewitnesses have related seem to match the little girl in the photo.

On Halloween 2009, my husband, Dan, and I went with our two newest investigators with the Macoupin County Ghost Hunters, Chad and Debbie Musgrave, for our first sleepover investigation at the Eldred House. At that time, no one had spent the night in the house since the 1960s. After the guests finish walking through the property, we normally meet with all the investigators in the kitchen to tell the paranormal history of the house. We had a full house that night, jammed with people who wanted to sleep in the house or camp in the yard (even though it was only 30 degrees outside!) and Dan and Debbie couldn't fit into the kitchen. As they stood in the dining room, both of them heard a noise from the staircase. When they looked up, they saw a black shadow lean over the handrail and look toward the crowd in the kitchen. The shadow quickly drew back and we heard footsteps retreat up the steps. Dan rushed to the second floor to see if we had left anyone upstairs only to find the rooms empty. Someone asked why a ghost would show itself with so many people in the house. The answer was easy – the Eldred family had always enjoyed festive gatherings in their home and having a group of people there was just like one of the parties they had thrown in the past!

The stories about the Eldred House go on and on. Dozens of investigators have had their own experiences here over the last several years. There are also stories that have been passed on to us from people who live in the area. For example, one of the neighbors told us that they have seen a woman standing in the window. On another occasion, they saw a woman walking across the lawn. Others have told us about power tools going missing when repairs were being made on the house and an apparition of a man staring out of a second floor window. Several photos have been taken of the mysterious woman that local residents told us about. There is even a photo taken by Cindy Moscardelli, a MCGH team member, of a woman looking through a window into the house. The weird part is that the window was in the attic – it's two and one-half stories high with nothing for her to stand on.

There are several questions that still haven't been answered and I'm not sure if they ever will be. Is the house haunted by Alma Eldred? Did the salesman really die there and is reliving his last night alive? Is James still watching over his prize possession, the house he built with his own hands? I have seen enough to know that the Eldred property – both inside and outside – is haunted. You don't have to take my word for it; it's easy to visit this amazing place on a tour or on a private overnight at the house. Of course, no one can guarantee that you will see a ghost but I can say that I've never been there where *something* strange hasn't happened. To me, this is a playground for paranormal investigators, so when you're ready, come experience it for yourself.

HAUNTS OF THE CHENEY MANSION JERSEYVILLE, ILLINOIS BY KELLY DAVIS

One of the wonderful things about helping Loren Hamilton with overnight tours and ghost hunts is the privilege of meeting so many interesting people. I had the honor of meeting three wonderful ladies from the Jersey Historical society, Carol Senger, Eve Gardner, and Marsha Murray, when they attended an outing sponsored by the American Haunting Tours at the James J. Eldred House. Throughout the night, Carol Senger told me stories about a grand house in Jerseyville called the Cheney Mansion. I've driven by the house hundreds of times and I slowed down almost every time just to admire the beauty of the architecture. I never realized that I would someday be able to investigate the secrets of this beautiful place.

Originally known as Hickory Grove, Jerseyville was just becoming a community when the first part of the Cheney Mansion was built. Back in 1827, it was known as the Little Red House because it was painted bright red. A few years later the house was sold to A.L. Carpenter, who then sold it to the D'Arcy

THE CHENEY MANSION (COURTESY OF THE JERSEY COUNTY HISTORICAL SOCIETY)

family. Though marriage and inheritance, the house was left to the Cheney family in the years that followed.

The Little Red House, the first wood frame building in the county, was initially a home but later it became the town's first tavern, a stop on the pony express, the town's first school, its first bank and then a rest stop for stage coaches. Travelers on horseback or on foot who came through the area stopped into the Little Red House. In 1834, the people of the area decided to break away from Greene County and form their own smaller county. This was to lessen the hardship of traveling to register and record legal documents at the county seat in Carrollton. At that time, there were only three families and one single gentleman who lived in Hickory Grove. These residents, along with some nearby settlers, met at the Little Red House for the purpose of forming a new county. They were required to set up a form of government, including a militia, to elect a postmaster, and choose a name for the county and a location for the county seat. The county of Jersey (most of the local settlers came from New Jersey) was formed and the decision was made to change the name of the town from Hickory Grove to Jerseyville, which subsequently became the county seat.

The Little Red House continued to serve the community as a site for business until it was inherited by Edward D'Arcy. D'Arcy's father had been personal surgeon to George Washington and he left Edward large tracts of land. D'Arcy began to make changes to the Little Red House almost immediately. Years later, Edward D'Arcy's daughter Catherine married Prentiss Dana Cheney. Upon her father's death, Catherine inherited the Little Red House and 3,600 acres of fertile ground in Christian County. More changes were made to the house, using the wealth Cheney had made as a banker in New York, and the house soon became known by its more formal name of the Cheney Mansion.

The Cheneys' wealth and position made them the county's leading citizens, but they had many years of unhappiness as they tried in vain to have a child. After several miscarriages, their son, Alexander, was born when Catherine was 42 and her husband 46 years old. Alexander grew up to be a doctor, practicing out of the home, but he gained a reputation as an alcoholic and ne'er-do-well. He and his wife, Sarah, also had difficulty conceiving a child but in 1916, a son, Prentiss Dana Cheney II, was born. A nursemaid named Dorothy Hofsaes was hired for the boy and she lived with them in the mansion, where she was treated like family.

As he grew up, the people of Jerseyville grew to know young Prentiss (who was called P.D.) as an eccentric character. Raised by his mother, his nurse, and his spinster aunt Dorothy Barry, P.D. was pampered and spoiled. He was driven to school each day in a limousine and given everything he could possibly want. Highly educated, P.D attended Washington University in St. Louis but he never took a single exam or ever earned a degree. As it turned out, he never worked a day in his life. He instead devoted his time to drinking, chasing women and music. P.D. could play any kind of instrument and he turned the front parlor of the mansion into a music room where he could entertain his friends and whatever young ladies took his fancy.

His eccentric behavior stood out in the small town of Jerseyville. He never carried money and when he wanted something, he always told the shopkeeper to send the bill to his attorney. The attorney then applied the bill to the mortgage and sales of land P.D. owned in Christian County. When he received his inheritance, he had over 640 acres of land that had been given to him by his parents. When he died at the age of 56, he had only 320 acres and very little else. But even then, he was hardly destitute – his land holdings alone earned the estate nearly $3 million.

Odd stories lingered in the wake of PD.'s life, notably one concerning his true birth mother. P.D. was loved by all three of the women who raised him but many have pointed out the fact that there is little, if any, resemblance between the young man and Sarah Cheney, who was somewhat old for a first-time mother when P.D. was born. Family photos, however, show a close resemblance between P.D. and Dorothy Hofsaes, his nanny. Could she have been more than just a nursemaid to the boy? Was she "hired" to come live at the Cheney Mansion, bringing along an infant son, because the Cheneys unable to have a child of their own? Some believe that Dorothy was indeed P.D.'s mother, but if there was a secret pact, it died with Sarah and Dorothy and the truth will never be known.

It is the reason, though, that so many believe Dorothy's ghost still lingers at the mansion. Her spirit has been seen many times, always on the floor of the house where the family lived and where her own bedroom was located. This was uncommon at a time when hired help usually lived in the attic. But perhaps Dorothy was more than just a member of the household staff?

Arrangements were made for my first investigation at the Cheney Mansion on January 10, 2009. I arrived with Loren Hamilton and we brought along several other investigators, including Dan Davis, Shaun Lievers, and Amanda Davis. We arrived loaded down with equipment. Three ladies from the Jersey Historical Society, Carol, Marsha and Eve, filled us in on the house's history by taking us on a tour and telling us about other people's experiences there over the years.

The ladies told us about Dorothy, who had been seen several times throughout the years still wandering through the house. A young man doing some work on the house received the fright of his life while walking up the service stairs. Slowly taking the steps, he heard faint footsteps behind him. Turning, he saw woman wearing an old-fashioned dress who appeared to be in her mid-thirties. Her hair was in a bun and she was wearing glasses. She was also slightly transparent. When shown a photograph of some of the past occupants of the house, he quickly pointed out Dorothy as the woman that he had seen.

All three ladies told of weird experiences in P.D.'s bedroom at one time or another. They told us that on several occasions, they had placed their hands on P.D.'s original bed and felt it vibrate. Carol showed us how the walking cane hanging on the footboard unhooked itself and flew away, landing several feet from the bed. The cane belonged to P.D. Cheney. They said that there are times when the bed had been moved several inches to the left or right when no one was in the room. They said they often heard it scraping across the floor while they were sitting downstairs. All three of them had also seen the ghostly figure of P.D. standing next to the bed. P.D. was a heavy smoker and was known for falling asleep with a cigarette in his hand, leaving multiple burn marks on the floor. It's on this spot where all three ladies had seen him standing.

Moving on into the nursery, Eve told us a story that would haunt our team for the night. Some time before, the door to the attic had been left open while boxes were being put away. When Eve turned to look at the door as she was leaving the room, she saw a hand come from the attic stairwell that exited into the nursery. The hand grabbed the door handle and closed the door. We could only hope that something like this would happen again while we were there! We left the door open when we left the room.

As we were walking out of the nursery, Carol told us that on several occasions, a stuffed rabbit that was sitting on a rocking chair had moved by itself from one side of the chair to the other. All of us made a mental note of the rabbit's position. Dan made it his mission to see thr rabbit move. When I asked who could be playing with the rabbit, Carol told me they believed two little girls haunted the residence, one black and one white. No one could locate any information about any female children dying in the home, but many staff members said they had heard them singing on the second floor.

The last room on the second floor we visited was known as the "drunken room." The room had very little furniture in it and was used solely as a place where P.D. would be locked up for the evening when he returned from the tavern and was making a fuss. Oddly, before we heard the story or even the name of the room, several of us became dizzy when we walked inside.

After that, we went downstairs to the basement. It was there where one of the mansion's secrets was revealed in 1950 when it was discovered that the Little Red House had been a station on the Underground Railroad. A small hiding place in the basement connected to a tunnel that led to a log home across the street. In 1950, while workers were doing repairs on the home's foundation, a tool accidentally broke through the foundation into an underground vault or cave that the owners did not know existed. Since the slave room has been uncovered, people have reported seeing shadows moving along the wall and voices being heard coming from the direction of the secret room.

The last active spot that we visited was the office. It contains the original bank vault from when the house served the town as a bank. On several occasions, witnesses have seen a man and a young boy standing in the back of the vault staring out at them.

As we returned to the main floor, Carol told us of water faucets turning on and off by themselves, dining room chairs moving on their own, phantom footsteps throughout the house, items going missing or moving, radio stations being changed on their own, a mannequin moving or failing to appear in photos when pictures are taken in the music room, people being touched by unseen hands, and the sighting of a ghost dog in the basement.

We scattered the cameras throughout the house and after an hour or more of setting up, we decided to take a break. Amanda placed herself at our command post to watch the three cameras that were up and running when she suddenly began to hop up and down, unable to talk. She finally blurted out, "The door is closing!" This is a statement that caught us totally off guard. We rushed to the screen to see the nursery door firmly swing shut on its own. Thankfully, we had aimed a camera on the door to see if we could catch the hand that Eve had witnessed. However, I put the camera in the wrong spot, since a bed was also visible in the lens and a hoaxer could have easily manipulated the door to make it look like something paranormal had occurred. In addition to going upstairs to check for drafts, we also moved the camera to a different location that would catch the whole door. I hoped for the best, praying that the door would close again. I would not be disappointed – it happened several more times that night!

Attempting an experiment, we sent the guys up into the nursery. Dan and Shaun sat on the floor, eyeballing the stuffed rabbit that still rested in the right hand corner of the rocking chair. All was quiet until Shaun tapped Dan on the arm and pointed to the bed. The bed ruffle moved out and lifted up as if someone was peeking out. Upon looking under the bed, they found nothing, no air ducts, not even a dust bunny. That was about the time when Dan heard the sound of someone walking up the service stairs with hard soled shoes. Remembering the story of Dorothy appearing in that same stairwell, he jumped up to find that no one was there.

Wanting to see if the same response happened when the girls went upstairs in the nursery, we decided to go up and try an EVP session. Armed with a voice recorder, a hand-held video camera, and my digital camera we headed up. Asking the typical questions, I looked down at my camera just in time to see a shadow rush in front of the screen. Before I could say anything, Marsha said, "Oh wow... I just felt a cold breeze rush right by me." I was starting to make me wonder who else was in the room with us!

Then Carol said, "What's that?" Looking out in the hallway, across to the other landing, we saw a black figure pass in front of a lighted window. I immediately went into the room, which used to be Dorothy's bedroom. Feeling a cold chill in the air, I began to snap a few photos. Suddenly, my camera would not take another picture. I kept changing modes and still couldn't get the shutter to work until I put it in manual mode and quickly snapped off two shots facing the closet. The first photo shows the chair and the closet as we saw it that night. The second photo showed a white mass moving across the photo but you can still see the outline of what looks like hair though the white mass. To this day, I keep asking myself "How close was that spirit to me?"

Rounding up the investigators from the nursery, I checked the rabbit one more time and was the last to leave the room. At this point, I was dumbfounded. We had so much activity in such a short period of time, I started to doubt what we had seen and experienced. I returned downstairs to show Loren and Dan the strange photos in Dorothy's room, unable to explain what I had captured. And of course, I updated Dan on the status of his rabbit.

We ended the investigation and Loren and I sent everybody out to wrap up the cords and unhook the cameras. A few minutes later, Dan yelled down to us to come to the nursery right away. We found him staring down at the rocking chair where the rabbit had moved to the middle of the chair. Being the last one out of the nursery, I recalled the rabbit was still in its earlier position on the right side of the chair. It had apparently moved on its own!

Convinced that the Cheney Mansion was worthy of further investigation, we returned on May 9, 2009, attempting to recreate anything that could have caused the amazing events of the previous January. The night was very quiet. We opened and closed doors, looked under the beds, worked with lights and cameras and looked for any plausible explanation for what had occurred months before. We found no explanations – and nothing out of the ordinary happened that night. Subsequent visits turned out to be more active, though, and I am convinced that the Cheney Mansion is truly haunted. By whom it remains to be seen, but we are working on it.

MEISSNER SCHOOL SPIRITS
BUNKER HILL, ILLINOIS
BY KELLY DAVIS

After years of living in St. Louis, I decided to move to the small Illinois town of Bunker Hill. It turned out to be a wonderful change and I soon discovered that the place had a fascinating history. The earliest inhabitants of the area were the Peoria, Kickapoo, and Winnebago Indians, whose camps have been found near the north end of town at Washington Street and West Morgan. One area of town was once known as Wolf Ridge because of the numerous wolves that once lived where North Washington and Fayette streets are located. The town's name is taken from the battle near Charlestown, Massachusetts, which occurred near the start of the Revolutionary War.

In 1834, county surveyor Luke Knowlton entered eighty acres of land in the county registry in what is now the center of Bunker Hill. On December 25, 1835, the town's three founding fathers, Moses True, John Tilden and Robert Smith came together to plat a town and to improve the surrounding countryside. The small settlement of Lincoln, just outside of Bunker Hill, was abandoned, prompting Moses and partners to establish a new town that became Bunker Hill in 1837.

A town square was built and and the Bunker Hill Military Academy was established. The school was open for a short period of time but closed as a military academy from 1862 to 1869 due to the fact that all of the students volunteered to fight for the Union during the Civil War. The academy housed the Bunker Hill public school until after the Civil War, when it became a military academy again. The school remained open until 1914.

For Abraham Lincoln buffs, Bunker Hill houses one of four statues of Lincoln sculpted by William Grandville Hastings. In 1904, Captain Charles Clinton, formerly of Company B of the first Missouri Voluntary Cavalry, donated the statue to the citizens of Bunker Hill in honor of the local veterans who served in Company B during the Civil War. The statue was unveiled in front of 7,000 onlookers by Mary True, daughter of one of the town's founders.

Bunker Hill has seen more than its share of tragedy. More than a century after its founding, two tornadoes ripped through town in ten years, both causing massive damage. But the second storm claimed more than just buildings.

On March 18, 1948, at 6:45 a.m., an Force 5 tornado tore through town. The deadly storm developed into a tornado just as it hit the Alton area, striking Fosterburg and claiming sixty buildings and ten lives as it continued to build up its speed. As it clipped the neighboring town of Woodburn, several homes were destroyed and four people were killed. This massive storm then headed right for Bunker Hill. It's said that eighty percent of the town was destroyed. Nineteen people were killed, 165 were injured and a reported $1.5 million worth of damage was done to the small town of 1,500 people. The storm continued on after it left Bunker Hill, taking three more lives in Gillespie. When all was said and done, 44 people had been killed, 300 injured and several million dollars in damage had been done.

MEISSNER SCHOOL AFTER THE DEADLY TORNADO

One of the few buildings that were spared from the storm was Meissner School. After the storm had passed, the school was used to house a first-aid center and a temporary morgue for the 19 bodies of the locals who were killed in the storm. Personal cars and trucks were commandeered to take the injured to Alton and to surrounding area hospitals. The dead were left behind in the school until the injured had been treated.

The storm brought the whole town together. Farmers used their tractors to move debris from the streets and volunteers repaired homes and covered broken windows. An emergency food line was set up at Bahn's grocery store, which had sustained less damage than others in town. Local organizations began to mobilize to assist in search and rescue.

During the storm, all five of the town's churches were destroyed. On March 28, at 11:00 p.m., two of the local ministers came together to preach to 500 residents and volunteers about unity and survival while using a bulldozer as a pulpit.

Years after the storm, stories of the "Gray Lady" began to surface from Meissner School. Students at the school told of seeing a mysterious woman walking the corridors whom they took to be one of the victims of the tornado. The children and even some of the teachers, began to see and hear things they couldn't explain. After listening to my son tell me these stories and having the inquisitive nature of a paranormal investigator, I wondered if there was any truth behind the tales. Could it be the older students were having fun scaring the younger ones by telling them that their classrooms had once held the bodies of the storm victims? Over the years, I heard that most students pinpoint their own classroom as being the former temporary morgue.

But my interest went beyond the tall tales told by the students. I also heard stories told by workers at the school who spent evenings alone in the building. For instance, a janitor was pulling a trash can down a hallway one evening when he heard the faint sound of footsteps behind him. Turning to see who was there, he heard his name being called by a woman's voice. He searched the building but found he was alone. He quickly finished up his task and left but he never forgot the incident.

Another report came from a teacher was sitting in her classroom late in the evening, finishing up her teaching duties, when she looked up to see a woman walk by the door. The woman walked with her head down and the teacher couldn't see her face. The teacher quickly followed her down the sixth grade hall and toward the cafeteria. When she addressed the stranger, asking if she was looking for someone, she received no response. The teacher turned her head for a moment and when she looked back, the woman was gone. When the story got out, it sparked the interest of the student body. They put out a dare to two of their teachers: if the students were able to raise enough money for a local charity, the teachers would stay the night in the school. The students raised the money as required, but the teachers didn't experience anything paranormal.

How the spirit got the name "Gray Lady" is unknown, as is her identity. Is she the spirit of a woman who died in the tornado of 1948? Or, is she a former teacher who loved the school so much that she still walks its halls? I don't think we will ever know.

Looking for more evidence of the Gray Lady, I asked Loren Hamilton, his wife, Roseanne, and Bill Alsing to join my husband Dan and me at an investigation at the school. Bill and I went up to the second floor where the library was. We sat in there for quite a while when we heard a voice yell out in the hallway. I looked at Bill and he nodded to acknowledge that he heard it too. I checked everyone's location, and no one had yelled. I came back into the library to tell Bill that I had found nothing out of the ordinary and we decided to move to another room. Having left the library ahead of Bill, he summoned me back to show me a trash can that he had tripped over directly in the same path that I had walked just a minute before. Luckily, Bill had his camera on when he came into the room, upon reviewing it we found that the trash can had been sitting several feet from where it was found when he tripped over it.

Could it be that an entity moved the trash can to let us know it was there? Or, could it be a spirit of a child playing games? I'm not sure anyone will ever know. That night was the only time we experienced activity at the school but combined with its history, it certainly is a supernaturally intriguing place. Does the Gray Lady still walk the hallways? No one can say, because the school closed in 2009. If the Gray Lady still walks there, she walks alone, likely missing the children over whom she watched for so many years.

STRANGE TALES OF GREENE COUNTY

THE GREENE COUNTY HANGING TREE
WRIGHTS, ILLINOIS

The story of the hanging tree, and the phantom that haunts it, has been told in Greene County for more than a century. The strange tale of murder and the macabre used to be recounted to misbehaving children as a ghoulish bedtime story. It involved a corpse that was used to frighten wrongdoers as it hung from a post at the railroad station. It remains today as one of Illinois' strangest tales of crime and a lingering ghost.

Dr. Charles MacCauliffe was the sole physician in the small town of Wrights in 1879. While he was a respected and generally well-liked man, it did not save him from death at the end of a rope after he committed murder one night. MacCauliffe and his brother-in-law, a man named James Heavener, were drinking one evening in the town's only saloon when they got into a heated argument. Fueled by too many drinks, the fight became so intense that MacCauliffe went behind the bar, grabbed a shotgun that the owner kept there, and fired both barrels into Heavener's chest. His brother-in-law was killed instantly and when he saw what he had done, the doctor panicked, threw the shotgun on the floor and ran from the saloon. He left Heavener lying on the floor in a growing pool of his own blood.

As MacCauliffe ran, a group of men who witnessed the murder chased after him. They quickly found the doctor hiding in a nearby barn and took him into custody, delivering him to the town constable. Wrights was not large enough to have its own jail, so after some discussion, the constable and several of the men decided to take Dr. MacCauliffe to nearby Carrollton. They loaded him onto a wagon and started out into the night.

Not far from town, the wagon rolled past a large oak tree at the edge of Hickory Grove Cemetery. As the men looked up into its branches, they decided that they would hang the doctor right then and there. With the full approval of the constable, they tied a rope around MacCauliffe's neck and stood him up in the back of the wagon. Ignoring his pleas for mercy, one of the men slapped the horse on the hindquarters and it jerked forward, pulling the wagon out from under the struggling doctor's feet. He hung there, his feet kicking and his body twitching, as he slowly strangled to death.

Later on, the constable and some of the men in the lynching party spread the story that a mob of men had surprised them, took the doctor away, and hanged him from the cemetery oak tree. Of course, most folks knew this was not the case because after the hanging, all of the men involved had gone home to bed. If the doctor really had been taken away from them, they would have scoured the countryside for his abductors. Even though no one believed their story, no arrests were ever made for the doctor's murder.

Most of the local people found out about the lynching the next morning. A group of children were walking along the road near the cemetery and saw MacCauliffe's body still hanging there, gently twisting in the breeze. They became frightened and ran home to tell their parents. Several adults went back to the cemetery and cut down the corpse. There was a lot of discussion about what to do with the body. At some point, it was loaded onto a wagon and taken to the railroad station in town. With the rope still knotted about its neck, the corpse was hoisted up on a pole and left on display as a warning to passersby about what happened to lawbreakers in Wrights.

The body became quite an attraction and people traveled from nearby towns to get a look at it. The late Vera Harr, a resident of Carrollton, recalled, "My mother was born that year and grandma wasn't allowed to see the body for fear that the baby would be marked for life." Finally, after several days, the corpse was cut down and buried in an unmarked grave in the southeast corner of Hickory Grove Cemetery. The doctor was laid to rest with

DR. MACCAULIFFE'S SIMPLE GRAVE IN GREENE COUNTY'S HICKORY GROVE CEMETERY

74

no ceremony whatsoever and no one was present at his burial, save for the two men who dug the grave. However, a local farmer, John W. Flowers, decided that MacCauliffe's grave should be marked.

From the nearby woods, Flowers dug up a small cedar tree and planted it next to the doctor's grave. He also mixed some cement and creek sand and created a small, stone monument. Using the metal nameplate from the door of the doctor's office in Wrights, he embedded it in the wet cement. The plate read simply "Doctor MacCauliffe." Below it, Flowers scratched out the words "Died 1879." The plate is still readable today but the lettering that was cut into the stone has faded to almost nothing.

Later, a marker was placed on the old hanging tree, telling the story of the murder and the lynching that followed. Unfortunately, the tree blew down in a storm a few years ago, bringing at least one eerie story to an end.

For decades, stories were told in Greene County advising against walking the road beneath the hanging tree at night. It was said that on certain nights, the ghostly figure of Dr. MacCauliffe could be seen hanging from a branch overhead. As he swayed in the wind, his body twisted until trespassers could see his face. If his eyes opened, the legend stated, then you were bound to die within the year. It was a warning of death that most superstitious local residents went out of their way to avoid.

NIGHTS IN THE HAUNTED MANSION
THE LEE-BAKER-HODGES HOUSE
CARROLLTON, ILLINOIS
BY LOREN HAMILTON & KELLY DAVIS

There is one house that is hard to miss as you travel through the small town of Carrollton It sits in the town square and catches the eye of those who pass by it. Home to the Greene County Historical and Genealogical Society, the Lee-Baker-Hodges house has expanded over the years with the growing town. Carrollton, established in 1821, is the county seat of Greene County. There is a town square with a courthouse in the middle. Although it"s a beautiful structure, this was not the first courthouse in Carrollton.

A merchant named J.W. Skidmore purchased the northwest corner of the square and two additional lots, where he erected a two-room building in 1821, the same year that the county and the town were plotted. In December of that year, the town needed a location to hold trials and hear legal cases, so the town fathers approached Skidmore and asked if they could have the use of one of the rooms to hold court for $4 each month. He agreed but later ran into financial problems and sold the property to Samuel Lee.

Samuel Lee is remembered today as one of the most esteemed men in the county's history, serving as a county clerk and recorder in the early years of Carrollton. Lee went on to become a circuit clerk and a justice of the peace. In 1824, he married Mary Ann Faust, Skidmore's 16-year-old sister-in-law. As his fortunes improved, Lee began working to expand Skidmore's two-room building to the south and to turn it into a grand mansion. When Lee died in September of 1829, he directed in his will that the mansion be completed to his wife's standards and used as her home. His wishes were carried out by Moses Stevens, who built the second courthouse across the street from the mansion in 1832.

The house, designed in Federal style, became home to the widowed Mary Ann Lee and her two young children. It was a lonely home until the young woman met an up-and-coming lawyer named Edward Baker. Soon to become a friend and colleague of Abraham Lincoln, Baker married Mary Ann and moved

THE LEE-BAKER-HODGES HOUSE

her and her children to Springfield in 1835. The next year they sold their lovely "Brick Mansion House," as it was described in the deed, to Dr. Orange Heaton. The Baker family moved west to the new state of Oregon in 1860, where Edward Baker would later be elected as a U.S. Senator.

At Lincoln's inauguration in March of 1861, Baker, known for his oratory skills, made the shortest public speech of his career with these words: "Fellow citizens, I introduce to you Abraham Lincoln, the president-elect of the United States." At the start of the Civil War, he organized the California Regiment and was commissioned as its colonel. He was killed on October 21, 1861 during the battle of Bull Run in Virginia, making Mary Ann a widow once again.

In March 1850, Dr. Heaton sold the Carrollton house to Charles Drury Hodges, who served as a county judge, circuit judge, a representative in the U.S. Congress and an Illinois state Senator during his long political career. In 1854, Hodges added a second floor to the east end of the house, incorporating it into a two-story Italianate style wing. It became a showplace and was called the finest house in town.

Judge Hodges passed away in 1884 and his wife continued to make the mansion her home until her death in 1899. The next year, their son, Beverly C. Hodges, converted the house into an office building. The house remained in the Hodges family for seventy years and was eventually sold to Dr. N.D. Vetter, who used it as his offices, in 1921.

In 1980, the home was listed on the National Register of Historic Places and its lease was transferred to the Greene County Historical and Genealogy Society two years later. Members of the local society work tirelessly to preserve and restore the home, doing research into its past occupants and collecting artifacts from the history of the house and the town of Carrollton.

Which may explain why the house seems to be haunted...

There are a variety of reasons why houses become haunted, but in some cases, a haunting can be caused by objects that are brought into the place. Often referred to as "possessed possessions," these objects seem to have ghosts attached to them, usually the spirits of those who owned them in the past. It's believed that this is what has caused the mansion to become haunted.

Each room of the mansion has a different theme. One room is a bank from the early 1900s, another a Victorian bedroom, another a sewing room containing a spinning wheel, and so on. All of the treasures have come to the house from various donors and it seems that some of them have brought other things along with them. There have been footsteps and voices heard in the old kitchen area, along with cold chills experienced throughout the entire house. Visitors and staff members have reported weird experiences in the mansion.

In early 2010, an amazing photo was taken in the house. My friend Del Dawdy and I were hosting a ghost hunt that included about fifteen ghost hunters and a few members of the historical society. About halfway through the night, I was asked my opinion of a photograph taken in the upstairs Victorian bedroom, which was in disarray at the time. New items and clothing had been donated to the house and there were racks of clothes and boxes scattered all over the bedroom.

The photo was taken of a strange glare that appeared in the mirror attached to the dresser. There was also a four-poster bed with a quilt in the room, a chamber pot, and other items from the Victorian era. I examined the photo and at first believed that it was merely the camera's flash hitting the scratches and dull spots where the mirror had been cleaned over and over for a hundred years. In the mirror was the reflection of a short, heavy woman holding a purse.... But, who was she?

I didn't think any more of it at the time but after looking at the photograph and checking the guests, I realized that the reflection was not of anyone in the house that night! I tried to duplicate the picture, thinking that perhaps it was a reflection of the scattered clothing and items in the room, but I couldn't do it. Knowing that the woman in the picture was not anyone in my group, I went downstairs to speak with the historical society members to see if they recognized her. They took one look and a friend of mine spoke up immediately and flatly stated that it was the owner of the furniture that had been donated to be placed in the room – and that she had been dead for some time!

Unfortunately, believing that it showed nothing more than a reflected camera flash, the guest deleted the photo from his digital camera and it was lost for good. It was one of the most amazing pieces of evidence to point to the idea that the Lee-Baker-Hodges Mansion is haunted and while it was lost, we continue to return to the house in hopes that something of the same caliber might show up again.

THE PETRIFIED LADY OF GREENE COUNTY
WALKERVILLE, ILLINOIS
BY LOREN HAMILTON

It was a Sunday morning, April 22, 1894, when Bub Howard of Walkerville came upon a surprising discovery while walking through the woods during an early morning hunting trip. He was a half mile southwest of town when he came upon what appeared to be a human foot sticking out of the mud in a ravine. As he reached into the mud to pull out the object, it broke off in his hand. An hour later a rescue party had uncovered the body of a woman — the petrified lady of Greene County.

The body was perfect except for part of the foot that had broken off. The lady appeared to be in her thirties, and there were no visible signs that her death had been caused by violence. Her right arm was extended along her side, while the left was draped across her middle. The fingers of both hands had long fingernails and were extended flat against her body. She measured five feet, eleven inches in height, and she did not have the characteristics of the Native American people who inhabited the river valley years before.

The body was found in a ravine composed of yellow clay, mixed with a great amount of sand. Around the burial site, was a scattering of brush and thickets of scrub trees. The trees were so entwined that roots had to be cut away from the body before it could be extracted from the mud. The roots and the darkened condition of the exposed foot led rescuers to believe she had been buried for a long period of time.

After the story of the hunter's discovery circulated around the area, there was speculation about who the woman was and where she came from, but one story seemed to be the most acceptable and feasible to the people of Walkerville.

Many years before, an elderly hermit lived in a cabin deep in the woods southwest of Walkerville. He was unsociable when he made his rare visits to town for provisions. One day, as old-timers remembered, a woman accompanied him on his trip into town. She seemed to be subservient to the old man, and never spoke or made eye contact with anyone when she was with him.

Months later the old man came to town alone. Hunters who used the woods near the hermit's cabin reported that the woman was no longer around, having disappeared as mysteriously as she had arrived. Rumors began to circulate that the old man had murdered his companion, but before authorities could investigate, the cabin burned to the ground in the middle of the night. No human remains were found. People speculated that the hermit had set the fire and left the area to move west. Further speculation claimed that he buried the woman's body nude so the few Native Americans still residing in the area wouldn't dig her up for her jewelry or clothing.

The body of the petrified lady was put on display for 15 cents, first in Walkerville, and then on South Sandy Street in nearby Jacksonville, in the building that now houses the Moose Lodge. The men who claimed to own the body failed to get rich with their morbid business. In August of that year, the body was sold to a group from Alton who took it on tour for several years, displaying the unidentified petrified lady at county fairs across the state.

Eventually, she disappeared from history and what became of her remains a mystery.

THE LITTLE DRUMMER BOY OF GREENE COUNTY
WHITE HALL, ILLINOIS
BY LOREN HAMILTON

Edward Hager grew up and worked on his family's Greene County farm until he was sixteen. On November 13, 1861, he joined the 61st Illinois infantry as a drummer. Three full companies mustered on February 5, 1862 from Carrollton to Benton Barracks, Missouri.

Hager's drumming set the cadence for marching. His position provided a communications channel between the commanding officer and the troops. But Hager was anxious to be a direct player in the battles of the Civil War. Some time between leaving with the 61st Infantry from Benton Barracks and arriving in Pittsburgh Landing, Tennessee, on March 26, 1862, Hager enlisted as a Union soldier. Records show he was a private with Company A.

The infantry unit fought with success until April 6 when it was involved in two battles that resulted in much loss of life and many injuries. Among the injured was young Edward Hager. Just a few days shy of his six-month anniversary with the infantry, he was wounded at the Battle of Shiloh, near Pittsburgh Landing.

He returned to White Hall to recover from his wounds but his health began to fail. On May 30, 1862, he died and was laid to rest in the White Hall cemetery. A marker honoring his military service was placed at his gravesite and remains in place today. It tells the story of how, in the heat of battle, Edward Hager traded his drum for a rifle to help defend his country.

But there is another story that most visitors to the cemetery don't know.

As prairie winds blow through the cemetery and the full moon lights up the sky, a shadowy figure dressed in a Union uniform is often seen standing behind the trees and the sound of a single drum can be heard in the distance. On those nights, the little drummer boy returns to perform for the troops.

GHOSTS OF THE GREENE COUNTY ALMSHOUSE NEAR CARROLLTON, ILLINOIS
BY LOREN HAMILTON

I've been very fortunate as a paranormal investigator. I have travelled to many of the well-known haunted locations that have been seen on television. I can list the Queen Mary in Long Beach, California, the Bird Cage Saloon in Tombstone, Arizona, Lemp Mansion in St. Louis and the Ohio State Reformatory in Mansfield, Ohio, as just a handful of places I've visited to look for ghosts.

So, I'm sure I disappoint many when I am asked that popular question, "What is the MOST haunted location you have visited?" My answer is: the former poor farm in Greene County, Illinois, and the building that once housed the county's poor and indigent — the almshouse. It sits desolate in a rural area northeast of Carrollton. You won't find it on a map or on a TV show about ghosts or on a haunted tour, but it never disappoints me as a place of distinction to visit. I think everyone interested in the paranormal feels connections to the places they visit, and the spirits are more active to certain people. For whatever reason, the spirits who inhabit the almshouse definitely enjoy talking to me.

In 1819, the Illinois General Assembly passed the Almshouse Law, popularly known as the Pauper Bill, mandating the public care of people who could not support themselves and their families. Persons who fit the definition were placed at one of the county "poor farms." Only three poor farm almshouses are left standing in Illinois, as of this writing. The word "standing" is used loosely when I speak of the one in rural Greene County. Years of neglect, nature's elements and vandalism have taken their toll on the once-stately structure.

The Greene County almshouse was a three-story building with a large basement. There were numerous outbuildings on the property, as well as extensive farmland that provided food for the residents and income to maintain the operation. The Greene County almshouse was in operation from 1842 to 1950. For 108 years, it took in the poor, orphans, the insane and those who suffered from ill health. It even had a tuberculosis wing.

Unwed mothers and their children made up the majority of the population. The average number of residents at any given time was between fifty and sixty. They worked the land, tended the livestock, worked in the kitchen and performed housekeeping duties to pay for their room and board. County records are sketchy as to how many individuals and families actually called the building home, but many

THE GREENE COUNTY ALMSHOUSE

people passed through its doors and, if they were lucky, a situation would present itself that would allow them to move on to better things. Otherwise, they lived and died at the local almshouse. Those whose lives ended on the property were buried in unmarked graves. Records for that information are also scarce; a large percentage of those individuals are lost and forgotten to their families.

By 1950, welfare and other social service programs eliminated the need for the poor farms. The almshouse in Greene County was later used as a nursing home, with its final use being that of a senior citizen center. The cost of upkeep eventually became unreasonable and the doors were closed for the last time in 1986. It now stands silent as it gradually crumbles into the prairie.

I first visited the almshouse in 2005. My wife and I were invited to attend a meeting to discuss a purpose for the building. My daughter-in-law and her husband, Stacy and Chad Shutz of nearby White Hall, are very active in local projects to benefit the history and progress of the county.

When I first laid eyes on the house I immediately felt despair. I could sense the hopelessness and sadness the former tenants must have felt, cast out by their fellow man and far from the bustling and thriving county seat of Carrollton. My wife took pictures of the building and the surrounding grounds. Inside, before the meeting started, I took a look around and was appalled at the vandalism — staircase railings gone, windows broken, bathtubs torn out and missing. Graffiti covered every wall, with names and messages from non-caring visitors written in every room.

When we arrived, it was a hot and humid summer afternoon, but before the meeting started, clouds rolled in and it became a dark and stormy evening. With open windows and holes in the roof, the group moved to the Carrollton courthouse for its meeting. My first visit to the almshouse was a short one.

At the courthouse I introduced myself as a member of the American Ghost Society and an Illinois Hauntings tour guide, and asked for approval to investigate the house. I received a nod to investigate the house, but I could not invite others to tour the old house. Safety was the main issue, but also the board wanted to discourage thrill-seekers who might do additional damage.

I invited a friend and fellow AGS member, John Winterbauer, to join my team of investigators. By then, I'd had time to look at the pictures my wife had taken of the property. There were shadows where there should be none, streaks of light and a dark cast over the house at a time of the day when the sun had been out and the sky was cloudless.

When the team approached the gate, a feeling of being watched came over us. When anyone looked at a particular window on the second floor, an image seemed to jump back into the darkness of the room. Once inside, we got the feeling of not being alone while we set up our equipment.

We experienced strange spikes on the EMF detectors, sudden temperature changes on each floor, strange sounds of background voices and footsteps. The most eerie sounds were of scratching coming from within the walls. John and I checked and rechecked each floor and could not determine where the sounds were coming from. After hours of this activity, we noticed red, piercing eyes showing in the video camera that was trained on the summer porch. We discovered a family of raccoons who had taken up residence and were not happy to find their home invaded by outsiders. We left with enough footage to give us a good review of the building.

Several months later, I presented my findings to the board that was overseeing the almshouse. News of my investigation had leaked into the community and I was inundated with stories from locals who had visited the house in the middle of the night -- most with liquid courage for reinforcement. None the less, the stories matched the images we found on our video and the sounds reported were similar to those we experienced.

For the second visit to the almshouse, my team included a local high school science teacher. It was the middle of the day and the sun was shining. As the teacher examined dates on the floor of one room of the basement, I went into the next room by myself. I heard footsteps above me and I could actually see the floorboards bending under the weight of someone walking overhead. By the length of the strides, it would seem this was a tall person, not a stray pet or a wild animal. I grabbed my friend and we went outside. We circled the house and continued to hear someone walking inside. After we summoned the courage to re-enter the house, we found nothing to relate to the sounds of footsteps. I still wake up hearing those sounds and try to come up with an answer to explain them.

In the summer of 2008, I visited the almshouse with my paranormal partner Kelly Davis and members of her Macoupin County ghost hunting team. This is a friendly, knowledgeable and sharing group. It included Kelly and her husband Dan, their children Amanda and Dylan, and their friends Rose, Dave and Kevin.

Soon after entering the building, they experienced the feeling of being watched. Images appeared in windows, phantom footsteps were heard and unexplained shadows were seen.

Early in the evening, Amanda, Kevin and I sat in the basement, in the same room where I had stood when I had heard the footsteps walking overhead. We sat in solitude with our electromagnetic field meters and asked specific questions of a past resident. We were able to narrow down the year and the facts behind her life in the house. We also spoke of her presence inside the house while her human remains lay in an unmarked grave down the path. During the conversation, we could sense her presence and saw her shadow lurking a few feet from us, peering at us, but afraid to come closer.

On the second floor, Amanda and I saw a shadow that ran into a small room. As we moved to the doorway, strong readings were received by both of our meters. Repeated requests for the entity to come out were ignored. We walked out of the room and re-entered it and then we sneaked in from a door that led to the sun porch. Again, we were evaded when we came within four feet of the shadow.

Our team physic, Rose, joined us upstairs. She felt the spirit was that of a small boy, possibly seven or eight years old, who had died in the home. He was curious, but afraid of our presence. After a short break, we repeated the procedure and after several unsuccessful tries, I chastised the boy for running away from us. As we entered the room again, and my voice rose in anger, I felt a small ice-cold grip on the hand that held my electronic meter, yanking my hand down. The meter flashed red. I tried to remain professional, but the reality of what just happened soaked in and it hit me like a ton of bricks. I had experienced a variety of sights and sounds on visits to haunted places, but this was the first time someone or something had reached out and touched me.

After we were home and reviewed the video and audio evidence, I became chilled as I heard a small boy's laughter at the same time the cold hand had reached out to touch me.

Since that visit, strange things have started to happen in my home. They are playful things, but strange nonetheless. Even though I have not returned to the almshouse, I wonder if the spirit of my young playmate came home with me!

TALES OF HAUNTED JACKSONVILLE

ILLINOIS COLLEGE

School spirits are not all that uncommon on the prairies of central Illinois. There are a number of schools and universities that boast haunted dorms and spirit-infested theaters, but few of these halls of learning can compare with the number of ghosts that are alleged to wander the campus of Illinois College. There is a very good chance that it just may be the most haunted school in the state!

Illinois College was founded in 1829 by Reverend John M. Ellis, a Presbyterian minister who felt a

"seminary of learning" was needed in the new frontier state of Illinois. His plans came to the attention of a group of Congregational students at Yale University, seven of whom came westward to help establish the college. It became one of the first institutes for higher learning in Illinois. The first two men to graduate from the college were Richard Yates, who became the Civil War governor of Illinois and later a U.S. Senator, and Jonathan Edward Spilman, the man who composed the now-familiar music to Robert Burns' immortal poem, "Flow Gently,

Sweet Afton." Both men received their baccalaureate degree from Illinois College in 1835.

Nine students met for the first class on January 4, 1830. Julian Sturtevant, the school's first instructor and the second president, reported, "We had come there that morning to open a fountain for future generations to drink at." Shortly after, Edward Beecher left the Park Street Church in Boston to serve the new college as its first president. He created a strong college and retained close intellectual ties with New England. His brother, Henry Ward Beecher, preached and lectured at Illinois College, and his sister, Harriet Beecher Stowe, was an occasional visitor. His brother, Thomas, graduated from Illinois College in 1843. Ralph Waldo Emerson, Mark Twain, Horace Greeley, and Wendell Phillips were among the college's visitors and lecturers in the early years.

In 1843 and 1845 two of the college's seven literary societies were formed. Possibly unique in the Midwest today, these societies have continued in their roles as centers for debate and criticism. Abraham Lincoln was one of many speakers appearing on the campus under the sponsorship of a literary society.

Illinois College also became heavily involved with the abolitionist movement as President Beecher took a very active role. At one point, a group of students was indicted by a grand jury for harboring runaway slaves. Illinois College was also a well-known station on the Underground Railroad and a number of tunnels can still be found leading to the Smith and Fayerweather houses on the campus.

In the years following the Civil War graduates contributed with distinction to the national scene. Among these was William Jennings Bryan, who within fifteen years after graduating was the Democratic candidate for the U.S. presidency in the race with William McKinley. He continued with a prominent role in politics even after being defeated in the election.

There were many other prominent graduates of the school over the years and it has maintained an outstanding scholarly program. Not surprisingly, it has also maintained close ties to the supernatural world, as well. Like with many other historic spots in Illinois, the events of the past have certainly left their mark on Illinois College. These events come back to "haunt" students and faculty members today and there are many who have encountered the ghosts of yesterday face to face.

One place where strange events have been reported is in Beecher Hall, which was built in 1829. This two-level building is now used as a meeting hall for two of the school's literary societies, Sigma Pi and Phi Alpha. The Sigs meet on the upper floor and the Phis meet in the lower part of the building. The majority of the encounters here seem to involve the groups who frequent the upper floor. The most commonly reported events are ghostly footsteps that can be distinctly heard in one room, always coming from

A VINTAGE PHOTOGRAPH OF BEECHER HALL

another. If a curious witness follows the sound, the footsteps will suddenly be heard in the other room instead.

Years ago, this was a medical building and cadavers were stored on the upper floor. Some believe that this may explain the ghostly activity. Campus legend has it that the students were not actually supposed to have the cadavers that were secreted away in the building. Supposedly, they were so dedicated to collecting medical knowledge that they stole corpses from local hospitals and cemeteries, introducing the art of "body snatching" to Illinois College. The corpses were said to have been hidden in the attic until the stench of decaying flesh alerted college officials to their presence.

Other legends claim that the ghost is that of Williams Jennings Bryan, who has returned to haunt his old school. He was a member of Sigma Pi and was often in the building during his years at Illinois College. There are others who say that it might be Abraham Lincoln's ghost instead. He was an honorary Phi Alpha and while he did not attend the school, he spoke at Beecher Hall on occasion. In addition, William Berry (Lincoln's partner at new Salem), William H. Herndon (his law partner), and Ann Rutledge's brother, David, all attended Illinois College.

Another allegedly haunted spot on campus is the David A. Smith House, built in 1854. Today, the structure is home to three of the women's literary societies, the Gamma Deltas, the Chi Betas and Sigma Phi Epsilon. There is a parlor for all of them but the Deltas use a room on the main floor while the Betas and the Sig Phis have rooms on the second floor. The attic is used by all of the groups and there is also a dining room, a kitchen and an apartment at the back of the house.

There are several versions of the historic legend concerning the ghost in this house, but all of them claim that she is the daughter of the original owner and that her name was Effie Smith. The story goes that Effie was being courted by a young man from town and they became engaged. When he proposed to her, he gave her a diamond ring and she was said to have scratched the stone against her bedroom window to see if it was real. When she realized that it was, she etched her signature into the glass where it remained for many years afterward. The window has recently been removed and this small and unusual piece of history has been lost.

Then, the story begins to take different paths. In one version, David Smith disapproved of his daughter's fiancée and he locked Effie into a closet one day when the man came calling. Fearful of her father's wrath, the young man hid himself in a small room that was only accessible from the attic. For some reason, he nailed himself in and later died there. According to students who have been in the attic, the nails are still visible there today on the inside of the door. It is said that when Effie learned of her lover's cruel fate, she threw herself from an upstairs window and died in the fall.

In the second version of the story, Effie's young man went off to fight in

THE DAVID SMITH HOUSE

the Civil War. Every day, Effie climbed up to the attic and sat in a rocking chair by the window, watching for him to return. When she learned that he had been killed in battle, she committed suicide by jumping out of the attic window. Yet another variation of the legend has Effie being jilted by her lover, at which point she committed suicide. Regardless of what happened, the story stands that she has since returned to haunt the house.

Effie's rocking chair is still in the attic and the stories say that if you move it away from the window (where it sits facing out), then leave the attic and return later, the chair will have returned to its original position. This window is located in a storage area for the Chi Beta society and every year, they test the chair and discover that the story is true. One young woman walked into the room one day and the door suddenly slammed closed behind her. It is also not uncommon for cold air to suddenly fill this room, even though for years, the windows were painted shut. It was said that an icy cold wind would often come from the window that had Effie's name etched on the glass.

Another reportedly ghostly location is Whipple Hall, which was constructed in 1882. The spectral occupant of this place is known only as the "Gray Ghost." The upper part of the building serves as a meeting hall for the Alpha Phi Omega society and the Eta Sigma chapter, which is a national service fraternity, as well as the location of the security office. The lower part of Whipple houses the meeting hall of the Pi Pi Rho Literary Society. The building's basement is only accessible from the outside and is divided in half. One side was a classroom when this was Whipple Academy, a college prep school.

Perhaps the most famous sighting on campus of the Gray Ghost occurred to a girl who was leaving a Pi Pi Rho party one night and had to retrieve something from the Alpha Phi Omega hall. She had been drinking (but later insisted that she was not drunk). She said she had started climbing the curved staircase and as she reached the middle of the curve of the stairs, she looked up to the top landing and saw a man standing there. He was dressed in gray and she quickly realized that he was not a security officer. As she peered into the shadows, she also realized something else -- he had no face! She began screaming and ran back down the staircase and out of the building. Due to the noise of the party, no one heard her

WHIPPLE HALL

screams and the revelers wouldn't learn of the strange experience until later.

A room that is located on the third floor of Illinois College's Ellis Hall is also rumored to be infested with ghosts. According to reports, no one lives there if they don't absolutely have to. Rumor has it that a girl hanged herself in the room's closet around 1986 after failing to get a bid from a literary society. It is said that doors open and close on their own, appliances and radios turn on and off and that windows have a habit of going up and down under their own power. Or at least that's one version of the story....

Other students and alumni of Illinois

FEYERWEATHER HOUSE

College claim that the girl who haunts Room 303 was a young woman named Gail who died of natural causes in the room. Apparently, her parents were aware that she was terminally ill when she went to school, but since attending college had always been her dream, they allowed her to go anyway. She died while living in Ellis Hall and a small plaque is mounted on the door of the room in her memory. It is said that her ghost is a mischievous one, opening doors and hiding things. Legend has it that if third floor residents lose anything, they will call out to Gail and ask her to return it. The missing item is usually found a short time later.

A former student at the college who lived for two years in Ellis Hall, wrote to tell me of her experiences while living below the "haunted room." She said that she often heard knocking sounds coming from the other side of the wall, even though there was nothing there. It was the outer wall of the building and there were no trees nearby.

The college is said to have other haunted places, but stories from some of these sites are much sketchier. One of them is Fayerweather House, a residence hall for women. It has been said that windows and doors open and shut on their own there and that lights turn on and off without explanation. Stories say that a girl hanged herself in the house, committing suicide in the closet of Room 5, which is located on the stairway landing between the first and second floors of the house. "Susie," as she has been called, is noisy and can often be heard walking around the house, opening doors in the middle of the night and scratching on walls.

The stories also maintain that while the attic of the Fayerweather house has been converted into dorm rooms, they are never used. It has been said that the rooms were closed when too many strange things started to happen to the students who lived there. One of my correspondents wrote that she had a sister who lived in Fayerweather who told her of doors slamming and lights turning on and off, as well as objects that would fly about in the rooms.

Another haunted site is Sturtevant Hall, one of the most famous spots on campus. Recent stories say that a ghostly young man in a Civil War uniform is sometimes seen here. In addition, it is said to be nearly impossible to find someone who is willing to spend the night in the north tower of the building due to strange noises that haunt the place. Before it was made into classrooms, the building housed the Pi Pi Rho Literary Society. Members of the society still maintain that toilets in the hall often flushed by themselves.

Crampton Hall, which was built in 1873, is also believed to be home to a ghost. The residence was built to house 69 men and it was named in honor of Rufus C. Crampton, a former professor and president of the college. According to the story, there was a male student who left a party one night and was later found hanged in his closet. Rumors still state that he was hanged in a way that he could not have done it himself. His former room is believed to be haunted.

And apparently closets in Crampton Hall are as mysterious as the stories that revolve around them. One student told me of three of the residents who were waiting for a fourth friend to get ready so that they could all go somewhere together. Finally, they tired of waiting and went to check on him, only to find that he was hanging upside down in the closet, stark naked, and so frightened that he was almost incoherent. The student went on to say that he lived in Crampton Hall for one semester and would never live there again. One night, he said he fell asleep with his lights on only to be awakened by a noise. When he looked up, he saw a man standing there looking at him. The man quickly turned and vanished into the closet.

A VINTAGE PHOTOGRAPH OF CRAMPTON HALL

Another resident haunt can be found in the McGaw performing arts building. It has been reported that you will never find anyone who is willing to be alone in the auditorium at night. The place is allegedly haunted by the ghost of a man dressed in clothing from the 1940s. People on the stage are said to glimpse him out of the corners of their eyes.

Rammelkamp Chapel allegedly has a haunted basement. Some of the students tell stories of classroom doors that open suddenly and then slam shut, sometimes in the middle of lectures. The classrooms are located on both sides of a long hall. By looking out the door, it is possible to see into the classroom across the hall. One day, during a class, a student reportedly became quite upset when she looked across the hall and spotted a woman in white in the adjoining classroom. This would not have been so strange if the woman had not vanished in front of her eyes!

NIGHTS AT THE OUR SAVIOR RECTORY
BY LOREN HAMILTON

A few years ago, while I was doing research and putting together the Haunted Jacksonville Tour, it was suggested that I include the old Catholic Church rectory on the tour. I had heard some of the stories about the house, which served as a home to the priests of the parish for over 100 years but, not being of the faith, I thought little more about it. Later, when I began to hear more about the place, I became intrigued.

Reverend Francis F. Formez lived in the Our Savior Church rectory on East State Street for 59 years and many in the parish believe he still lingers there today. After his death in 1960, there were reports of people smelling men's cologne in the rectory when nobody nearby was wearing any, of a radio that turned on by itself to Cardinals baseball games, and the appearance of an apparition or two.

Altar boys from the church were responsible for cleaning the rectory. They had all heard about the haunting and some of them were apprehensive about going inside, especially after one young man encountered what he took to be the ghost of Father Formez. The boy was cleaning the priest's old bedroom when he had the feeling he was being watched. With trepidation, he turned to see an elderly man peering into the window with his hands pressed against the glass next to his face. The young man bolted in terror, vowing never to return. When I heard that story, I initially chuckled to myself, believing that someone was playing a trick on him. But when I later learned that the room was on the second floor where no living person could have stood outside and looked in, the story suddenly became more credible. Since the church didn't object to me adding the rectory to the tour, it soon became one of our visitors' favorite spots.

The rectory has an interesting history in Jacksonville. The land on which it is located was first purchased by William S. Jordan and his wife, Elisa, on November 12, 1823. On November 2, 1835, the Jordans sold most of the land to John J. Hardin, an attorney and a contemporary of Abraham Lincoln who moved to Jacksonville in 1830. His mother had been widowed when Hardin was thirteen and she later remarried Porter Clay, brother of Henry Clay. In 1832, Hardin was appointed state's attorney. He was a member of the Illinois House of Representatives from 1836 to 1842, and entered into the United States Congress in 1843. David A. Smith was his law partner. Hardin saw action in both the Black Hawk War and the Mexican War. He led the first regiment of Illinois volunteers and was killed in the battle of Buena Vista in Mexico on February 23, 1847. His body was brought back to Jacksonville and laid to rest in the East Cemetery.

After Hardin's death, Smith, acting as executor of the estate, sold most of the property to Richard Yates, who was governor of Illinois during the Civil War. He was the first graduate of Illinois College in Jacksonville and studied law under Hardin. Yates' public career included six years in the Illinois Legislature, another six as senator and four years as governor. He died in St. Louis on November 28, 1873 while serving as commissioner over the Cairo and Fulton Railroad.

It was Yates who would sell the rectory property to James Ewing on December 3, 1849. Ewing was a carpenter by trade and would be the first to build on the property. On July 4, 1865, he sold the new structure to Elbert Sharp, his sister, Elizabeth Berry, and their father, Martin Sharp for $3,400. Elbert had come to Illinois with his father from Tennessee in 1828. They settled on a farm northeast of Jacksonville before purchasing the home at 462 East State Street. Elbert became a carpenter and then entered the grocery business in 1872. When Martin Sharp died in 1872, Elbert brought his father's share of the house and later bought out his sister's share in 1884. Elbert died in a tragic accident in 1885 and his wife, Mary, remained in the house until 1895. At that time, the house was purchased by the Catholic Church for $5,000.

And this is where the events that lead to the haunting began.

In August 1895, the home was torn down to make room for the new rectory that would stand next to Our Savior Catholic Church, which was built in 1868. The first to inhabit the rectory was Father John W. Crowe. Father Crowe first came to Jacksonville to serve the parish in 1892. While work was done building the rectory, Father Crowe lived in the Yates mansion that stood to the east of the church. The Dominican Sisters bought the former governor's home and it was being used as a convent. When the convent was moved to nearby Springfield, the house was sold to Father Crowe to use a rectory. Father Crowe lived in the Yates mansion until the new rectory was finished in 1896. At that time, the old Yates home was remodeled and converted into a hospital. It opened as Our Savior's Hospital in November 1896.

The rectory is a two-story Queen Anne structure made of brick and stone. It has spindle work with a hipped roof and lower cross gables. A large wrap-around porch surrounds the first floor and a full basement lies underneath. Father Crowe lived there until his death in 1916.

He was succeeded by Reverend Formez, who had served as assistant pastor since 1901. It was during his tenure that three bells were installed in the tower of the old church and the church acquired an organ. Both the bell and the organ were moved to the new church, which now stands east of the rectory, in 1977.

The last priest to live in the rectory was Monsignor Michael Driscoll, who was installed as pastor after Father Formez's death in 1960. It was through his efforts that the new church was built and the parish would also see a new convent and a new high school. He passed away in the rectory before it was closed in 1995. At that time, a plan was put together to save the rectory. It was remodeled and is now listed on the National Register of Historic Places.

The rectory became a fascinating stop on the tour. I always told the story of the altar boy and the ghost of Father Formez, pointing out the window where the eerie vision appeared. During one memorable tour, screams and gasps of amazement occurred before I could point out the window where the face was seen. As I was telling the story, the window blinds opened and the image of a man was seen peering down at the group. Needless to say, I lost control of the tour and things were in chaos for the rest of the night. On another tour, my wife, who doesn't share the same belief in ghosts that I have, also saw the image of a man looking out of the window – not once, but twice!

Members of the local parish are divided as to the identity of the rectory's resident ghost. Some feel that it is Father Formez who lingers here, while others believe that it might be one of the other longtime residents of the rectory, or perhaps even a guest who spent time there. Besides Father Formez, the other name that I most often hear mentioned is that of Monsignor Driscoll, who not only died in the building in recent years but who also expressed a belief in the spirit world. Those who knew him often remember that he believed a person would smell the scent of lilac or lavender when a spirit enters a room.

In recent years, the rectory has become one of the oddest and most active locations for ghost hunts offered through the American Hauntings Tours. Based on my own experiences, and those of our guests, I have come to believe there are multiple spirits in the house. I personally believe that it's the ghost of Monsignor Driscoll who watches over the house. Much of the activity in the house occurs in the room where he died. I have recorded knocks and conversations, and felt an unexplained cold chill in that room.

I have had many investigators tell me they felt ill and short of breath when they entered the room, without having any prior knowledge of the house or what occurred there.

During one EVP session, we were answered with loud knocks from the table when asked for a sign showing that we were not alone and the image of a man was seen standing by us in the video. During the middle of the session the outside door slammed itself shut as if someone was leaving in haste.

The Our Savior Rectory is a compelling and spooky place. Is it as haunted as so many people claim? Find out for yourself, but keep in mind that this is a place that has caused many non-believers to embrace the possibility of the supernatural. The same thing just might happen to you!

GHOSTS OF THE HOCKENHULL BUILDING
BY LOREN HAMILTON

I'm often asked while hosting the Haunted Jacksonville tours, "So, what makes Jacksonville so haunted?" A quick look around the old downtown shopping district answers that question: the town's history. The reminders of past centuries still stand there, including the towering Hockenhull Building on the east side of the square.

Robert and John Hockenhull came to Jacksonville in 1839. They had been apothecaries in England and they opened a small drugstore on the city square. Early success in this business would lead to another store on East State Street that sold everything from farm implements to fine silverware. This would be the first location that would be dubbed the Hockenhull Building.

In 1866, Robert Hockenhull, along with Raymond King and Edward Elliott, opened the Hockenhull, King and Elliott Bank, which stood where the former US Bank stands now. By this time, Robert had purchased a home on Grove Street, where the Barton Stone retirement home is now. He went on to become a trustee for Illinois College and the All-Female Academy (later MacMurray College). Jacksonville had been good to the Hockenhull family. In fact, business had been so good that in 1891, the building that we now call the Hockenhull Building was constructed on the east side of the square. It still looms over the city today, although much has changed about the old square.

In those days, the downtown square was traversed by cable cars that transported passengers to and from the area businesses. Times were prosperous and the downtown flourished, as it did during my formative years growing up in Jacksonville. Men could buy a suit and pick up tools for the house and garage. Ladies could get their hair done, furnish the house and buy dress for Saturday night. Families could eat at the Woolworth lunch counter or at any of the restaurants that were found downtown. A person could also pick up a medical prescription or toiletries from the downtown Walgreen's, which later moved into the space where the Hockenhull drug store was once located. Retail business was alive and well downtown and a significant number of Jackonsonville's residents lived there as well. Many of the downtown stores had apartments above their shops. Walgreens was no exception and there were a number of apartments on the second and third floor of the Hockenhull Building.

Tragically, disaster struck on a cold winter night in early 1966, when a fire that started in one of the apartments swept through the Hockenhull Building's second and third floors. There were few safety measures in the building – no smoke detectors, fire alarms or fire escapes. Seven people failed to escape, suffocating on the thick smoke that was spawned by the blaze. Their bodies were later found among the charred walls of the Hockenhull Building's upper floors.

The 1970s and 1980s brought about a decline to downtown Jacksonville, along with other downtown

A VINTAGE PHOTOGRAPH OF THE HOCKENHULL BUILDING

business districts around the country. Much of the new businesses in town chose to locate along new roads that bypassed the old square and the downtown became empty and desolate. For years, memories of better times were recalled and ghost stories were told about the now-empty buildings. You could stand in the plaza and almost hear the voices and bustle in the winds of change that had come upon Jacksonville.

By the middle 1990s, those with a feeling of nostalgia for yesterday began returning to downtown and the revival of the old square began. Art galleries were among the first to return. My friend Sean Meek was one of the first to see the downtown's future. He purchased the Hockenhull Building with plans to open a co-op gallery offering the work of local artists. Being the local "ghost guy," I was invited to walk through the old building with a reporter from the local newspaper one weekday afternoon as part of a story regarding downtown revitalization. I decided to bring along a small electronic meter with me, just to see what would happen. Walking through the building's upper floors was like a trip back in time. I saw some reminders that the local Jaycees had held a Halloween Haunted House in the old building, as well as charred remains of clothing from the 1966 fire still left behind in a closet.

I was also witness to other, more disconcerting things, like mysterious spikes on my electronic equipment, even though there was no electricity on the upper floors. We also saw strange shadows in the hallways – shadows that should not have been there. It was almost as if the former residents were coming out to see who had invaded the long-empty space.

Of course, I wanted to do an official investigation. Sean agreed and I wasn't disappointed with what I found. On one of my first investigations there, I left a video camera to record any activity that might take place while no one was in the building. While going through the long process of reviewing the tape I noticed something odd at the end. The tape shows me coming back to claim the camera and being followed by an odd glowing mist that trailed me down the hallway. At the same time, the screen vibrated with each shot. I can assure you that I felt nothing at the time and was completely alone in the building. That strange event, along with other results from investigations and reports from the artists downstairs, led me to include the Hockenhull Building on the Haunted Jacksonville tour.

The downstairs artists reported odd things while working there. Office equipment suddenly turned off and on and the sounds of footsteps joined talking and laughter coming from the empty upstairs. Were the former occupants making their presence known to the new arrivals in the building?

I invited others to join me at the location to see if they sensed anything strange and odd things happened time and time again. During two years of regular visits at the Hockenhull Building, guests stated that they saw weird shadows where no shadows should be, and some said they had seen a woman with long hair in the bathroom mirrors that had been left behind in the old apartments. Others heard voices busy in conversation while some experienced physical issues like nausea, dizziness, headaches and blurred vision as soon as they entered.

Eventually, Sean started construction on the upper floors, hoping to rent out the apartments again. At that point, the ghost hunting visits stopped. It was during this time that Jacksonville's downtown began coming back to life. New businesses, night clubs and restaurants joined the art galleries to make the square a thriving place once more.

Over the course of the next few years, I received many requests to lead investigations at the Hockenhull Building. People continued to hear the stories and witness strange movements from the upstairs windows, but because of the construction work being done there, I reluctantly turned down all of the requests.

However, in the summer of 2010, I was asked for suggestions about haunted locations by Carl Jones, who teaches a paranormal class at Lincoln Land Community College in Springfield. Carl is an excellent investigator as well as an instructor. I knew if anyone should get the chance to see if the ghosts of the past were still present, it should be Carl and the group from LLCC. Sean agreed with me that it was time to revisit the Hockenhull Building.

Carl's group experienced some of the same activity that past visitors had encountered, along with some disembodied voices that were caught on audio tape. A second visit by LLCC verified the same results and gave me enough proof to put the Hockenhull Building back on my list of locations for public investigations on a very limited basis. We have the chance to search for the resident ghosts a couple of times each year. Some of the investigations have included hearing weird knocks, strange voices and sudden drops in temperature.

There is now a pet shop located on the first floor of the Hockenhull Building. The art gallery is a thing of the past. I have not heard whether or not the new tenants hear strange sounds coming from upstairs the way that the artists did. The future of the place is uncertain and suggestions have ranged from loft apartments to retail space, so only time will tell.

COFFEE, WINE AND GHOSTS
BY LOREN HAMILTON

You often hear of "dream teams" in sports, but on a humid July evening in 2006, I put my own dream team together for a paranormal investigation in Jacksonville.

The location of interest was the Due Gatti Coffee House, on the south side of the downtown square. My team was headed by my friend, author Troy Taylor. Joining us was John Winterbauer of Springfield, and Len Adams and Luke Naliborski, leaders of the Alton Hauntings tours. Everyone in the group was an officer of the American Ghost Society, so my expectations were high, to say the least.

The owners of the coffee house, the name of which is Italian for "Two Cats," were eager to tell us of the giggling they heard coming from the kitchen on a daily basis, the movement of objects and the clanging noises that seemed to come from the second and third floors.

The building that housed the coffee house was constructed in the early 1800s, like much of downtown Jacksonville. The downtown square is a dream location for both history buffs and ghost hunters. Over a period of more than 150 years, the Due Gatti building was home to many different types of businesses. It has been a restaurant and coffee house on more than one occasion but also a confectionary, a bank, and a flower shop, to name a few others. Inside, the visitor's gaze is drawn to the high ceiling, the large mirror behind the bar, and the narrow length of the downstairs — which seems to stretch farther than the space it actually occupies. There is a winding metal staircase, an old telephone booth that now acts as a storage closet, and a walk-in safe that has guarded money for generations.

We unloaded our equipment while it was daylight. We came prepared with EMF detection meters, thermometers, video cameras and audio equipment. We filled all three floors with yards of cable wire stretched across the floors. It was Sunday evening and the coffee house was closed, so it was an ideal time for our investigation. The weather was hot and the team was uncomfortable from the humidity so we took frequent breaks outside during the evening to escape the steamy air inside.

At this point I would like to tell you we had some unusual experiences, but we did not. I would like to report we saw the ghost of Abraham Lincoln playing gin rummy with Mark Twain, but we did not. As much as we pleaded, the spirits refused to come out. Pardon the pun, but it was a dead night. We rolled up our cable and put away our toys. We were not looking forward to reviewing our tapes but we did because they ran during our breaks, and we couldn't discount the possibility that something interesting had been recorded. We did get some quiet voices on the audio and some laugher that sounded like it came from a small child coming from the kitchen area.

The highlight from our balmy July night was a hidden door found in the basement, behind a wall. It appeared to lead nowhere. In the early 1900s the Jacksonville square was a round-about for cable cars and there were tunnels running underground but I could not find this door on any of the plat maps I reviewed of the downtown area. A psychic friend, Angelic Ross from Danville, visited the building and sensed that a murder had taken place on the property, probably during Prohibition. She felt the body was still buried under the basement floor. Had the doorway once led to a hidden room used by bootleggers? We will never know.

When I first started the Haunted Jacksonville tours, we left from Due Gatti, even though the investigation did not produce overwhelming evidence. Due Gatti was sold before the second tour season. New owner Joe Racey renamed the popular eatery The Three-legged Dog. He and his daughter, Beth, welcomed me back on a few occasions, but they don't believe the spirits have remained in the building. In fact, the new owners may wonder if the spirits were ever there.

Street construction to recreate the round-about pattern on the Jacksonville Square has kept me away from the coffee house more than I would like. But when the dust settles and the square once again looks like it did when the bank or the confectionary store brought customers to downtown, or in the early coffee house days, I'll be back to visit again.

Hopefully we'll find out if the ghosts have stayed behind or not.

THE EMPORIUM DEPARTMENT STORE
BY LOREN HAMILTON

There is a business located on the downtown square in Jacksonville where cash registers ring, parents are heard scolding their children for running down the aisles and customers try to barter with the store clerks. The place is the old Emporium Department Store, and the sounds heard there are quite interesting, considering the fact that the store closed for business in 1978!

The original building where the Emporium came to be located was erected in the early 1900s, but it would not open its doors as the Emporium until 1928. It was a huge place, a true department store of the day, and carried everything from clothing to toys and even fine furs. The store was three stories high, rising from a basement that was used for receiving shipments of merchandise. Eventually, an annex was built on one side. Oversized windows looked out on the street, holding mannequins and displays of the latest merchandise, just like Marshall Field's in Chicago and Macy's in far-off New York. It became *the* place to shop in Midwestern Illinois.

The Emporium flourished at a time when Illinois downtowns were bustling and busy. In Jacksonville, the square was host to JC Penny, Sears, S.S. Kresge, Woolworth's, three drug stores, three movie houses and a myriad of shops and eateries. For fifty years, the Emporium was a solid fixture on East State Street

94

but as time passed, Jacksonville's downtown, like so many others, began to fade. The streetcars vanished as the lines were pulled up and paved over. Soon, the walk from the parking lots to the front doors of the stores became longer as one company after another faded into memory. When bright and shiny chain stores began to open on the edge of town, the final nails were driven into downtown's coffin. In 1978, the last customer walked out of the Emporium.

But the building was not yet silent. Kruwag's Furniture, operated by Harold Waggoner, moved into the space in the late 1970s and operated for more than two decades. They specialized in one of the popular items of the era – the waterbed. In 2001, they closed their doors and joined the other new stores on the edge of Jacksonville. The old Emporium building was now empty.

Over the course of the next five years, the building remained empty, save for the rats. Nature was not kind to the structure and it looked as though the place might be lost for good. In early 2006, though, Joe Thomas bought the building with great plans to turn it into a center for troubled teenagers. He purchased it for a remarkably low price, only to discover later that year that the deteriorating building cost more to repair than he could handle. Even renting out the three apartments in the upstairs annex didn't bring in enough revenue to keep pace with the onslaught of work that was needed. Later that fall, he surrendered and the building was up for sale again.

Growing up in Jacksonville, I knew the history of the Emporium building – and had heard the ghostly legends of the place. Legends say that in the middle 1950s, a repairman doing a routine inspection of the elevator got too close to the edge, lost his footing, and fell down the shaft three floors to the basement below. The fall turned out to be a fatal one and stories stated that the repairman's ghost never left. Voices were sometimes heard and things moved about and I wondered if it was his intelligent spirit lingering behind or perhaps just some memory from yesterday. I became determined to find out.

The first two times that I visited the building, I saw nothing of a paranormal nature. I did get an odd feeling when left inside by myself, but was it something ghostly, or merely my imagination? I knew that I needed a larger team to tackle such a large place and we got the opportunity to check it out during the week after Christmas in 2006. We made plans to spend an entire Friday night and I assembled a team of four men and three women. In times past, Christmas was the store's busiest time of year and I hoped that the energy of the season would make the night a productive one.

I arrived at 7:00 p.m., two hours before the rest of the team. I opened up the building and turned on the lights and heat so that we could be comfortable during the night. Problems began right away when I was unable to open the old lock. It took a lot of twisting and turning, and a little grease, but it eventually yielded. The place smelled of mildew and old carpets and I heard water dripping as it seeped through a crack in the ceiling. I hunted for the light panel and found that all of the switches were still labeled from the days of the Emporium. I flipped a switch and found that it still turned on the old neon sign outside, half of which still miraculously worked. I was the first person to flip that switch in more than 25 years! As I walked through the place, I looked around at the relics of yesteryear. I saw the cabinets where furs were stored and the catwalk behind the walls where loss prevention officers could keep an eye out for shoplifters. I also found a 1948 edition of the *Chicago Sun-Times*, countless antiques and the skeletal remains of rodents and birds that had gotten into the building but couldn't get out.

As I wandered around, I started to get the uncomfortable feeling of being watched. I started to think that I was not alone. That was enough to convince me to go downstairs and wait for the others to arrive.

When the team arrived, we assembled our gear. We had come prepared with EMF meters, Geiger counters, tape recorders, a video camera, and four digital cameras. I gave the newcomers in the group a short introduction to ghost hunting, advising them to be aware of all of their senses and to let everyone know if they saw, felt, heard or smelled anything unusual. After that, we walked through the building so that everyone would know where the steps and doorways were located after we turned the lights down low.

We started our investigation in the old apartments. The first two were uneventful, but then we entered the third and all of our equipment began to light up. As we walked through the bedroom and hallway, we got extremely high readings on our instruments and all of us felt that we were not alone in the room. We took a number of photos to examine later and then headed back downstairs – where we found the lights had been turned back on for us! I turned them off and as we proceeded through the first floor, we found no activity.

After that, we went down to the basement, where shipments had once been stored and where the worker had once plunged to his death in the elevator shaft. We made our way to the spot where he died, but it was eerily silent on this night. The basement was filled with narrow passageways that led nowhere and doors that opened into closed walls. Over the years, the city of Jacksonville had gained a reputation as an important point on the famed Underground Railroad and we wondered if perhaps these hiding places and tunnels had once been part of the system. That mystery remains unsolved, as does the source of the strange activity that we experienced there. All of our meters picked up anomalous readings in some of the tunnels and again, we wondered if we were alone.

As we went back upstairs, headed for the second floor, we discovered that the first floor light was on again! I turned it back off and then we went up the stairs. We explored the upper floor for about an hour and then as we started back downstairs, I passed by the old elevator. Suddenly, my EMF meter came to life in a flurry of lights and sound. Just then, we all heard a loud bang from inside the elevator shaft. It was as if someone was behind the doors, knocking to get our attention – or perhaps to get out! A few moments later, the knocking stopped as abruptly as it started. We were all more than a little unnerved by this time. Our camera batteries were drained, our meters had gone quiet and we were shaken by the strange sounds. We decided to go downstairs and regroup for a few minutes and, of course, we found that the light had turned on by itself for the third time. I decided not to bother turning it off again.

We remained in the building for another two hours but experienced nothing else out of the ordinary. Whatever had been there with us was gone – or maybe it had gotten bored and didn't want anything else to do with us.

I visited the building one last time in the summer of 2007 but didn't return again to visit whatever spirits might remain. As of this writing, the bottom floor is occupied by a tavern. I did stop in one day to see if they had experienced anything strange and the sister of the new owner came up to me and asked, "Are you that ghost guy?" I told her that I was and she went on to tell me about the weird happenings that had occurred while the work was being done to set up the tavern. She said things moved around and vanished during the remodeling. They often came in each morning to find recently hung drywall lying on the floor. Tools were moved and hidden and she even stated that on one occasion a "force" held back a worker's arm as he was trying to nail some woodwork onto the wall.

The old elevator shaft where the long-ago worker died has been removed and pool tables fill the first floor, banishing the old department store to a distant memory. I still think about the store when I pass by on the street and think about what the place used to be --- and I think about the spirits that may still linger on the second floor. Do they still walk the floors there, like the downtown shoppers of yesterday, or have they faded into memory as well?

THE STRANGE CASE OF NATHANIEL VAN NOY
MENARD COUNTY, ILLINOIS
BY JOHN WINTERBAUER

Should one travel the back roads of Menard County in central Illinois you may find yourself on an old road that parallels the Sangamon River as it runs through one of the county's most scenic valleys. It is a peaceful place now; there is nothing left to remind the passerby of the strange and tragic events that took place here in 1826.

In the lives of the early pioneers events sometimes occurred of such magnitude that they were used to mark time. The murder of Peggy Van Noy was just such an event. For years afterward, residents would recall significant events starting with the phrase, "Two years before Van Noy was hanged..."

To start from the beginning, Nathaniel Van Noy and his wife, Peggy, came to the area that is now Menard County but at the time was part of a much larger Sangamon County, around 1820. They settled on a small tract of land about five miles west of Athens that came to be known as Van Noy Settlement. The peaceful valley in which the Van Noys made their new home was comprised of primeval forest intersected by the road from Beardstown to Springfield, the main artery for traffic through the area.

Nathaniel built a comfortable cabin on the south side of the road and a blacksmith shop on the north where he began to ply his trade, catering to locals and travelers. All seemed well enough with the Van Noys with the strange exception that Nathaniel was rarely home. The blacksmith would be gone for great lengths of time and upon his return would have plenty of money - this despite not firing his forge for weeks on end.

Apparently this curiosity didn't alarm his neighbors as they still came to Van Noy when they needed work done. On August 27, 1826 a local man and his young daughter made the trek to Van Noy Settlement to find the forge once again cold and the shop deserted. Curious, the father and daughter crossed the road to the Van Noy cabin where they beheld a horrific sight. There, in a pool of blood, lay Peggy Van Noy. Her husband was nowhere to be found.

The man sent his daughter back through the forest for help. Local historian John C. Harris wrote of the adventure years later: "A great aunt of mine, then a small girl, was among those sent out to summon the neighbors to the Van Noy cabin, and she used to tell of how fearful she was on that mission as she passed through the primeval forest lest a lurking Indian or Van Noy himself would jump out from behind a tree and kill her."

Several men arrived at the cabin and settled down to await the return of Nathaniel Van Noy. Hours passed and at some time during the vigil the men discovered the secret of Van Noy's mysterious wealth. Hidden on the homestead were the implements of counterfeiting. Later it would be revealed that Van Noy would make up a batch of phony cash and then travel to distant towns to spend his bogus money, receiving real currency back in change. For the men waiting at the cabin, this discovery cast serious suspicion on Nathaniel's role in the death of his wife.

Late in the night, Van Noy returned and was corralled by his captors. The blacksmith was visibly agitated and claimed to have spent the day stalking a deer that he had shot and wounded. Upon being questioned about Peggy's death he tried to shift blame to the Indians of a nearby village. This, apparently, was not satisfactory to his captors and Van Noy was turned over to Sheriff John Taylor.

THE PRESENT-DAY SITE OF THE VAN NOY SETTLEMENT. THE CABIN WAS ON THE RIGHT, VAN NOY'S SHOP WAS ON THE LEFT

Sheriff Taylor notified Judge John Sawyer who immediately called a special session of the Sangamon County Circuit Court. A grand jury was impaneled and sworn in to hear the case. Sufficient evidence was found to try Van Noy for the murder and a jury was called to hear the case.

Bowling Green, future friend to Abraham Lincoln, was selected as foreman of the jury, which also consisted of Samuel Lee, Jesse Armstrong, Levi Gordon, Thomas Parish, Erastus Wright (who, coincidently, was the first school teacher in Sangamon County), William Vincent, Philip Fowler, John Stephenson, Levi Parish, James Collins and George Davenport.

The trial of Nathaniel Van Noy commenced on August 28, 1826 with Attorney General James Turney representing the people. James Adams and I.H. Pugh acted for the defense. There is no record of the testimony for either side but it's not presumptuous to imagine the defense was weak and evidence against Van Noy overwhelming because, despite his "not guilty" plea, it only took a day for the jury to find him guilty of the gruesome crime. On August 28, 1826 jury foreman Green read the verdict, "We, the jury, find the defendant guilty in manner and form as in the indictment against him is alleged." At 9:00 the next morning Judge Sawyer issued the following ruling, "It is adjudged and considered by the Court that the said defendant Nathaniel Van Noy, having been found guilty of the murder of his wife, Peggy Van Noy, by the jury impaneled and sworn in this cause, be remanded to the jail of the County and there kept until the twentieth day of November next and that on said twentieth day of November next between the hours of twelve of the clock and four of the clock in the afternoon that the Sheriff of said Sangamon County take the body of the said Nathaniel Van Noy to some convenient place in said County and that the said Sheriff cause the said Nathaniel Van Noy to be there hanged by the neck until he be dead."

In less than three days Van Noy's fate was sealed and he was removed to the county jail to await his execution.

Murder and counterfeiting would seem to be enough to make this story noteworthy, however as Van Noy awaited his date with the gallows a series of strange events began to take place that would make any pulp fiction writer green with envy. It seems a Springfield doctor by the name of Addison Philleo claimed he had developed a device that if applied to a corpse immediately after death would reanimate the body. Dr. Philleo approached Van Noy in his cell and the two struck a bargain. Nathaniel Van Noy sold his corpse to Dr. Philleo, apparently with the belief he would be brought back from the dead shortly after his hanging.

November 20, 1826, the day of Van Noy's hanging, dawned clear and bright. A long procession formed at the county jail. Men, women and children proceeded through Springfield to a hollow near the site of the present state capital building to witness the spectacle. The wagon carrying Van Noy was driven beneath a simple crossbar supported by two posts and the prisoner was asked if he had any last words. According to Reverend R.D. Miller in his history of Menard County, "The murderer, who was a most excellent singer, asked permission of the sheriff to sing. Being granted the privilege, he stood on the platform, or cart, and sang in full, round tones that old hymn, composed by Dr. [Isaac] Watts, the first verse of which is: "'Hark! from the tomb a doleful sound; my ears attend the cry.'"

Miller added that Van Noy sang the entire, rather lengthy, song before a Methodist minister asked for prayer and offered Van Noy's soul to God. At that point a black hood was placed over his head, the noose was slipped around his neck, the horses bolted forward and Van Noy swung.

The body dangled for five hours before being cut down. Apparently Sheriff Taylor had heard of Dr. Philleo's deal with Van Noy and had decided not to turn over a fresh corpse. Dr. Philleo, thwarted in his experimentation, began an autopsy on the spot. This revolted onlookers so much that the good doctor was forced to move to a nearby building to finish his work.

One of Van Noy's last public statements was that he had buried a quantity of gold beneath a tree in the valley near his cabin. For years people searched for Van Noy's gold but to this day it has never been found.

By 1832 Dr. Philleo had relocated to Galena in northern Illinois where he published the *Galenian*, the only paper north of Springfield. When the Black Hawk War broke out that spring Dr. Philleo attached himself to the battalion of Major Henry Dodge as a war correspondent. As Dr. Philleo was the only newspaperman with the army his reports were published across the country.

As Dr. Philleo chronicled the campaign of Major Dodge he always referred to him as General Dodge, which gave readers the impression that Dodge was in command when in reality it was General James D. Henry. The reports were never officially corrected and the result was that for many years thereafter histories asserted that Dodge, and not Henry, was in command.

A single martial deed can be attributed to Addison Philleo during the Black Hawk War. One day a scouting party came upon two of Black Hawk's warriors who attempted to flee. One of the Indians was killed in the chase. A short time later Dr. Philleo came across the body and scalped the Indian. For many years he displayed the scalp as evidence of his valor. Dr. Philleo died in January 1841 in Tampa Bay, Florida.

As Van Noy's story passed into legend, the old homestead became a place to be feared by travelers on the road. Several pioneer memoirs recall hastening the horses as they passed by the former home of the Van Noys for fear of lurking ghosts. It is interesting to speculate on the thoughts of the young Abraham Lincoln as he traveled the route during his time in New Salem. As it was the most direct route to Athens and Springfield, he would have gone that way often. The house was standing as late as the 1850s before mention of it stops in the accounts of area settlers. Some say it was standing well into the twentieth century but there is no evidence to support this claim.

Shortly after the Nathaniel's hanging, tales of the spirit of Peggy Van Noy wandering the fields around her old home began to circulate. One story tells of a traveler who passed by late one night only to be startled by the sounds of a woman's screams coming from inside the dilapidated house. The man, unaware of the building's violent past, dismounted and ventured inside to assist the obviously distraught woman.

After a few minutes of searching the premises, the man was unable to locate the woman. Perplexed, he returned to his horse and continued his journey. When he reached the Hall Tavern in Athens he told his story and only then did he learn about Peggy Van Noy's horrific murder.

Others reported seeing the spectral form of a woman floating through the trees around the ramshackle cabin. While I can find no particularly interesting accounts, it is said that all the witnesses believed the ghost to be that of Peggy Van Noy. These reports continued for years and the old Menard families have preserved many of them as part of family lore. The existing tales are several generations old and, unfortunately, many specific details have been lost over time.

One story concerns the irate spirit of Nathaniel Van Noy and was told to me by my great-uncle, George Whitney, when I was about eight. George was a local historian of note in Athens. I didn't realize it then and had I known I would have paid more attention. This, perhaps more than any other story I've collected, illustrates how fact and legend sometimes become blurred. The main protagonist of the tale, Alexander Hale, was a real man and a prominent resident of Athens. It is the inclusion of a real person that adds merit to a story such as the one my uncle told me all those years ago.

According to George's account, Hale and two unnamed friends made the trek from Athens to the Van Noy farm under cover of darkness to search for the hidden gold. The men set to work digging but several hours passed with no trace of the treasure being found.

Late in the night the young men noticed an odd glow coming from deep in the nearby woods. Believing it to be the lantern of a rival search party, they decided to sneak up on the other party and scare them away. As they quietly crept through the trees, one of the men entered a small clearing and came face to face with a man surrounded by an unearthly glow, who glared menacingly at him and raised a threatening hand in his direction. The would-be treasure seeker didn't wait to see what the spectral man would say; he ran, screaming in terror, back toward Athens.

His companions, having not seen the ghost, and shocked by this bizarre turn of events, ran after their friend. After catching up with him farther down the road, and hearing his unlikely tale, Hale and the other man wanted to keep searching for the treasure but the frightened man refused. Eventually, the others relented and accompanied their terrified partner home.

The next day Hale and the other man returned to the scene to collect their tools and look for signs of the mysterious "glowing man." Finding no sign of him, they returned to Athens and there the story ends...or does it? The next year Hale, in partnership with John Overstreet, erected a large, brick flourmill in Athens at a cost of $11,000, no small sum in 1856. I'll put it to the reader as George put it to me...with a wink. Isn't it fun to speculate where the money for the venture might have come from?

Today the valley seems quiet. One of the few remaining stretches of the old Beardstown road still passes the site of the old Van Noy homestead. Sometimes I drive through this peaceful valley and wonder if Peggy still wanders these fields or if some unsuspecting soul may yet encounter the ghost of Nathaniel himself as he still protects his ill-begotten gold. Or maybe, just maybe, the ghosts are quiet now because a couple of entrepreneurs from Athens left Van Noy with nothing to guard but an empty hole beneath a tree.

TALES OF GHOST HOLLOW RANCH
CASS COUNTY, ILLINOIS
BY JOHN WINTERBAUER

The original inhabitants of central Illinois, if the lore is to be believed, knew of certain places where the spirit world was a little closer to our own. In these places they held their religious ceremonies and buried their dead. To those of us in the modern world, these old beliefs seem a bit quaint. But what if they were right? And what if those places still hold power today?

Above the bluffs of the Sangamon River, hidden away amongst the rolling, wooded hills of Cass County is the fifth-generation farm of the Wagoner family, now run by Rich Wagoner, who has turned the ancestral farm into a retreat for those who enjoy a simpler way of life. This is Ghost Hollow Ranch.

The rustic beauty of the 120-acre spot has changed very little since Rich's great-great-great-grandfather first took up residence here more than a hundred years ago. The only modern improvements to be seen are Rich's small cabin, a combination bunkhouse and stable, and a large fenced corral where horseback competitions are regularly held; the rest is given to nature and riding trails.

Ghost Hollow Ranch is a tranquil, out-of-the way place but, as the name implies, it is also a very haunted place; what's more, its hauntings are only now being fully explored. To date there have been two organized investigations by members of the American Ghost Society (with hopes of more to follow) and they have yielded some fascinating results. There will be more about those later, but first we need to explore the history of this location and introduce you to its ghosts. As you will see, they are as varied a group of spirits as you will ever hope to find!

LOOKING DOWN GABBY'S ROAD TOWARD MILLER'S CREEK IN GHOST HOLLOW

The hauntings of Ghost Hollow Ranch are for the most part the result of tragedy. As those familiar with ghosts and hauntings know, untimely, violent deaths often leave ghosts behind. This is certainly the case here!

Illinois was settled from south to north with the first permanent white settlers arriving in the central part of the state around 1818. Many passed through the area prior to that date; most of them were trappers and hunters who wandered into the area which, until their arrival, had been the exclusive hunting grounds of Native America tribes like the Kickapoo, Pottawatomie and Winnebago. While the intrusion was unwelcome, the two factions managed -- unlike whites and Indians in other parts of the country -- to live in relative peace.

Tales of Indian ghosts in the area are plentiful. One woman who lived near Tallula (south of Ghost Hollow) claimed that one morning, as she made breakfast, she looked out the window and watched as a man, clearly an Indian, walked through her backyard and vanished before he reached the property line. Another person talked of encountering the wandering spirit of an Indian one evening while camping along the Sangamon. Several accounts have been reported of ghostly Indians around Cass and neighboring Menard County, generally they are fleeting glimpses of shadowy figures in the woods.

The Mound Builders were in the area long before the Indians we recall today; evidence of their culture can be found near Lewistown to the north at Dicksen Mounds. In the area that it today encompassed by Ghost Hollow Ranch the tribes consisted mainly of migratory people who subsisted by agriculture and hunting in the rich river bottoms. Not far to the east of Ghost Hollow is a prominence known today as Shickshack Hill.

By 1833 the natives of this area had been induced by treaty to surrender their traditional lands and move west. One Indian who remained behind, and became familiar with the incoming white settlers, was Shickshack, a Winnebago chief who had been in the area since around 1812. On the hill that now bears his name he lived a peaceful life with his two wives, Lo-lo and Mah-qua-la, and their four children.

Shickshack was on good terms with his white neighbors but, as game dwindled and his hunting grounds shrank, he became resolved to the fact that the Indian's days in the area were numbered. In 1827 the old Indian saw a steamboat on the Illinois River for the first time. The noisy, smoke-belching machine convinced him that he couldn't ever live among these new settlers and, it is said, he moved north.

During the Black Hawk War in 1832 several members of Abe Lincoln's company from Sangamon County recalled running into Shickshack near Dixon's Ferry, where they had a pleasant visit with their old neighbor. At their parting they shook hands and Shickshack continued his northward migration; some say he ended up in Wisconsin but, the fact is, he simply disappears from history.

Shickshack became somewhat of a legend in the area. Even after the bulk of the tribes had departed; lone Indians wandered through from time to time and usually the settlers claimed these figures were Shickshack. One hunter claimed to have stumbled across the old Indian and, becoming startled, shot him and dumped the body in a frozen pond. There are few traces of the Native Americans around the area today. Their burial mounds can be found along the bluffs of the Sangamon River and the old-timers recall where their villages once stood but obvious signs of these proud people have vanished...unless, of course, you consider a golf course near Petersburg that derives its name, Shambolee, from a long-forgotten Indian who once lived in the area.

That Ghost Hollow Ranch was home to Indians is evidenced by the mounds they left behind of the property and the artifacts that are still sometimes are found there. Six large mounds ring the west side of the ranch. In the early 1900s one was partially excavated and the burial treasures removed but the bodies left intact. These mounds have yielded some interesting results with K-II EMF meters and other equipment. During one investigation in 2009, Kelly Davis recorded significant electronic activity at one mound in particular, evidence that was replicated a year later during our second investigation.

What makes this activity interesting is that there are no power lines or manmade objects that would produce these types of readings anywhere near the hill. Furthermore, Kelly received specific answers to her questions as she conducted the tests on the hill. While to date, nothing more concrete has been recorded it remains an interesting, mysterious place.

ONE OF THE BURIAL MOUNDS IN GHOST HOLLOW THAT HAS BEEN THE SCENE OF ODD ACTIVITY

A few years ago a worker on the ranch was walking through the woods near the mound that had been excavated; as he rounded a bend in the path he came face to face with a man he knew instantly was the ghost of an Indian. The ghost stared straight ahead and started to make a motion of some sort with his hands before he vanished before the shocked employee.

As far as is known, the first white settler on the acreage that now encompasses Ghost Hollow Ranch was a trapper who came here in the mid-1800s. Sadly, his name is lost to history but his spirit still lingers and is the one ghost at the ranch who may inadvertently scare you if you visit!

The old man's cabin stood where there is now a parking lot for the stable and corral and his still-functioning well is nearby. In those days people didn't travel much; they planted themselves in one spot and took what they needed from the land around them. This circumstance led to a booming trade for some entrepreneurial types who would pack as many goods as they could carry into a wagon and travel around the countryside hawking their wares. One such huckster was a regular in the neighborhood.

This man came to the trapper's cabin one afternoon and, as was the custom when no one had hard cash, he negotiated the trade of some of the trapper's goods for some of his own. The deal was done and the peddler rode away. Not long after the old trapper began to think he had been cheated in the deal and he began to watch for the peddler's return, which was always announced by the distinctive, noisy clanging of the goods on the wagon.

Weeks passed and word got out that the old man was angry and looking for revenge, so the peddler, it is said, avoided the area as best he could. But one stormy night, the peddler made a fateful error.

Lost in the storm, and drunk some say, he erroneously turned down the road that led past the trapper's cabin (the modern Gabbys Road, which still follows the same route through Ghost Hollow). Once down the road there is no room to turn, even today, as the bluffs rise high on both sides.

The trapper heard the loud, unmistakable wagon and rushed out into the night to face his nemesis and confront him over his perceived grievance. Meanwhile, realizing his mistake, the peddler urged his horses

THE STRETCH OF ROAD WHERE THE GHOSTLY TRAPPER IS REPORTED

on faster. The trapper reached the road just as the wagon thundered by and he lunged to grab the bridle of one of the horses, only to be pulled beneath the wagons wheels and crushed to death.

What happened to the peddler is unknown but ranch guests today still encounter the old trapper near his homestead.

On more than one occasion Rich has had frantic people pound on his door to tell him an old man has just thrown himself in front of their car. Upon further inspection they find no damage to their car and no sign of the man; he simply vanished.

Others report strange occurrences with the electronics in their car while coming down the road. Radio reception gets fuzzy, dash lights inexplicitly dim and headlights go out completely. Cars have been known to stall on the spot. While all this can't be attributed without question to a ghost, it does make the spot in the road a weird location where investigators have been able to record strange, unexplained spikes in the electromagnetic field.

Rich's great grandfather, Breeze Wagoner, purchased the property after the old trapper's death around 1860. Although the elder Wagoner has never been seen I often wonder if the man who started the farm still wanders its grounds. His manner of death certainly shows his tenacity!

Breeze was a muleskinner who made his way to Illinois a few years before he bought the property. One afternoon he and his mule boarded the ferry that crossed the nearby Sangamon River. The mule, a cantankerous creature, got spooked during the ride and started to kick and buck, inflicting significant damage to the craft.

At the other side Breeze and his destructive mule disembarked and went about their business, returning late in the afternoon to cross the river. The ferryman told Breeze his return fee would be a dollar, significantly higher than the passage over. When asked why, he replied it was to cover the damage the mule had done on the first trip.

Breeze thought the price unfair and refused to pay. An argument ensued and finally Breeze declared he'd rather drown trying to swim his mule across the river than pay such an exorbitant fee. And that's exactly what he did. The mule swam to safety; Breeze was lost in the current.

One ghost you may encounter lost her husband in a similar manner and she waits for him to this day. Her name is Mrs. Miller and she is the most famous ghost at the ranch, the one whom visitors are most likely to encounter as she has been seen repeatedly over the years.

Mrs. Miller's story begins in the 1950s. She and her husband were neighbors to the Wagoners and often used the road in front of the house while going about their business. The creek at the bottom of the hollow is called Miller's Creek and even today, it can quickly become a raging torrent during heavy rains. It was a common problem when Rich's grandpa lived on the land and Rich remembers the floods from when he was a boy. It was a dangerous place during a storm because the water rose so rapidly.

The creek was spanned by a questionably constructed lumber bridge that consisyed of several boards set across the creek with no rails or safety features of any kind. Mr. Miller was riding home on a skittish horse in a downpour and, despite the ankle-deep water rushing across the bridge, he decided to brave it. Partway across, Miller's horse spooked and he was thrown from the saddle into the fast-moving water and swept away. His body was never recovered.

Mrs. Miller was a broken woman after that; she returned often to the spot to look in vain for her husband's body. This sad ritual was played out for several years until the widow joined her husband in death. But, as it turns out, even death didn't bring the long-hoped-for reunion as Mrs. Miller has returned to continue her watch.

Rich's grandpa and later, Rich himself encountered the spirit of Mrs. Miller on the bridge where her husband died. She wears the plain clothes of a farmer's wife and stands looking into the woods only to vanish seconds later.

Guests near the house have reported a woman, presumably Mrs. Miller walking through the parking lot and into the stables. One man told me he awoke one night while sleeping in the bunkhouse to see a woman walking through the room. Startled, the man started to ask who she was and what she wanted but before he could get the words out the woman disappeared!

Once Rich even encountered the ghostly woman in his house when he glanced up to see her standing there. She looked him straight in the eye and abruptly vanished. Although he was startled, Rich simply accepted the fact that he might share his home with a ghost and went about his day. Mrs. Miller hasn't been seen in the house since but Rich believes she often takes or moves things, including a pair of glasses that were a gift from his mother.

In recent years Mrs. Miller has also been seen serenely rocking in the chair on the front porch of Rich's house. The only suggestion I can offer, and one that I hope is right, is that she may have come to peace with the fact her husband is gone and now she, like many visitors to the ranch, is enjoying the peacefulness the place offers.

Another occurrence in the area of the bridge that people have reported over the years are strange lights floating along the road and out in the woods. This was a phenomenon I hoped to capture on film during an overnight investigation in 2010. That night I, along with several others, had

MILLER'S CREEK

an encounter that may very well be related to what others have been reporting for years. During the night I took another investigator, A.J. Jenchel, out into the woods to investigate the mound that had been disturbed in the early 1900s. We were trying to find a hint of the Indian ghost.

Failing in our mission, we made our way back through the woods and, coming to Miller's Creek, we decided to follow it out to the bridge and try to find Mrs. Miller.

As we walked along with our flashlights A.J. and I realized there were people on the bridge. We thought our lights might be mistaken for something paranormal so we began to talk a little louder to ensure we weren't mistaken for ghosts.

We reached the bridge and found David Lowery and Chris Mason who had, in fact, seen our lights. They had been on the bridge for several minutes and had seen several lights floating through the trees. They said the light from our flashlights was markedly different in appearance than what they'd seen. Several minutes passed as we discussed these weird lights when suddenly, from about twenty feet up the road, I noticed a light. It was about the size of a basketball and had a weird, bluish glow surrounding it. This light approached us very slowly and then, within seconds, it blinked out and didn't reappear. Chris saw it as well, and confirmed it was the same as what they'd seen earlier.

What was this light? It's hard to determine if it's the ghost of Mrs. Miller or perhaps a roaming Indian spirit. Maybe it's something else altogether, natural or otherwise. Hopefully future investigations will offer some answers to this puzzle; until then it's just another of Ghost Hollow's many mysteries.

Finally we come to a ghostly encounter with special meaning to Rich because it involves a horse unlike any he has known before or since. The horse's name was Dark Eyes and, if you're lucky, you may meet him yourself if you visit the ranch.

Dark Eyes came into Rich's life in the early '90s his owner was sent to prison and needed someone to watch over his horse. Rich took the animal and quickly realized this was a special horse. He developed an instant bond with Dark Eyes and spent the next year taking him to horse shows and competitions. When home at the ranch it wasn't uncommon for Dark Eyes to escape his stable and run out into the nearby alfalfa field. Unlike some horses, Dark Eyes would come running back when Rich called his name. It became a friendly game between the two.

Dark Eyes performed well at events, eventually winning a World and Congress Championship. Rich and the horse had a great year but their short-lived relationship came to an end when Dark Eyes' rightful owner was released and came to claim his horse. Reluctantly Rich sent Dark Eyes home and thought he'd never see him again. It was sheer coincidence that brought the two friends together again a few years later.

While on a trip to northern Illinois Rich happened to see an ad for a horse event in Ottawa, Illinois, so he made an unscheduled detour. Upon arrival he met several people he knew from the circuit and quickly learned that Dark Eyes was there with his owner.

Rich sought the horse out and, when he finally saw his old friend, his heart sank. The horse looked terrible, sick and neglected. He would later learn that Dark Eyes had been badly mistreated. When Dark Eyes saw Rich he perked up. "He seemed almost happy," Rich told me. Rich and the owner talked and all the while Dark Eyes nuzzled Rich's hand; it was a good meeting for both of them. Rich made an offer to buy the horse, but it was rejected.

Fate came knocking again about a year later when once again again, Dark Eyes' owner was about to be sent to jail. The man made Rich the same offer as before: he could watch Dark Eyes for the duration of his imprisonment but after that the horse would be returned. Rich, unable to face the parting again, reluctantly refused. Not long after that, he learned that Dark Eyes had died.

Rich mourned the horse like an old friend. When he tells the story now, many years later, you can still hear the sorrow in his voice. It is that deep sadness that Rich believes may have led to a recurring event at Ghost Hollow that he believes is caused by the spirit of Dark Eyes.

It began one quiet summer night a year or so after Dark Eyes died. On a ranch, it's not uncommon for horses to escape the stables or corral; Dark Eyes did this frequently. At Ghost Hollow, the animals often make their way to the large alfalfa field just beyond Rich's yard. That night Rich heard, as he sometimes did, a horse out in the field. He went out to search for the animal and was unable to find it. Upon inspection, he found all the horses in the stable. He wondered if it had been his imagination but when he heard the neighing of a horse in the field again he knew without a doubt that it was Dark Eyes.

To this day Rich listens for his old friend and others claim to have heard the mysterious sounds of a horse that isn't there. Rich wonders, "Could this be something I wanted so badly that, somehow, I caused it to happen?" While the power of suggestion certainly can apply in this case, is it so hard to believe that in death, Dark Eyes has returned to a place he loved in life? There are numerous reports of ghost animals in the investigative files of paranormal researchers all over the world.

Ghost Hollow Ranch has its share of mysteries. The ghosts here are as much a part of the land as the trees and the creeks. They, like the ranch itself, offer an insight into a simpler time, and while we may never fully solve all of the mysteries, Ghost Hollow is a place that will remain a haven for those who long to escape the modern world and possibly even the physical world itself.

THE LEGEND OF TOWANDA MEADOWS
TOWANDA, ILLINOIS

Those of us who have traveled along old Route 66 north of Bloomington, Illinois, have seen the house nestled eerily in the cornfields off in the distance. We have wondered about it, just as travelers on the old Alton & Chicago Railroad did decades ago. The brick Italianate mansion seems out of place on the Illinois prairie, looking mournfully toward a highway and a railroad line that seem to have passed it by, leaving it stranded in the distant past. The house has been crumbling there for many years – lost, abandoned, seemingly forgotten and, some say, haunted by the tragedies of yesterday. It is a house of realized dreams, great fortune and premature death. In that respect, it is strangely suited to the shadowy corners of Illinois.

The grand house that came to be known as Towanda Meadows, was built in 1874-1875 by William R. Duncan, a pioneer farmer and stock raiser who came to Illinois in 1863. When Duncan erected the mansion, it was said that he purposely set out to make it so impressive that it would be noticed by travelers between St. Louis and Chicago. He attained his objective, building a spacious mansion with six fireplaces, a winding staircase with hard-carved walnut spindles, and walls that were more than a foot thick. But Duncan was destined to enjoy the luxurious house only for a short time; not long after it was completed, death and tragedy came calling.

William Duncan was born in December 1818 in Clark County, Kentucky. Raised by wealthy parents in the slave state of Kentucky, William became rich after his father's death in 1836. Under the terms of his father's will, the family's slaves were set free, which convinced William to remain loyal to the Union when

A VINTAGE PHOTOGRAPH OF TOWANDA MEADOWS

the Civil War began to rage years later. Eventually, the political division in his home state caused him to move north to Illinois.

William had a brother, Thomas, and two sisters, Elizabeth and Sally. In their father's will, Sally was described as being unable to care for herself, suggesting that she was mentally ill. If so, it was a condition that would return to haunt the family in later years as William's second son, James, was declared insane by a McLean County court in 1882 and sent to the Jacksonville State Hospital.

William married his first wife, Nancy Redmon, in 1835 when both of them were only seventeen years old. She died in 1848 and William married a second time a year later. His new wife was a widow named Mary Chorn Quisenberry. She and William had four children, Nannie, Henry, James and Mary Elizabeth.

In late October 1863, William sold off a large portion of his cattle and moved his family to Illinois. They traveled by train and ended up in Towanda, likely renting a home owned by Nathan Sunderland on property that Duncan eventually purchased in December 1865. The start of the family's new life in Illinois was shattered by the death of Mary Duncan on February 23, 1864. William was devastated by the loss of yet another wife and the children were heartbroken, especially Mary Elizabeth, who was only three years old at the time.

Late in 1864, William, now 45 and widowed twice, traveled back to Kentucky where he took a third bride, Sarah Ann Bean, age 29. Sarah was wealthy in her own right and the two signed a pre-nuptial agreement of sorts, giving her control over her own money, an arrangement that was unusual for that time.

The newlyweds returned to Illinois and William begin building his cattle business and amassing a fortune. He brought a number of experienced cattlemen with him from Kentucky, including a number of free black men who had worked for his family for years. In 1866, he became a member of the advisory committee of the McLean County Agricultural Society and was appointed to audit the treasurer's books. In some of the minutes of the society's meetings, Duncan is referred to as introducing some of the finest breeds of foreign cattle to the area. He formed an alliance with a number of other forward-thinking farmers in the region who advocated the improvement of crops and livestock through selective breeding and other scientific means.

Tragedy visited the Duncan family again on June 16, 1868 when twelve-year-old Henry drowned in a pond on the family's property. He was buried next to his mother in a small home plot, although the bodies were later moved to Evergreen Cemetery in Bloomington. During his son's funeral, a grieving William had the grave of his second wife, Mary, opened so that he could say goodbye to her one last time.

A few years later, construction was started on Duncan's three-story mansion. The house was unlike anything that had been seen in the area and locals came from far and wide to watch the building take shape. William welcomed sightseers, which bolstered his reputation as a kind and generous man. Most regarded him as one of the county's foremost residents, and he was in great demand as a speaker for the state agricultural society, and at the September 1875 meeting of the National Agricultural Society, which was held in Cincinnati.

Towanda Meadows was completed in 1875 but sadly, William lived in the house for less than a year before his death in October 1876 at the age of 57. At the time of his death, he was returning home from the state fair in Ottawa, Illinois. He had been depressed for some time, following the death of his last remaining sister, Elizabeth. Many blamed his melancholy for the fact that he was unable to shake off a severe cold that he contracted at the fair. After becoming ill in Ottawa, he was put to bed at the home of his friend Abner Strawn and remained there for several days. Feeling better, he departed for Towanda, but only made it as far as Normal before he collapsed. He was taken to the home of relatives and died with his third wife, Sarah, by his side.

Duncan never saw his beloved Towanda Meadows again. He was buried on the property next to Mary and Henry until Sarah had their remains exhumed and moved to Evergreen Cemetery.

Sarah remained at the farm for a time with the remaining eight children. They had little time to mourn as squabbling, tragedy and death continued to plague the family. Soon after the death of her father, Nannie, William's oldest daughter with his second wife, Mary, filed a lawsuit on behalf of herself and her siblings against Sarah and her children. She was seeking a portion of her father's substantial estate and the courts divided the land into parcels. Nannie later became a schoolteacher and married Franklin Barnes, a successful farmer, in 1878. They had a daughter, Lucy, who was born in 1880.

Like other members of her family, Nannie was doomed to an early grave. In 1884, her health began to fail (although it's not listed in the records, she likely suffered from tuberculosis) and Franklin, very concerned about his wife, sold his farm and moved his wife and daughter to Pomona, California. He hoped that the mild climate might improve Nannie's health. Unfortunately, she continued to decline and as she neared death, she told her husband that she wanted to return to Illinois to live out her final days. She passed away while they were on their way home and she was buried in Evergreen Cemetery.

Tragedy struck the family again in 1896 when Nannie's daughter, Lucy, died from consumption (the old-fashioned name for tuberculosis) in her father's Bloomington home. Lucy died on the day before her sixteenth birthday. Her father later moved to Towanda, where he served as the town's postmaster for a number of years. He remarried and later died in November 1905.

William and Mary's third child, James, was only eighteen when his father died in 1876. Nelson Jones, a friend of James' late father, was appointed by the court to be his guardian. James lived each winter in Texas, where he raised horses that he brought back to Illinois for sale. In September 1878, James married Flora Dillon of Bloomington and his guardianship was ended. In February 1880, James and Flora had a son, Levi William, and moved into a home next door to James' sister Nannie and her husband, Franklin. James worked hard to improve the farm and was soon worth quite a bit of money. He began importing horses from overseas and established himself as a successful dealer. A second son, Floyd, was born in November 1882.

Tragedy touched James and his family in 1883, when James, Flora, Flora's sister, Ida Dillon Harding, and other members of the Dillon family traveled to France for both business and pleasure. James planned to arrange for the purchase of a number of horses and to see the sights with his family. As they were preparing to make their way back across the Atlantic, Ida became seriously ill and was unable to depart for the return trip. James and Flora and another couple made the trip so they could care for the horses but three others remained behind with Ida, who died a few days later.

This was the start of a terrible time for James and his family. In three years, James went from a prominent businessman to a severely depressed and mentally ill young man. His malady struck in his late twenties and was likely an onset of bipolar disorder, for which no diagnosis existed at the time. On July 7, 1886, Flora's father, Levi Dillon, filed a petition with the court indicating that James, then 28, was insane. He asked the authorities to investigate the allegation. As was customary at the time, a warrant was issued for James' arrest and he was taken to the Illinois State Hospital for the Insane in Jacksonville. He was judged unfit to manage his personal estate of more than $20,000. Levi was first appointed as conservator, but he was later replaced. There was controversy about what happened to James' money while he was in and out of the insane asylum but accusations were made in particular against Levi Dillon. When James was eventually released from the hospital his remaining property was restored. James and Flora divorced in December 1891. The couple's older son was raised by James and Floyd was cared for by Flora. What happened to James after his release from the hospital and subsequent divorce is largely unknown. In 1891, he was lsited in public records as working at a livery stable in Bloomington. Soon after, he vanished from history.

Mary Elizabeth, William and Mary's youngest child, was in Kentucky when her father died. She had been living there with her uncle, James Chorn, and his family. In 1881, she was in Illinois visiting friends and family when she met Ellis Dillon, Flora's brother. The two fell in love and despite being two years older than Ellis, Mary Elizabeth married him in December 1883.

The couple later moved to Wisconsin, where Ellis enrolled at the University of Madison to train to become an electrical engineer. They had four children, Carl, Lula, Helen and Dorotha and apparently lived a happy life for many years. Then, in September 1918, Mary was granted a divorce from her husband on the grounds of cruel and inhuman treatment. According to her testimony, she and Ellis had lived together in the same house for five years but they never ate together or slept together and Ellis refused to speak to her. She was unable to cite a cause for this treatment. Ellis was ordered to pay her $50 a month in alimony while she remained unmarried. Ellis later moved to Montana but what became of Mary Elizabeth is a mystery.

After William's death, Sarah and her five children remained at Towanda Meadows only a short time before returning to Kentucky. Sarah died of pneumonia in February 1922 at the age of 86; she never remarried.

In 1882, Sarah sold Towanda Meadows and her remaining 100 acres to F.M. Jones, who later sold it to D.W. Kraft of Normal. Over the years, the old mansion had gone through a succession of owners and during the twentieth century, tenants occupied the grand old home. The fireplaces were bricked up, the second and third story windows shuttered, and it was left to decline in the wind and weather of the Illinois prairie.

It was the tenants who lived in the house who told strange tales of ghosts and lingering memories. Many of them spoke of footsteps on the stairs and in the hallways, of whispers, the sound of a woman weeping and knocking at the front door during the wee hours of the night. Every one of these weird happenings can be directly tied to the mansion's tragic past with a woman crying for a lost child and the fateful knock that summoned Sarah to the bedside of her dying husband. History has left an impression on this creaking old place and past events seem to be replaying itself over and over again.

One former resident of the house once told of his encounter with a spectral woman on the second floor. He was only a boy at the time but clearly remembered exploring the upper floors of the house when he was living there with his family. In one of the closed-off bedrooms, he clearly saw a woman standing and gazing out of the window. When he gasped at the sight, the woman quickly turned around and then vanished in front of his eyes. He never forgot the incident but who the woman might have been in unknown. Despite the efforts of local researchers, no Duncan family photographs have ever turned up.

Do phantoms still linger at Towanda Meadows? No one can say for sure. For years, it has been in the hands of absentee landlords but efforts to restore it may someday succeed and life may be breathed back into the once-glorious home of William Duncan. Will restoration work manage to bring the spirits "back to life?" Only time will tell.

MURDER & MYSTERY AT AIRTIGHT BRIDGE
COLES COUNTY, ILLINOIS

Spanning the muddy and churning waters of the Embarras River in east central Illinois is the rusted and creaking expanse known as Airtight Bridge. It has been considered an unsavory place by locals for many years, more likely because of its reputation as a drinking spot for teenagers and Eastern Illinois University students than for anything connected to the supernatural. But this did not stop the ghostly tales from being told. Visitors to the remote spot told of eerie cries and mysterious, mournful weeping even though this tales seemed to have no connection to the history of the bridge.

All of that changed in 1980. It was in October of that year when a grisly discovery was made at Airtight Bridge that would create a terrifying history of unsolved murder, horror and connections to one of the most notorious serial killers in modern American history.

If Airtight Bridge wasn't haunted before that October, it certainly had a reason to be in the years that followed.

The old steel bridge that earned such infamy in later years was built in 1914 along the only road that

AIRTIGHT BRIDGE

ran between the town of Ashmore and the unincorporated towns of Bushton and Rardin. Designed by Claude L. James and built by the Decatur Bridge Co., locals claimed that it earned the name "Airtight" because of the unnatural stillness that travelers experienced as they crossed the span, but according to the Coles County Historical Society, the name came about because of the way that the air settled in the wooded valley where the road was located. Regardless, the bridge crossed the Embarras River in such a remote spot that few people ever journeyed there by accident.

Thanks to its secluded location, the bridge became a popular drinking spot and a hangout for the Illinois chapter of the Sons of Silence Motorcycle Club, an outlaw biker organization that was founded in Colorado in 1966. The bridge's unsavory reputation continued in 1977 when the body of a drug overdose victim was found nearby. But the gruesome event that occurred in 1980 was bad enough to send even the Sons of Silence in search of a new place to party.

On October 19, the nude body of a young woman was found floating in the Embarras River, just a few yards downstream from Airtight Bridge. The body was missing its head, hands and feet, which caused the investigation to be dubbed the "Airtight Torso Case." It was the last in a series of murders of young women in Coles County that went back nearly a decade. It turned out that the Airtight Torso Case was unrelated to the others but, like the earlier crimes, it remains unsolved.

The body was discovered on a Sunday morning by William and Tim Brown, brothers who lived near Urbana, Illinois, who were in the area on a deer hunting trip. They took the road down to Airtight Bridge at around 11:00 a.m. and as they crossed the metal span, they noticed something strange in the shallow water below. They quickly pulled over to the side of the road, where they encountered a local farmer named Victor Hargis, who was on his way to help his son dig a well. The brothers pointed out what appeared to be the remains of a woman and Hargis and William Brown climbed down to the river's edge to take a closer look.

Hargis passed away in 2004 but his son, Victor, Jr., later recalled his father's reaction to the discovery. "You could hardly tell it was a woman because the head was gone," he said. "It's hard to believe someone would do something like that."

Hargis immediately returned to his truck and drove home to call the Coles County Sheriff's Department. Chief Deputy Darrell Cox, who was at pistol practice at the time, received the call and was the first law enforcement officer on the scene. It took him nearly twenty minutes to drive the back roads from Charleston, but he was very familiar with the area around Airtight Bridge since it was part of his regular patrol. Years later, Cox, who went on to become the county sheriff, vividly remembered what he saw that day. "I could tell when I got there that it was missing its head and feet. I remember when I first saw it standing on the bridge; it didn't look like a person."

Other officers soon arrived and the bridge was cordoned off as a crime scene. It wasn't long before word spread of the dismembered body and newspaper and television reporters rushed to the secluded spot. Such horrific crimes rarely occurred in the rural area and thanks to this, the case became a sensation, grabbing headlines for many days to come.

Investigators worked late into the night, scouring the bridge and the surrounding area for clues. Scuba divers were sent into the river and officers tramped through the woods but the missing body parts – which the coroner stated had been severed cleanly – were never found. Coles County Coroner Dick Lynch described the woman as being in her twenties, rather flat chested, and "not in the habit of shaving." He added that she had dark auburn hair, was approximately 5 feet 9 inches tall, and weighed around 130 pounds. Although Lynch was of the opinion that she had been murdered elsewhere and her body dumped at the bridge, he was unable to determine a cause of death. Sheriff Chuck Lister agreed with Lynch's findings, stating that he believed the woman had been murdered and dismembered and then taken to Airtight Bridge, where the body had been rolled down the bridge embankment to the water. The remains were sent to Springfield to be examined by pathologist Dr. Grant Johnson at Memorial Hospital. He was able to determine that the murdered woman had type A-negative blood, shared by only 6.3 percent of the U.S. population, but he failed to find anything conclusive because of the advanced decomposition of the body and the fact that the head and extremities were missing.

The torso did not have any major scars, tattoos or birthmarks that might offer any clues to the woman's identity. The pathologist was also unable to come up with a cause of death, or even a definite time of death. The remains had not been spotted in the river the night before the discovery but Dr. Johnson believed that she had been killed quite some time before that. In fact, he estimated that she had been dead for more than 48 hours before she was found. She had been murdered, he believed, and her body left somewhere else before it was placed in the river. With her hands missing, it was impossible to tell if she had struggled with her killer. There were no drugs, poison or alcohol in her system and no evidence of rape or other types of violence. Sadly, it appeared that she had been pregnant at one time and had likely given birth. Somewhere, investigators grimly realized, was a child who was missing his or her mother.

The discovery of the victim's rare blood type was a major clue in a case that was otherwise woefully lacking in solid leads. A check of missing person reports led nowhere and the investigation grew cold. On October 23, the sheriff's department called off the search at Airtight Bridge. Both police investigators and news reporters continued to delve into the case, running down every possible clue and checking into every theory, no matter how thin. Nothing turned up and the story eventually vanished from the headlines. Almost a year after the remains were discovered, the unidentified young woman was laid to rest in Mound Cemetery in Charleston. Her grave was marked only with the words "Jane Doe."

The case was largely forgotten for the next several years. Then, in the middle 1980s, interest was revived when a convict named Henry Lee Lucas confessed to the murder. Since his death in 2001, Lucas has earned a reputation as either one of the most prolific serial killers in history – or one of the greatest frauds. According to Lucas, between 1975 and his arrest in 1983, he and an accomplice named Otis Toole roamed the country, murdering at least eleven people before being arrested in Texas. While in prison, Lucas confessed to between 350 and 600 homicides! Investigators from all over the country brought him their cold cases and Lucas claimed to have committed one after another. A task force was set up to investigate his claims and has since been criticized for sloppy police work, accepting Lucas' claims at face value and helping him to perpetrate what many believe was a long-running hoax. Although initially sentenced to die, his sentence was commuted to life in prison by then Texas Governor George W. Bush. Lucas later died in prison from natural causes in 2001. Whether or not he committed all – or perhaps any – of the murders he confessed to remains a mystery. Most researchers believe his claims were wildly exaggerated but that he certainly killed more than eleven people.

One of the many murders that Lucas confessed to was the Airtight Bridge case. Almost as soon as he took credit for it, the Coles County Sheriff's Department eagerly announced the news. Sheriff Lister announced at a press conference that the Airtight Killer had been found and that an indictment would be forthcoming. According to Lucas, he was unable to remember his victim's name but he did remember the bridge. He had picked up the woman in East Texas and brought her to Missouri, he said, where he had killed and dismembered her. He said he left her torso at Airtight Bridge but had dumped the other parts of the body at other locations, which were then searched by the Illinois State Police. No trace of the woman's head or limbs was ever found. The grand jury refused to return an indictment in the case and it fell apart completely when Lucas recanted and claimed that he had not committed the murder.

The Airtight Case went cold again. It would not be until 1992 that a real break occurred. On November 20, the sheriff's department finally announced the name of the victim – Diana Marie Small, a resident of Bradley, Illinois. She had disappeared from her home a short time before her body was discovered over 100 miles away in Coles County. Detective Art Beier of Coles County and Detective Steven Coy of Bradley had been able to piece together the clues and reveal what had happened to Diana. She had never turned up in missing person reports because she was never reported missing. Her husband told the police that he wasn't worried because she had left home before. No other relatives knew that she was missing either. Diana's mother and sister had joined a fundamentalist Christian sect and moved west, where they fell out of touch with Diana and her husband. More than ten years later, her sister, Virginia, left the church and tried to get in touch with her estranged family. That was when she realized that Diana was missing and soon after, filed a missing person report. Detective Beier saw the report on a national listing, recognized the description of the Airtight victim, and contacted the Bradley police. A DNA match confirmed that Diana had finally been found.

Tragically, her murder has never been solved. Coroner's reports in 1980 were correct when they stated that Diana had given birth. She had a daughter named Vanessa who was only two years old when her mother disappeared. She had no idea what had happened to Diana for many years since her father refused to talk about it. Diana's case was re-opened in 1995 but her husband would not talk to detectives. Since that time, the case has gone cold once more.

In October 2008, the anonymous stone that marked Diana's grave was replaced by one etched with her name, bringing one part of this mysterious case to an end. However, most feel that it will never be completely over until the tragic young woman's killer is finally found.

The identity of the murderer remains a nagging question in this story – but it's not the only one. Does the spirit of Diana Small still linger at Airtight Bridge? Some claim that it does, but others say that the bridge was haunted long before she was slain. So, if the ghost that walks the old steel bridge is not Diana's, then whose restless spirit remains there? Perhaps there is more dark history to Airtight Bridge than any of us know...

THE MURDER OF REBECCA HOULDEN MENARD COUNTY, ILLINOIS BY JOHN WINTERBAUER

Over the years I've collected countless ghost stories from all over central Illinois. In every case I make an effort to tie the ghostly events to an event or series of events in the past. This story, I believe, may have some bearing on the ghostly encounters reported in one particular little graveyard.

The headline in the *Athens Cyclone* newspaper screamed:

JUSTICE AVENGED!
Charles Houlden, who murdered his helpless wife in cold blood on the 22nd day of March, 1884, tendered a rope by 12 Good and Lawful Men and True, After a Fair and Impartial Trial...

On March 22, 1884, Charles Houlden, a resident of rural Menard County, intimated to a neighbor that he planned to kill his wife, Rebecca. The neighbor later recalled, "He would have been better satisfied and that something startling would occur in that vicinity some day."

That evening, something startling indeed occurred on the Houlden farm. It is an event that remains unparalleled in its cruelty and consequences in the history of Menard County.

Charles Houlden was born in England in 1836 and later immigrated to America with his sister. He eventually settled in the Rock Creek precinct of Menard where he adopted the life of a farmer. He was described as, "an ordinary average Englishman and a widower" in the *Athens Cyclone* of 1885. He was a man of rather heavy build, 5 feet 7 inches tall, weighing 140 pounds. His sharp chin and nose gave him Romanesque features, and his sunken, gray eyes were framed by "iron gray hair, whiskers and mustache."

Rebecca Hines was a neighbor of Houlden. Not long before, her third husband, Samuel Hines, had died, leaving the widow with three children and an 80-acre farm to tend by herself. Houlden, seeking the land more than the companionship of a wife, began to court Rebecca, and they were married not long after.

The couple began to argue almost immediately. They fought, it seems, over control of the farm. The newspaper noted that their home quickly became a place of "disputes, quarrels and bickerings." The fights were violent and often came to blows. The Houldens quickly became the source of much gossip in the neighborhood. Eventually, it was said, Charles agreed to buy Rebecca out and give her a divorce.

A murder trial was being held in nearby Petersburg about this time. It was a distraction to many who attended the trial as a form of entertainment. On March 22, Charles Houlden spent the day at the courthouse, leaving as the trial went to the jury. Later that evening one of Houlden's neighbors, Joseph Sutton, met Charles on a lane near his farm. Sutton had stayed at the courthouse for the reading of the verdict and Houlden inquired as to the outcome, "Not guilty," said Sutton.

"Anybody can come clear if they have the money," was Houlden's reply. Sutton continued on his way home and Houlden went inside for supper with his wife, her daughter, and her thirteen-year-old son, Oscar.

During the meal Rebecca noticed something odd about the way her husband was looking at her, "Charley, what are you looking at me for?" she asked.

Without a word, Houlden pushed away from the table and went to the door where, just outside, he had earlier placed an ax. In a frenzied rush, he lunged at his terrified wife who only had time to scream before the ax descended toward her head. The quick-thinking Oscar threw himself at his stepfather and managed to hit his arm, deflecting the killing attack on his mother. Rebecca received a glancing blow that immediately left a bruise. The daughter ran from the cabin for help.

By now, the crazed Charles was blinded with rage and again raised the ax. Oscar again managed to grab Houlden's arm but not before the weapon made contact just above Rebecca's left eye, leaving an ugly gash. Oscar grabbed the ax and tossed it out the door into the night.

Houlden then jumped astride his fallen wife, crushing her to the floor with his full weight. As she begged for mercy, Houlden drew a dull knife from his pocket and began systematically sawing away at her throat. Blood sprayed across his arms and chest, seeming to spur Houlden to more savagery. As his mother lay dying at the hands of her husband, young Oscar struggled with the killer in an attempt to wrest the knife from his bloody hands.

Finally, Charles began waving the knife at the unarmed boy, who had no choice but to back away to spare his own life. Houlden stood and, believing his wife dead, began to leave the scene. But then he noticed Rebecca rise to her hands and knees and begin crawling toward her son. Though badly wounded, she was still alive!

Houlden howled in fury and again jumped on the woman. Seizing her hair tightly in one hand, he wretched her head back, exposing her already brutalized neck while he renewed his attack.

Soon, his grisly task was accomplished and he fled into the darkness beyond the cabin. Rebecca "fell with her head hanging over the front doorstep a bleeding corpse," according to a newspaper report. A short time later, the daughter returned with an older brother and found young Oscar in a state of shock, sitting beside the lifeless form of their mother.

Arrested shortly after the killing, Charles Houlden was locked in the Menard County Jail in Petersburg and charged with the murder of his wife. He was held there until his trial commenced in March of the next year.

Edward Lansing and N.W. Branson acted for his defense, while an imposing team of lawyers represented the prosecution. The defense attorneys entered a plea of insanity and the trial began. After both sides rested, the case went to the jury on March 11. It was late in the day, nearly 5:00 p.m., but it took only fifteen minutes for them reach a verdict of guilty of willful, deliberate murder. Two hours later, they reached a unanimous decision that Charles Houlden was to "be hanged by the neck until he is dead."

The execution was set for May 15, 1885, and Charles Houlden was returned to the jail to await his date with death. His was to be Menard County's first, and as it turned out, last, public execution.

THE CRACK OF DOOM
In the Prime of Life and Excellent Health, Dropped into the Arms of the Grim Monster, May 15, at the End of a Rope...

Early on Friday May 15, people began pouring into the little hamlet of Petersburg, reminding one citizen of a circus day. A crowd, estimated at over 1,000, soon gathered in the yard of the county jail where inside, Charles Houlden waited to meet his maker.

The hanging was scheduled to occur inside the jail, out of sight of the masses. When exactly Houlden would die had been kept a secret from everyone except for the people "lucky" enough to have tickets to enter the jail and witness the event. At 11:30 a.m., they arrived and were ushered into a small room adjoining the jail to await the summons of Sheriff Michael T. Hargrave.

Houlden had been allowed to select the hour of his death. It was to occur at 12:10 p.m. and shortly before that, Sheriff Hargrave entered the condemned man's cell and read the death warrant. Houlden, dressed in a new black suit, black slippers and crisp white shirt, listened silently.

The sheriff then led Houlden from his cell into a hallway at the south end of the jail. There a scaffold, with an upright on each side, running floor to ceiling and spanned by a simple crosspiece, had been erected. A six-foot by six-foot platform containing a trapdoor was reached by a short staircase. The walls of the hallway enclosed the device on three sides, reminding one witness of a speaker's platform at a picnic.

Hargrave tied the prisoner's hands behind his back and ushered him up the stairs to the platform, where a chair had been placed. From this vantage point Houlden could clearly see the dirty rope that hung from the upright that would soon end his life. Several visiting sheriffs joined Houlden on the platform and sat slightly behind him on a bench provided for their comfort. Hargrave asked Houlden if he had any last words. "No," the prisoner replied. With that, the noose was slipped around his neck. He appeared emotionless as a black sack was placed over his head to mask his death agony from the witnesses.

Sheriff Hargrave sat on the bench behind Houlden as the condemned man was moved onto the center of the trapdoor. In Hargrave's hand was the rope that ran to the trigger of the apparatus. The pins that had locked the trap in place were removed and seconds passed...

There was no sound in the tightly packed hallway. Finally, Hargrave pulled the rope, dropping the trapdoor and with it, Charles Houlden. A dramatic newspaper article described him as "dropping with a dull, blood- stirring thud, his neck was broken. Aside from drawing his legs up and straightening them down again, there were no further movements of his limbs, or body. In the prime of life and in vigorous health, Houlden stoically stood between two worlds [and if consciousness is eternal] experienced the realities of each."

Fifteen minutes later, Charles Houlden, the first --- and last ---- man executed by the county of Menard, was declared dead.

There is no record of where the county buried Charles Houlden. His wife was buried in a rural cemetery not far from the homestead she shared with her murderous husband. Today, she rests peacefully beneath the grass in this out-of-the way place.

The cemetery where Rebecca Houlden is buried is haunted, possibly one of the few legitimately haunted cemeteries in Menard County. For years, people passing by or visiting the old graveyard have experienced a variety of paranormal activity that, if the stories are true, suggests there's something about the place that is not quite right.

Can these events be accredited to the restless spirit of Rebecca Houlden? Could it be that the county chose to bury her killer in an unmarked grave in the same ground? Perhaps it is something else altogether, but the tales from this old burial ground are numerous and varied.

Sitting a quarter-mile or so off one of Menard's many twisting back roads, the little cemetery is barely discernable under the best of conditions. At night, or during the months when the corn is high, it can't be seen from the main road at all.

The first burial was made there in 1858. It was a family cemetery then, but over the years it has changed ownership and names on several occasions. One researcher, the late Jim Toal, made a record of all the grave markers in the early 1980s and, using the list created from that research, 45 of the stones he noted are now entirely gone. Although the burial records of this cemetery are intact and appear to be complete, it is possible that the removal or destruction of these stones may play a part in the hauntings that are reported here.

Upon entering the grounds, one is immediately moved by the silence of the place. Surrounded by tall cornfields on one side during several months of the year, the acre and a half or so that makes up the cemetery is framed by dense timber on the remaining boundaries. It is not particularly eerie and nothing leaps out that says "haunted!" but close examination of the grounds offer some suggestions that could explain the strange stories that have been uncovered about the site.

Two areas in particular show evidence of unmarked burials. The southeast corner, where Rebecca Houlden lies, is the most prominent. There are very few stones in this area although sunken ground and strips of concrete remain to show where graves are located.

Could this be why the graveyard is considered to be haunted? Many researchers believe that graves that are purposely, or accidentally unmarked can cause paranormal activity.

The most common event reported here is that of mysterious balls of light that float among the old gravestones. These lights have been reported for many years and the reports are fairly consistent. One account will serve to describe what witnesses have seen while driving along the road at night.

"The graveyard is way down a lane in the woods," a young woman named Jeni told me. "We were coming home from a basketball game in Athens, my boyfriend lives out there and I was taking him home. I hate driving out there anyway because it's so dark and the roads all twist around. I always worry about hitting an animal or something, so I pay extra attention and drive really slow there.

"We came up the hill and Robbie said, 'Hey look at that' and he pointed out the window toward the [old cemetery]'."

What the two teenagers saw appeared to be lights weaving around out amongst the stones. Not sure of what they looking at from a distance, they stopped to get a better look.

Jeni continued: "He thought someone was out there screwing around. These lights were red and there were four or five of them. We sat there for maybe ten minutes before they blinked out and didn't come back."

Robbie became obsessed with what they'd seen that night and often walked to the graveyard from his home. He made several visits before he saw the lights again.

"One night, Robbie called me and said he and his friend and gone over there on their bikes and had seen the lights. They rode down the lane to just before the cemetery then they got off their bikes and sneaked up thinking they were going to surprise somebody."

The boys saw the lights from a closer vantage point than on the previous sighting. They claimed they were independent balls of light zipping around in the cemetery and just inside the tree line to the north. There was, according to Robbie, no sign of another human being on the grounds. After a few minutes, the boys made a hasty retreat and, upon his return home, Robbie called his girlfriend.

"He did sound kind of scared, out of breath and excited. I believed him when he said he saw these lights," Jeni said. Not long after Robbie witnessed the lights again and, this time, Jeni was with him.

"This time we just drove down there and sat at the end of the lane. The lights didn't go away and it was freaky because you could see them in the headlights of the car. They were like these balls that were just flying around. There were only a couple that night and they were still red. It was weird and surreal, not really scary, just strange. When they went out we left," she said.

Until Robbie left for college a year later, Jeni often accompanied him to see if the lights were floating in the cemetery. Only one other time did they witness the event after that second night. The results were similar to their first encounter, as they saw the lights only from the road that last time.

Jeni and Robbie are braver than most witnesses who have reported these weird lights. Most people don't dare to travel down the long, dusty road to see what waits at the other end. Are these lights ghosts? Probably not, more than likely they are a naturally occurring phenomenon that has yet to be explained.

My own theory is that as a ghost gathers the energy that is required to manifest itself, it drains the area around it of any electricity it can. This "feeding" often results in the appearance of odd balls of light that are akin to static electricity.

These strange balls of light would be enough to suggest that some form of paranormal energy lingers at this cemetery but other reports exist that are both chilling and, to a ghost hunter, worthy of further examination. Consider this account, sent by a young man who is a former employee of Menard County and who, in years past, mowed the grass in the county's cemeteries:

There are a couple of those old cemeteries out there that creeped us all out but [that one] was one of the worst. We always felt like people were watching us there, like they were in the woods or something. We only saw something weird one time.

We were about half done with the graveyard and about ready to knock off for the day. There was nothing odd about the place that day; I mean feeling-wise, it felt fine. Only then one of the guys stopped the mower and was looking off toward the back of the cemetery.

I looked and there was a guy there, young guy -- maybe twenty -- and he was walking into the middle like he'd just come out of the woods or something like that. Then he stopped and looked like he was going to go behind a tree or something. The other guy with the mower started up again and kept mowing so I did too. A couple of seconds later, I glanced over to where that guy had been and there was nobody there. He was gone and there was no way he could have got out of the cemetery from where he was in like two seconds while I looked away.

I got kind of nervous but not too scared really; it was just weird. Then later, some of the other guys said they had seen him too but none of us could figure out where he'd gone. He was like [magician] David Copperfield; he just disappeared right out of the graveyard!

Could these men have seen a ghost? It certainly is possible. It's also possible someone had simply walked into the cemetery or had been there all along and they had failed to see him earlier. Whatever the case, another witness made it clear, in no uncertain terms, that she believed she witnessed a ghost in the same area.

"My family is buried there," Marie informed me, "some of the earliest to come to the area. I do genealogy and have spent a lot of time in [that graveyard]."

One spring afternoon, Marie and her two young daughters had driven from Chatham to take pictures of the family stones. They had been in the graveyard about twenty minutes when one her little girls told her mother she needed a new roll of film.

Turning to go back to the car, Marie was startled by the presence of a man standing almost directly behind her, between her family and the car.

"He was a younger man," she said, when pressed she determined that he looked to be around thirty. "He had this look on his face like he was amused. I was scared because he had walked up on us so quietly. I said, 'Hello,' and he didn't respond and then I started to panic. Just a second after that he disappeared right in front of my eyes!"

Marie, now terrified, grabbed her daughters and led them quickly to the car and made her escape, rattled but unharmed. She reported that she has never returned to the scene of her shocking encounter, despite her husband's pleas to take him to the cemetery.

These reports are the only two I've received concerning full-blown apparitions in the graveyard. Many times people have told me about feeling watched (which coincides with the boys' sighting) or of strange, unexplained chilly breezes or cold spots in the grounds, which is said to be another indicator of ghost activity. One couple told me they'd heard whispers as they walked the grounds. They didn't stay long and were unable to offer further details as to what they thought they heard. Another woman told me she heard a woman call her name but could find no one else nearby.

The question I put to you is this: can all these people, without conferring with each other, be lying, mistaken or confused? It's possible, of course, but it's hard to imagine that all of these unconnected people could come to me with reports of ghosts, all of them stemming from this little-known graveyard. Possible, yes... just not probable, especially when Menard County offers many other, sometimes creepier, settings for fictitious ghost encounters.

Nothing in the record points to a specific identity for the mysterious young man who seems to be prowling the grounds but there are certainly many people buried there that could fit the description. Is it possible his mortal remains lie buried in one of the many unmarked graves and he's simply seeking some recognition? It might just be that Charles Houlden, a criminal if there ever was one, lies there as well. Thankfully, his appearance in life doesn't match the witnesses' description.

Spurred by the accounts I was hearing, I took a drive out to this isolated graveyard one afternoon a few years ago. It was a bright, sunny spring afternoon. The only sounds that day were the birds in the surrounding trees and the faint sound of an occasional car far up the road.

I'd visited the spot before on several occasions and had never encountered anything odd there. This day, I didn't feel anything strange and no mysterious figures appeared to me. It seemed like any other rural cemetery except that the odd stories came flooding over me. I have to admit I proceeded with a small amount of trepidation.

With a video camera set up at the west end of the grounds, I began to make my way through the gravestones, snapping pictures as I went.

As stated, Rebecca Houlden's grave is unmarked. Jeanne Weaver, an active Menard County genealogist/historian, had told me she remembered Rebecca's gravestone and it was there when Jim Toal did his research. However, there is nothing there now to commemorate the unfortunate woman but an empty field. I passed the afternoon scouring the grounds for hints of forgotten graves. I found much evidence of missing stones but, from a paranormal standpoint, the day was a bust. Until....

Later that night I loaded the pictures from my digital camera into the computer and began to examine them. In one frame, a streak of light, preceded by a white ball of light is clearly seen near the last resting place of the unfortunate Rebecca Houlden.

There was nothing extraordinary about the graveyard that day. No odd EMF readings, nothing to make me think I wasn't alone. Still, that weird picture gives me pause. Is it possible that Rebecca or some other unfortunate soul (or souls) still wander the grounds?

Unfortunately, the computer that this photograph was stored on was later destroyed and all attempts to photograph or film an anomaly in this cemetery since have been fruitless. I will continue with the hope that something reveals itself to me.

Since that day, I've visited the graveyard on several occasions. Each time I wander the grounds I carry Jim Toal's list and quietly read the names from the missing stones with the hope that someone decides to answer.

Of course, I honestly don't know what I'd do if someone did...

"AULD LANG SYNE"
GHOSTS OF THE COLISEUM BALLROOM
BENLD, ILLINOIS

Located just off what was once the original path of Route 66 in downstate Illinois is the legendary Coliseum Ballroom. Its long and often mysterious past has been linked to big band history, bootlegging, gangsters, murder and more and it continues to stand as one of the great old landmarks of the region. The ballroom is no longer the dancehall that helped to create its notoriety, but it still manages to attract people from all over the region who come looking for a little history – and for its resident ghosts.

The old Coliseum was built in the small town of Benld, a once-prosperous mining community that became a central Illinois melting pot of nationalities, made up of men who came to work in the local coal mines and their families. Situated in the middle of three mines, Benld furnished homes, churches, schools, and more to the immigrants who settled the area. They came from many countries, including Austria, Bohemia, Croatia, England, France, Germany, Greece, Ireland, Italy, Lithuania, Russia, Scotland, Slovakia, and Sweden.

The history of the area began in the late 1800s with the arrival of the Dorsey family, who settled the Cahokia Township of Macoupin County. In the early 1900s, the Superior Coal Company, a subsidiary of the Chicago & Northwestern Railroad, bought 40,000 acres of coal and mineral rights from the Dorsey family and began to sink mines to furnish coal for their locomotives.

In 1903, the town of Benld was established, taking its name from its founder, Ben L. Dorsey. Legend has it that the name was actually a mistake. The story goes that a sign once existed outside of town that had Dorsey's full name on it. A storm came along and tore off the end, leaving the letters "Ben L. D." By default, this became the name of the town. No one seems to know if there is any truth to this tale, but it's an odd bit of possible history for this fascinating town.

Benld was laid out in the middle of the three mines and soon began to grow. The original town was platted so that North Sixth and Seventh streets would be the hub of the community, with growth spreading in every direction. At the western edge of town, a station as built and trolley tracks were laid by the Illinois Traction System. The Chicago & Northwestern Railroad also laid its tracks to the west of town, creating a surge of business toward Central Avenue, where a rail yard and a roundhouse were built, creating additional employment for the area. In 1916, a fourth mine, the No. 4, was sunk west of Benld and more people came to the area. By the early 1920s, the town's population had grown to over 5,000.

Benld boasted a racetrack, a football field where a professional team played, and a city band that consisted of coal miners who performed every Sunday, their only day off. Benld also had barbershops, blacksmith shops, dairies, a feed store, hardware and grocery stores, laundries, a hemp factory, a soda factory, a lumber yard, a bowling alley, a theater, taverns, and numerous other establishments during its heyday.

One unusual incident in Benld's history occurred on September 19, 1938 when a local resident named Edward McCain was surprised to find that this garage and automobile had been damaged by a falling meteorite. The meteorite, which was about four inches in diameter, fell from space and penetrated the roof of the garage. It ripped through the roof of the car, through the car's upholstered seat, and the floor of the car before coming to a rest on the garage floor. The "Benld Meteorite," as it came to be known, is now on display at the Field Museum of Natural History in Chicago.

But it wasn't a meteorite that gave Benld its lasting infamy; it was liquor. During the years of Prohibition, the town of Benld was home to more than forty taverns, which operated wide-open, even though it was against the law to sell alcohol anywhere in America. In Benld, alcohol wasn't just sold, it was also manufactured. In a wooded area east of town and along Cahokia Creek, was a place known locally as Mine No. 5. Of course, it was a not a coal mine at all but large, well-funded, alcohol distillery with three fifty-foot smokestacks and the capability to produce hundreds of gallons of whiskey each week. The distillery was one of the largest illegal operations of its kind in the United States at the time and it was owned either by gangsters from St. Louis or Springfield or by Al Capone himself. There are some pretty solid recollections of Capone actually visiting Benld later in the 1920s, so it's possible that the distillery was connected to his Chicago operations in some way.

Illegal liquor operations in Benld would also give birth to what remains as the town's greatest historic landmark, the Coliseum Ballroom. The large brick ballroom, with a main floor that could hold up to 800 dancers, was opened on December 24, 1924. It had been built for the grand sum of just over $50,000, an exorbitant amount for the time period. The Coliseum was constructed and operated by Dominic Tarro, a local businessman, but rumors spread that the funding for the project had come from unsavory pockets, namely those of gangsters who planned to use the ballroom as hideout for

THE COLISEUM BALLROOM IN 1924

syndicate gunmen and as a way station for liquor runners between Chicago and St. Louis.

And as it turned out, the rumors apparently had some basis in truth. In January 1930, Tarro was one of many people indicted by a U.S. Department of Justice investigation into bootlegging in central Illinois. Indictments were returned against the Corn Products Co. and the Fleischmann Yeast Co. for supplying materials for making liquor. In addition, 17 bootleggers were charged with conspiring to violate the Volstead Act, which enforced Prohibition as law. This was the first time that the government criminally charged the companies that made the supplies used in illicit distilling, but investigators believed that could make a case against them. Prohibition agent James Eaton was able to track more than 200 carloads of corn sugar that were sent from a St. Louis plant of the Corn Products Co. to bootleggers in Benld. He also believed that the Fleischmann Yeast Co. had sold products to distillers in Benld.

The alleged go-between for the bootleggers and the suppliers was Dominic Tarro, owner of the Coliseum Ballroom and, according to the indictments, the purchasing agent for the raw materials used in making liquor and a distributor for the illegal finished product. On January 30, Tarro posted a $30,000 bond and was freed from custody. Rumors began to circulate that Tarro planned to offer testimony about the Benld operations in exchange for immunity when a few days later, he disappeared.

On February 5, Tarro's automobile was found near Mason City. He left his home that morning in Benld and was on his way to see his attorney, but he never arrived. The car had been riddled with bullets and left on the side of the road. Tarro was nowhere to be found and while his lawyer publicly stated that he feared his client had been murdered, the prosecutor in the case surmised that he was hiding out because someone had heard that he planned to be a government witness. He was sure that Dominic Tarro would turn up soon, alive and well.

Tarro did turn up, on May 2, but he was neither well nor alive. His body was found in the Sangamon River and was positively identified by his cousin, Fazzio. His arms and feet had been tied together with wire, a strand of which had been looped around his neck to draw his head down almost to his knees. He had been beaten and the clothing stripped from his body before he was thrown in the river. The corpse was decomposed and the coroner surmised that the body had been in the water since the day Tarro had disappeared.

Dominic Tarro had learned the hard way that it didn't pay to turn informant against the mob.

Following his murder, Tarro's wife, Marie, took over management of the ballroom and in the years that followed, the Coliseum gained legendary status for the big name groups that were booked to play there. The ballroom drew top talent of all types, dating from the 1930s all the way into the 1970s.

Some of the bands and acts that played at the Coliseum included Sammy Kaye, Tommy Dorsey, Count Basie, Lawrence Welk, Duke Ellington, Lionel Hampton, and Guy Lombardo, who treated patrons to what became one of his signature tunes, "Auld Lang Syne." Years later, former customers would remember this song as a special favorite from the heyday of the Coliseum.

After the big band era, the Coliseum wholeheartedly embraced rock-n-roll. Performers that came during the 1950s, 1960s, and 1970s included Ray Charles, Ike and Tina Turner, Fats Domino, Chuck Berry, Chubby Checker, the Everly Brothers, Jerry Lee Lewis, Bill Haley and the Comets, Fleetwood Mac, Ted Nugent, Bob Seger and many others. People came from all over the state, to see the acts that Marie and later, her daughter, Joyce, booked into the Coliseum. The ballroom had the largest dance floor in the state of Illinois, outside of Chicago, and could seat hundreds on the main floor and the balcony.

The place enjoyed great success for many years, especially after Joyce Tarro took over operations after her mother's death in 1955. She was a tough, hard-headed businesswoman who, her friends always said, would never back down from a fight. She had a habit of carrying around the ballroom's weekend receipts

123

THE COLISEUM WAS USUALLY PACKED EVERY WEEKEND DURING THE HEYDAY OF THE BALLROOM.

with her, which could amount to several thousand dollars, a fact that was commonly known in the small town of Benld. But what was also well known was the fact that Joyce also carried a gun, and she was not afraid to use it. Unfortunately, the gun was not enough to save her life in February 1976.

The winter of 1976 was a bad one in central Illinois. A series of heavy storms blanketed the area with snow in early February and business was slow at the Coliseum. As it turned out, this was a good time for Tarro to get away. A friend of hers, Bonnie Anderson, had recently purchased a winter home in Fort Lauderdale, Florida, and after hearing about it, Tarro decided to do the same thing. Patty Ferraro, a young woman who had been living with Tarro for two years as a companion and assistant, flew down to Florida with her over the first weekend in February. Tarro had an appointment to see a home and after touring it, decided to buy it. She and Ferraro then decided to take a few extra days in the sunshine, far away from the cold weather in Illinois.

But while Tarro was enjoying the warm Florida weather, events were being set into motion in Chicago that would eventually lead to her death.

Just before St. Valentine's Day, Tarro received a call in Florida that informed her about problems back home at the Coliseum. One of her key employees was seriously ill and so Tarro decided to cut her vacation short. She had planned to stay in Florida until Monday, February 16, but she decided to get back home before Saturday night, which was expected to be a busy night at the Coliseum. There was going to be a Valentine's Day dance and the Guild, a popular local band, was providing the music. A huge crowd was expected and Tarro didn't feel right about leaving the staff short-handed.

Tarro and Ferraro made it back to Illinois and during the afternoon of February 14 and they went to nearby Litchfield to visit one of Tarro's relatives, who was in the hospital. On the way, the women stopped at a store and Ferraro bought Tarro a new watch because she was having trouble reading the time on her old one. They returned home later that day and got dressed for the evening. Tarro wore checkered slacks, a white shirt, a black jacket, and her black wig. She finished off the outfit with a .25-caliber automatic, which she clipped to the waistband of her slacks. They drove to the ballroom in Tarro's 1975 black and white Cadillac.

The Coliseum was packed that night with over 800 people in attendance. Bartenders at all five of the ballroom's bars were kept busy throughout the evening. With admission prices set at $2.50 per person,

124

and thousands of dollars made from the free-flowing drinks, Tarro had a very good night.

The music stopped around 1:00 a.m. and the hundreds of partygoers and dancers filed out of the ballroom. Ferraro assisted Tarro in gathering the receipts and putting the cash into moneybags. Afterward, they relaxed at a table with a bouncer and a bartender to play cards while the custodians finished their work and the band packed up their equipment. They played for a little over an hour and then got ready to leave. Tarro stuffed all of the smaller moneybags into a large gym bag and then stuck a second pistol, a .32-caliber revolver, into her waistband. They walked outside, where one of the employees asked for a ride and climbed into the Cadillac. He was dropped off at his house and then the two women headed for Tarro's red brick home on North Main Street.

The streets of Benld were dark and silent as the Cadillac turned into the driveway. Ferraro picked up the gym bag and carried the money into the enclosed rear porch. Tarro walked across the landing to the kitchen door while Ferraro turned off the outside lights. The first sign of trouble appeared when Tarro began having trouble getting the door unlocked. When she looked down, she saw pry marks on the frame. She turned to Ferraro and told her that she thought someone had tried to break into the house.

Ferraro dropped the duffle bag. She asked, "Have you got your gun?"

Tarro pulled the revolver from her waistband and tried the door again. When she put her shoulder against it, the door swung open. She turned on the light and looked around, immediately realizing that someone had been in the house. A discarded moneybag was lying on the stove. Tarro took a couple of steps into the kitchen, with Ferraro close behind. She reached for the moneybag and that was when Ferraro saw a dark shape in the bedroom doorway. She screamed.

Tarro coolly raised her revolver and opened fire on the shadow. One shot went high and the other was aimed at chest level. Ferraro lurched backward as the person in the other room returned fire. Tarro grabbed her left side and Ferraro scrambled out the back door and ran to a neighbor's house, where she continued to scream as she banged on the back door. She turned when the back door of Tarro's house flew open and someone ran out to a car that pulled up to the house. The automobile roared away and Ferraro ran back to check on Tarro.

When she entered the house, she found her friend on the floor near the doorway to the living room. Blood was seeping through her blouse and pooling on the floor beneath her body. Ferraro snatched up the telephone and tried to call for help, but the wires had been cut. She hurried back outside and drove to the Benld police station.

Benld's Police Chief, Matt Sucach, was called at his home and joined officers Darrell Turcol and Tony Rives at Tarro's home. A call was also made to the Macoupin County Sheriff's office in Carlinville, about fifteen miles north of Benld. Deputy sheriff's officers and investigators from the county coroner's office were also dispatched to the scene. Officers knew that Tarro had fired several shots, thanks to Ferraro's report, but they discovered that she had not hit anyone. There was no blood at the scene but Tarro's and her shots were traced to bullet holes in the bedroom wall.

Tarro had been shot five times. Three bullets had penetrated her heart and lungs and two shots hit her left wrist and thumb. Officers deduced that there must have been two intruders. The women saw one of them when they entered the kitchen and Tarro fired at him and missed. The other man was apparently hiding in the bathroom and shot Tarro from the side. She had staggered into the living room, where she was found. The gym bag that had been filled with the Coliseum's receipts had been left on the back porch; the killers had grabbed it during their escape.

While searching the house, investigators found a pistol that had been left behind by the intruders. The guns that Tarro carried were still with her and while she had other weapons locked in her bedroom, all of them were revolvers. The discarded gun had been a 7.65-millimeter semi-automatic pistol. Officers found six empty shell casings from it. The killers had taken the money, but they left evidence behind.

The intruders had ransacked the house, pulling open drawers and breaking things as they searched for cash and valuables. Glass jars that had been filled with coins were empty and jewelry was missing, but they had missed a white envelope on Joyce's dresser that was stuffed with $20 bills.

Investigators for the Illinois State Police arrived a few hours later and began taking fingerprint samples from the house. They checked the door that the intruders had forced open and paid special attention to an empty milk bottle in the kitchen and several cigarette butts that had been left in an ashtray. Neither Tarro nor Ferraro had drunk the milk or smoked the cigarettes, so officers knew the killers had been waiting for quite some time. They also lifted prints from the pistol that had been left behind, hoping for a match in their database.

Ferraro described the getaway car as being a dusty or dirty green vehicle. Almost immediately city and county authorities issued a warning for other jurisdictions across southern and central Illinois to stop cars fitting this description. Dozens of cars were pulled over, but no suspects were found. The police had only a vague description of the car and no description of the suspects at all. The investigation seemed to hinge on the evidence that had been collected from the house.

As the crime scene crew worked in the house, Benld officers canvassed the street and spoke to neighbors, but they found no witnesses. They later interviewed a number of people who had been arrested for armed robbery in the past, but these interrogations led nowhere. The biggest problem was that it seemed to be no secret that Tarro had been carrying large amounts of cash with her for years. All a would-be robber had to do was watch the comings and goings at the ballroom to know when Tarro was likely to have the most money. They could follow her home once, and then be waiting for her the next time. The greatest hope that investigators had was that the robbery seemed to have been carried out by someone inexperienced. Professionals didn't leave guns and evidence behind.

The shock of Tarro's murder reverberated through the small town of Benld. Nearly everyone in town knew and liked her. Her family had been in the area almost from the town's beginning and despite her father's questionable connections, and terrible murder, the family was respected and admired. No one could believe that a cold-blooded murder like this could happen in such a peaceful town – or that anyone from Benld could be involved.

The investigation continued throughout the day; there were few leads, but then something strange happened around 3:00 p.m. Chief Sucach and Sheriff Richard Zarr were discussing the case in front of the Benld police station when a car pulled up. A man inside whom Zarr thought he recognized motioned to them and the sheriff walked over. The man was from Gillespie, a small community just north of Benld, and he had brought his teenage daughter to speak with the police. She had something to offer, possibly about the Tarro case, he explained, as they went inside the station.

According to the girl, a young woman she knew and two men she didn't recognize came to her home the night before. The woman, Mary Kay Hughes Conner, was from Gillespie. One of the men said that he didn't feel well and fell asleep on the couch while his friend watched a movie on the television. The girl and Conner walked in the kitchen and at some point, Conner told the girl that they were going to rob Joyce Tarro that night. The girl warned her that trying to rob the Coliseum was foolish because of the large crowd that would be there, but Conner shook her head and assured her that they had a plan. The conversation ended when one of the men walked into the kitchen and a few minutes later, the trio left the house.

As soon as they heard the story, police officers were dispatched to Gillespie to look for Conner. They knew she was 23 years old and had been in trouble with the law in the past. Officers soon discovered that she was believed to have gone on a trip. The girl who provided the information said that although she didn't know the two men who had been with Conner, she thought that Mary Kay told her they were from Decatur and one of them went by the nickname "Indian."

Sheriff Zarr called police in Decatur, and officers there recognized the nickname and went looking for a man named Roy "Indian" King. They knew that he was 25 and lived in Decatur, as well as in Litchfield and Hillsboro, which were closer to Benld. They also went looking for a friend of King's who matched the description the teenage girl had given to police. Officers soon learned that King was currently in the company of a 15-year-old runaway and his friend was staying with an older woman who worked as a dancer in a Decatur bar. Police were waiting for him at the tavern when he dropped his girlfriend off at work. He was picked up and taken to the police station for questioning.

The young man denied any knowledge of the robbery and murder in Benld. He asked to use the telephone and called his mother, who had just returned home from work. She came immediately to the station and talked to her son. After a few minutes, she left and then came back to the station with two revolvers. At the same time, her son had started to talk to the police.

According to the police, he told them that he had met Roy King earlier that year and they had struck up a friendship over their mutual interest in motorcycles. King reportedly introduced him to May Kay Conner and the conversation later got around to Joyce Tarro and the large amounts of money that she carried home with her. There was talk that the robbery had been planned before, but someone had backed out. He said King and Conner told him that Tarro always carried a gun and he that he told them that he wanted no part of it – at least not at first.

Then, in early February, he went to Chicago with a friend and lost money in a dice game. He borrowed $1,000 from a loan shark and had only a week to repay it. He had no luck selling his van or motorcycle and desperate to raise the cash, he contacted King and Conner and agreed to drive the getaway car in the robbery. He had to have the money by Sunday, so a Saturday night robbery was planned. The young man was supposed to wait in the car while the others broke into the house and waited for Tarro to return home. When she arrived, they were supposed to grab her from behind, threaten her with a gun, tie her up, and take the money. There was not supposed to be any shooting involved.

King borrowed a semi-automatic pistol from a friend and they went out and bought ski masks and rolls of duct tape to be using in tying up Joyce Tarro. A car was borrowed and the three of them headed for Benld at about 5:00 p.m. on St. Valentine's Day. He told police that he had a touch of the flu that day and when they stopped at the girl's house in Gillespie, he fell asleep on the couch. Afterwards, they had gone to a local bar for some drinks and then they shot pool for a few hours. At 10:30 p.m., they went to the

Coliseum Ballroom to make sure there were enough customers in attendance that night to make the robbery worthwhile. Satisfied, they drove around town for a while and then King and Conner were dropped off at Tarro's house while he found a nearby spot to park the car.

As his story continued, he explained that his friends had ransacked the house for about two hours as they waited for Tarro to come home. She arrived shortly after 2:00 a.m. with the receipts from the ballroom. He described hearing screams and gunfire from the house and knew that something had gone wrong. He started the car, drove to the house, picked up King and Conner and sped away. Conner was crying and King was shaking when they got into the car. He demanded to know what had happened and King told him that Tarro had started shooting as soon as she came in the door and they had to shoot her. He wanted to know if she was dead. King allegedly replied, "If she isn't, she ought to be. I emptied the clip into her. I know I got her twice in the shoulder blades." Conner told him that Tarro had almost killed her when she initially opened fire.

Back in Decatur, they stopped at a relative's house and the money was divided up between the three of them. He then reportedly met a man at a Decatur shopping center and paid him the $1,000 that he owed the loan shark. Afterwards, he told police, he met King, Conner, and the 15-year-old that King had taken up with and they rented a motel room on Eldorado Street.

Roy King went to a friend's house and purchased a motorcycle that he had been wanting for a long time. The price was $500 and the payment was reportedly made with $300 in $1 bills and $200 in change. The motorcycle was loaded into his friend's van, to be taken to another friend's house where they could check out the motor. On the way, the two of them stopped at the old Decatur dam on the Sangamon River (in what was then known as Hell Hollow), where the ski masks and a ring taken in the robbery were placed with the empty moneybags into the gym bag. The bag was then loaded with bricks and tossed into the river. Then, the witness told police, he went home and filed the serial numbers off the guns that had been used in the crime.

A large number of law enforcement officers, from several departments, were searching for King and Conner, but by early Monday morning, they became convinced the two had left the area. On Tuesday, the Illinois State Police received a call from the Eagle County Sheriff's Department in Eagle, Colorado, about 100 miles west of Denver. The Colorado officers reported that a young man had just walked into the sheriff's office and claimed that he had been kidnapped in Decatur, Illinois, and forced to accompany Roy King and Mary Kay Conner on a western trip. He said he had escaped from them after his car had broken down in Eagle. He reported that King's girlfriend, the teenage runaway, was also traveling with them. After the car broke down, the others planned to purchase bus tickets to continue their journey.

The information was sent west along the bus route to Salt Lake City, and at about 9:00 p.m., police in Grand Junction, Colorado, found the trio at a local café when the bus had pulled in for a rest stop. They were taken to the Grand Junction jail. Charges of burglary, theft and murder were filed against King, Conner, and their accomplice, who was still being held back in Decatur. The suspects in Colorado waived extradition and were returned to Illinois on Monday, February 23. A month later, a Macoupin County grand jury returned indictments against them for murder, armed robbery, robbery, burglary, and theft.

Roy King and Mary Kay Hughes Conner went on trial on June 9. Their getaway driver negotiated a guilty plea for robbery and was sentenced to two to six years in prison. In exchange, he appeared as a state's witness during the trial. Testimony and final arguments continued until June 23. That afternoon, State's Attorney Edmund Rees went over the evidence with the jury and demanded a guilty verdict. The jury went into deliberation at 12:40 p.m. and returned with a verdict less than three hours later. Both defendants were found guilty of murder, armed robbery, robbery, and theft. Conner broke down and wept as she was led from the courtroom.

Judge John Wright later sentenced King and Conner to serve 50 to 150 years on the murder charges, plus 25 to 75 years for the armed robbery and an additional 10 years for theft.

It was a fitting end to a bloody chapter in the history of Benld and the Coliseum Ballroom. This second violent death brought down the curtain on the Tarro era at the Coliseum.

Many feared that the ballroom would be closed for good after Joyce Tarro's death. In her will, Tarro had left the Coliseum to Bonnie Anderson, a former Benld resident who had gone on to become a singer and entertainer in Ft. Lauderdale, Florida. The ballroom was operated for a short time by Tarro's cousin, Bud Tarro, who owned a grocery store in town, but his tenancy was short-lived. After the Coliseum was closed for two months, Anderson began leasing it to Joyce Tarro's friend Ferraro and Hiram Franzoi, the owner of a construction company. Sadly, their occupancy of the ballroom would also not last for long. Ferraro had vivid memories of the night that Tarro was killed and she remained at the ballroom for as long as she could. She said, "It's not the same place with her gone, and the atmosphere to me, is different. The ballroom business isn't the ballroom business without Joyce."

As the years passed, times turned tough for the ballroom. New owners attempted to revitalize the place a time or two with music acts and even as a roller rink but it never again enjoyed the success of its earlier days. However, it was during these days of decline that employees began to report strange incidents in the old building. Eerie footsteps were often heard and shadowy figures were sometimes reported in dark corners. One former employee, George Luttman, who worked there from 1977 to 1981, told me that he often came in to clean in the mornings and on several occasions he saw people wearing outdated formal clothes who looked as if they were ready to swing to the sounds of Tommy Dorsey or one of the other big bands of the era. When approached, the figures always vanished.

The Coliseum fell into years of abandonment and further decline but then, in the late 1990s, it was purchased by Cheryl Hammond, her husband, Davey, and her father-in-law, David. They planned to open the place up again, this time as an antique mall and roadside attraction on old Route 66. They bought the building in October and had a lot of work to do before they could make their planned opening in February. Almost immediately, Cheryl later reported, she spotted a woman upstairs who should not have been there. She was unable to see her face, but she did notice that she was short and had dark hair. The woman was there one moment and gone the next. No one had any idea who she might be but Cheryl said she and others have seen her in the building

THE COLISEUM BALLROOM TODAY

many times.

Cheryl was not the only one to have strange encounters here. Customers, visitors and even antique dealers who came in to stock their booths reported a number of odd happenings. George Henry, a local resident who helped the Hammonds renovate the building, saw a man ascend a back stairway that the owners had blocked for safety reasons. When he went up the rickety stairs to investigate, he found that the bottom of the stairs was inaccessible. There was no way that anyone could have climbed up the staircase.

Dealers and customers experienced cold spots among the booths and in hallways and told of a misty woman who was often seen near a former bar area. In spite of the fact that the Hammonds had the place re-wired, lights frequently turned on and off without explanation. Others told of feeling a presence as the hair on the backs of their necks stood on end. They also talked of a breeze that moved past them as if someone had just walked by. In every case, no one visible was near.

Eventually, the Hammonds closed the Coliseum, likely discouraged by the lack of traffic that ventured off the interstate, and moved their operations a few miles south to a former school building in Livingston. The Coliseum was closed, dark, and empty for several years but has recently re-opened as an antique mall.

What events of the past still linger in this former gangland hot spot? I recommend, if you are hoping to find out for yourself, that you venture to the old Coliseum Ballroom in Benld. This is a place with a rich and colorful past and one that is sure not to disappoint even the most jaded crime – or ghost – enthusiast.

NORTHERN ILLINOIS

"BEHIND THESE WALLS"
HISTORY & HAUNTINGS OF JOLIET PENITENTIARY
JOLIET, ILLINOIS

The Joliet Penitentiary was meant to be the last stop for many of the thieves, killers, and desperate criminals who found themselves locked behind the prison's ominous walls. It was not designed to be a place of hope or rehabilitation, but a place of punishment for the men who chose to ignore the laws of society. The Joliet Penitentiary broke the bodies and minds of scores of criminals over the years of its operation and for many of those who perished there, the prison became their permanent home. There was no escape, these luckless souls discovered, sometimes even after death.

For more than forty years, from Illinois' statehood in 1818 to around 1858, there was only one state penitentiary in Illinois, located in the Mississippi River town of Alton. The prison was completed in 1833, but soon it deteriorated beyond repair, which was a major concern since the state's population was growing rapidly and along with it, the crime rate. During his inaugural speech in 1853, newly elected Governor Joel Mattson, a Joliet native, spoke out for the need of a prison in northern Illinois. By the middle 1800s, the population center of the state had shifted from southwestern Illinois toward the expanding city of Chicago. In 1857, spurred by scandals involving the horrific conditions of the Alton prison, the Illinois legislature finally approved a commission to scout for locations for the new penitentiary.

A VINTAGE PHOTOGRAPH OF JOLIET PENITENTIARY

Governor Mattson's friend, Nelson Elwood, a former mayor of Joliet, was appointed to the Board of Penitentiary Commissioners and it was Elwood who convinced the members of the board to build a prison at a site that was then two miles north of the city of Joliet. The location boasted a fresh water spring, proximity to railroads and the Illinois & Michigan Canal, and the city of Chicago. But the greatest argument in favor of the fifteen-acre site was the limestone deposits that lay beneath it. The deposits were so deep that no inmate could escape by tunneling out through them.

The penitentiary was designed by William Boyington in a style known as Castellated Gothic. Boyington had also designed several Chicago landmarks, including the Chicago Pumping Station and the Water Tower on Michigan Avenue. The structures were all of similar style and reminiscent of medieval construction, evoking castles and, of course, dungeons. The walls of the prison would be 25 feet high, six feet wide at the base and two feet wide at the top. Turreted guard towers anchored each corner of the site. The cellblocks were to be constructed in long rows, holding 100 cells in each one.

Construction on the penitentiary began in 1858. The workforce consisted of 53 prisoners that had been transferred in from Alton. They lived in makeshift barracks while they mined the Joliet-Lemont limestone quarry just across the road from the building site. Local private contractors supervised the construction and the prisoners. Quarry drilling was done entirely by hand and the huge blocks were hauled by mule cart to the road. A conveyor belt was later built to transport rocks to the surface. As work progressed, more prisoners were transferred to Joliet and assigned to work on the construction. There was no shortage of stone or labor and, in 1859, the first building was completed. It eventually took just twelve years for the prisoners to construct their own place of confinement. By then, the Alton prison had been completely shut down and all of the state prisoners had been sent to Joliet.

132

The Joliet Penitentiary contained 1,100 cells – 900 for the general population, 100 for solitary confinement, and 100 to house female inmates. At the time it was finished, it was the largest prison in the United States and was adopted as an architectural model for penitentiaries around the world, including Leavenworth and the Isle of Pines in Cuba.

Prisoners were housed in two-man cells that were six by nine feet, with no electricity, plumbing, or running water. Each cell had a pitcher for fresh water and a bucket for waste. The stone walls of the cells were eight inches thick with only a door and a small ventilation hole for openings. The cellblocks were built running the length of the middle of each building, away from any natural light. The cells were grim, confined, dimly lighted chambers that offered little hope for the men incarcerated in them.

THE QUARRY WHERE STONES FROM THE PRISON WERE CREATED BY THE MEN WHO WOULD BE INCARCERATED BEHIND THE PENITENTIARY'S WALLS.

Life in the new penitentiary was harsh and sometimes brutal. The plan for the Joliet prison was based on the dreaded Auburn System, which was created in Auburn, New York, in the early 1800s. The inmates at Joliet passed their days under a strict regime of silence, but were allowed to speak to their cellmates during the evening hours in quiet voices. Contact with the outside world was severely limited, and no recreational activities were offered.

Prisoners moved from place to place within the prison using a "lock step" formation, which was a sort of side step shuffle with one hand on the shoulder of the man in front. Inmates' heads had to be turned in the direction of the guards, who watched for any lip movement that signaled when someone was talking. The lock step formation also made it easier for one guard to watch over a larger number of prisoners. Floggings, being placed in the stocks, and extensive time in solitary confinement were common punishments for those who broke the rules. The inmates wore striped uniforms. Men who were deemed to be escape risks were shackled.

Convict labor, under constant discipline, allowed the Joliet Penitentiary to initiate factory-style working conditions at a profit. Lucrative contracts were sold to the highest private bidder, who then sold the products manufactured in the prison on the open market. Under the constant scrutiny of the guards, the prisoners were put to work producing an array of goods: rattan furniture, shoes, brooms, chairs, wheelbarrows, horse collars, and dressed limestone. The prison was also self-sufficient in most aspects of daily life. It had a thriving bakery, a tailor shop, a hospital, and a library, which was administered by the prison chaplain.

A prisoner's day began at 6:00 a.m. when he was marched into the prison yard to empty his waste bucket into the sewage ditch. He then marched into the kitchen, then back to his cell for a breakfast of hash, bread, and coffee. When the dining hall was completed in 1907, prisoners were allowed to eat communally, but in silence. Prisoners in solitary confinement received a daily ration of two ounces of bread and water.

The prison buildings were impossible to keep warm in the winter and very hard to keep clean, which made it a breeding ground for lice, rats, and various diseases. Tuberculosis, pneumonia, and typhoid were the main causes of death among inmates. Unclaimed bodies were buried in a pauper's graveyard, called Monkey Hill, near the prison on Woodruff Street.

The strict silence, unsanitary conditions, forced labor, and harsh punishments gave the Joliet Penitentiary a reputation as the last possible place that a man wanted to end up.

Prison reform was first introduced at Joliet in 1913 with the appointment of Edmund Allen as the warden. By 1915, the striped uniforms and the lock step formation were gone, and the rule of silence ended. Prisoners were allowed recreation privileges and a baseball diamond was built. Warden Allen also started an honor farm on 2,200 acres four miles north of the prison. Prisoners were allowed to work in the fields, and on the farm, as a reward for good conduct.

Ironically, Warden Allen, who lived in an apartment on the prison grounds with his wife, Odette, experienced personal tragedy, possibly at the hands of one of the trusted inmates. On June 19, 1915, Allen and his wife planned to leave on a trip to West Baden, Indiana. Mrs. Allen's dressmaker had not quite finished two of her dresses, and Odette persuaded her husband to go ahead and leave without her. Early the next morning, a fire broke out in the warden's apartment. When the prison fire department responded, they discovered Mrs. Allen dead, and her bed engulfed in flames. The fire was ruled as arson and a trusty, "Chicken Joe" Campbell, who had been Mrs. Allen's servant, was charged with the crime. Campbell was tried, convicted, and sentenced to death, despite the fact that the evidence against him was

(LEFT) REFORM WARDEN EDMUND ALLEN (RIGHT) THE ROOM WHERE ODETTE ALLEN, THE WARDEN'S WIFE, WAS KILLED IN 1915 -- MURDERED BY ONE OF THE INMATES THAT ALLEN'S REFORMS TRIED TO HELP (CHICAGO DAILY NEWS)

purely circumstantial. At Warden Allen's request, Illinois' Governor Dunne commuted his sentenced to life imprisonment.

Construction on a new prison, called Stateville, began in 1916 on the land where the honor farm was located. It was originally intended to replace the older prison, but the national crime sprees of the 1920s and 1930s kept the old Joliet Penitentiary open for more than eighty years.

During its time in operation, the prison housed some of the most infamous and deadly criminals in Illinois history. Some of them were already well known when they walked through the front gates while others gained their infamy inside the walls.

The first execution at the prison took place during the Civil War years, in the spring of 1864. George Chase, a convicted horse thief, attempted to escape from the penitentiary. When he was confronted by Deputy Warden Joseph Clark, Chase attacked him with a club and hit him in the head, killing the officer. Chase was re-captured, charged with murder, and sentenced to hang – turning a short sentence for stealing horses into the death penalty. Chase was hanged a short time later, becoming the first inmate to be executed at Joliet.

Famous Chicago gangster George "Bugs" Moran served three terms for robbery at Joliet between 1910 and 1923. After the murder of his crime mentor Dion O'Banion in 1926, Moran became the leader of Chicago's North Side bootleggers. His time in power lasted until 1929, when seven of his men were slaughtered by the Capone gang in the St. Valentine's Day Massacre. Moran turned to a life of petty crime and died in Leavenworth in 1957.

Frank McErlane was considered one of the most vicious gunmen in Chicago and before being sent to Joliet, was credited with killing nine men, two women, and a dog. Arrested for his part in the murder of an Oak Park police officer in 1916, he served one year at Joliet before trying to escape. He was caught and served another two years for the attempt. Shortly after the start of Prohibition, McErlane began running a gang with his partner, Joseph "Polack Joe" Saltis, on Chicago's south side. Later, they allied with the Capone gang against the south side O'Donnell Brothers. During the war with the O'Donnells, McErlane introduced the Thompson machine gun to Chicago and with it, killed at least fifteen men during the Beer Wars. McErlane was suspected to have taken part in the St. Valentine's Day Massacre, and he suffered serious wounds during a gun battle with George Moran in 1930. While recovering, Moran sent two gunmen to kill him, but McErlane pulled a revolver from underneath his pillow and began firing, driving off the surprised gangsters. McErlane was wounded in the gunfight, suffering two wounds in his injured leg and one in his arm, but he recovered. In 1932, he became ill with pneumonia and died within days.

Nathan Leopold and Richard Loeb, two college students from wealthy families, were sentenced to life imprisonment at Joliet in 1924 after kidnapping and murdering fourteen-year-old Bobby Franks. They had been attempting to pull off the "perfect crime." Warden John L. Whitman was firm in his assertion that the young men received the same treatment as the other prisoners, but his claims were nowhere near the truth. Leopold and Loeb lived in luxury compared to the rest of the inmates. Each enjoyed a private cell, books, a desk, a filing cabinet and even pet birds. They also showered away from the other prisoners and took their meals, which were prepared to order, in the officers' lounge. Leopold was allowed to keep a flower garden. They were also permitted any number of unsupervised visitors and were allowed to keep their own gardens. The doors to their cells were usually left open and they had passes to visit one another at any time. Loeb was stabbed to death by another inmate in 1936. Leopold was eventually released in 1958, after pleas to the prison board by poet Carl Sandburg. He moved to Puerto Rico and died in 1971.

George "Baby Face" Nelson also served time at Joliet. In July 1931, he was convicted of robbing the Itasca State bank and sentenced to one year to life at Joliet Penitentiary. He served two months before being sent to stand trial for another bank robbery. He was under armed guard and on his way back to Joliet when he escaped and went back to robbing banks with the Dillinger gang.

Another famous inmate was Daniel L. McGeoghagen, a racketeer, Prohibition beer maker and skilled safecracker. The McGeoghagen gang attempted to loot 300 safe deposit boxes in 1947, but when things went wrong, they ended up taking seven people hostage. A gun battle with the police ensued, leaving two people dead and two wounded. McGeoghagen was captured, tried, and sentenced to fifteen to twenty years at Joliet. He was paroled in 1958.

One of the more recent inmates at Joliet was serial killer John Wayne Gacy, one of Chicago's most notorious murderers. Between 1972 and 1978, Gacy tortured and killed 33 young men, burying 28 of them under his home. He was sentenced to death in 1980 and spent some of his time on death row in a cell at the Joliet Penitentiary.

The 1970s saw the rise of gang violence within the penitentiary's walls. The Gangster Disciples, the Vice Lords, the Latin Kings, and the P. Stone Nation all vied for power, leading to a riot in April 1975. A group of 200 P. Stone Nation gang members took twelve prison workers hostage and held a cell block for five hours. Herbert Catlett, a former member of the gang, attempted to intervene on behalf of the hostages. He was serving time for armed robbery and trying to turn his life around when he was released. When the hostages were eventually set free, Catlett was found with his throat slashed.

In 2001, the Joliet State Penitentiary was closed down. The crumbling old prison had finally been deemed unfit for habitation and all of the prisoners were moved out. But, as many who came to tour the penitentiary were soon to discover – the prison may have been abandoned, but it was certainly not empty.

The first mention of ghosts connected to the old penitentiary was not so much a story about the prison being haunted, but rather one of the inmates. That man's name was Adolph Luetgert, Chicago's "Sausage King." Luetgert was a German meatpacker who was charged with killing his wife, Louisa, in

"SAUSAGE KING" ADOLPH LUETGERT

May of 1897. The two of them had a stormy marriage and when Louisa disappeared, detectives feared the worst and searched the sausage factory that was located next door to the Luetgert home. In one of the vats in the basement, human bone fragments and a ring bearing Louisa's initials were found and Luetgert was arrested.

His first trial ended with a hung jury on October 21 after the jurors failed to agree on a suitable punishment. Some argued for the death penalty, while others voted for life in prison. Only one of the jurors thought that Luetgert might be innocent. A second trial was held and, on February 9, 1898, Luetgert was convicted and sentenced to a life term at Joliet. He was taken away, still maintaining his innocence and claiming that he would receive another trial. He was placed in charge of meats in the prison's cold-storage warehouse and officials described him as a model inmate.

By 1899, though, Luetgert began to speak less and less and often quarreled with the other convicts. He soon became a shadow of his former self, fighting with other inmates for no reason and often babbling incoherently in his cell at night. But was he talking to himself or to someone else?

According to legend, Luetgert began to claim that he was talking to Louisa in his cell at night. His dead wife had returned to haunt him, intent on having revenge for her murder. Was she really haunting him or was the "ghost" just the figment of a rapidly deteriorating mind? Based on the fact that residents of his former neighborhood also began reporting seeing Louisa's ghost, one has to wonder if Luetgert was mentally ill – or if the ghost had driven him insane.

Luetgert died in 1900, likely from heart trouble. The coroner who conducted the autopsy also reported that his liver was greatly enlarged and in such a condition of degeneration that "mental strain would have caused his death at any time."

Perhaps Louisa really did visit him after all....

In 1932, the Joliet Penitentiary gained statewide attention, and great notoriety, for a strange ghostly phenomenon that was allegedly occurring at Monkey Hill, the old pauper's burial ground on the property.

In the 1930s, the prison maintained a large field behind the compound for grazing cattle and a limestone quarry that served to provide the prisoners with hard labor. Nearby was the pauper's graveyard where the unclaimed dead were buried. The graveyard was a desolate place that was largely ignored by those who lived nearby. It probably would have never been talked about at all, if not for the fact that an unexplained voice began to be heard in the cemetery in July 1932.

On July 16, the night of a full moon, a woman named Mrs. Dudek was standing in her backyard, which adjoined the potter's field. As she was enjoying the cool night air on that summer evening, she began to hear a beautiful baritone voice singing what sounded like Latin hymns from a Catholic Mass. She called to her daughter, Genevieve, and the two of them took a flashlight and pointed it in the direction the voice was coming from. They saw nothing there.

The next evening, Mrs. Dudek's son, Stanley, and her husband, George, both of whom had been away the night before, also heard the singing. They searched the cemetery but found no one. They were unable to determine where the sound was coming from. News of the voice spread through the neighborhood and those who came to listen to what the Dudek's claimed to hear went away stunned. They quickly realized that the voice was not coming from someone's radio. It was a ghost, they said – a ghost in the old prison cemetery!

News of what was assumed to be a specter in the potter's field spread throughout Joliet and soon people from all over town were coming to hear the mysterious singing. Lines of cars filled Woodruff Road and then turned into the prison field, where neighborhood boys directed them to parking places. The procession began early in the evening each night since the voice began to sing around midnight.

After about ten days of this, word of the enigmatic voice had spread all over the Chicago area. Curiosity-seekers came from the city, from Indiana, and from the nearby cities of Plainfield, Lockport, Aurora, and Rockdale. The story was picked up in the local newspapers, and then in Chicago and Indiana, and, finally, across the country. The people of Joliet had a genuine mystery on their hands.

People soon began to come from as far away as Missouri, Wisconsin and Kentucky to hear the singing. According to the local newspaper, a man named Joshua Jones from Sickles Center, Missouri, was sent by a local contingent from his town. "Folks in my town read about this in the newspapers but they won't believe it until they hear it from me," Jones told a reporter.

The visitors to the old cemetery started off numbering in the hundreds and the groups of thrill-seekers soon began to grow into the thousands. From the beginning, the tourists attempted to uncover the source of the "ghostly" sounds, or at least the whereabouts of the person pretending to be a ghost. Whenever the singing began, the searchers rushed into the field, looking behind bushes, in trees, and even below ground for any hidden caverns. They looked for wires, loud speakers and concealed microphones, but found nothing. In spite of this, the singing persisted night after night and each night it was the same, the low, mournful calling of Latin hymns.

The skeptics who came in search of a reasonable answer went away confused. People soon began to accept the genuineness of the phenomenon as all attempts to prove it was a hoax had failed. Each night, thousands of people drove to the field and climbed the hill to what had once been a lonely graveyard. They sat on the flat gravestones, spread their blankets in the grass and brought along picnic baskets and thermoses of coffee. The crowds waited expectantly for the eerie voice and, for a time, were never disappointed.

Eventually, though, the voice began to miss its nightly performance. And when it did come, it was sometimes as late as 4:00 a.m., several hours after it had originally started. The faithful stayed and waited for it, though, huddled in blankets and sleeping in the chilly air of the early morning hours. They claimed the voice was offended by those who came only for thrills. It waited for the quiet, attentive listeners, who received a performance of prayerful hymns.

However, even the most devoted still searched for an explanation for the voice. Was it some sort of heavenly visitor? The ghost of a deceased prisoner? No one knew, but in late July, officials at the prison announced that they had an explanation for the singer. They claimed that it was merely an Irish-German prisoner, a trusty named William Lalon Chrysler, who was singing in joy about his upcoming parole. Chrysler had been convicted of larceny and had served four years of his term before becoming eligible for parole. Toward the end of his sentence, he had been placed in charge of late night inspection of water pumps at the nearby quarry. It was said that the mysterious singing was Chrysler intoning Lithuanian folk songs in English to relieve the monotony down in the depths of the quarry. The prison officials reported that the bare stone walls of the quarry were a perfect sounding board for enhancing and throwing Chrysler's voice to the hilltop more than a quarter mile away. They added that if there were a wind from the north, it would sound as though the voice was right inside the cemetery, where the crowds had gathered. The case was closed – there was nothing supernatural about the voice, they said, it was merely a trick of sound and the wind.

Many people went away convinced that this "official" story was the final word on the subject, but others were not so sure. Many believed that the prison officials were more concerned about getting rid of the crowds than with solving the mystery of the voice. For the entire month of July, thousands of people had encroached on the prison's property. The barbed wire fence that had surrounded the prison field was broken down and the cow pasture had been turned into a parking lot.

To make matters worse, Joliet police officers were unable to deal with the massive numbers of people who came to hear the voice. Local criminals began preying on the tourists, picking pockets and breaking into cars, while some of the less savory neighborhood youths began a car parking racket that extorted money from those who parked in the field. They began threatening motorists with broken windshields if they didn't pay protection money to keep their autos safe. The situation had become a far cry from the first days of the phenomenon, when neighborhood children were helping to direct traffic.

Since the prison officials were unable to stop the voice from being heard, they discredited it instead.

William Chrysler provided the perfect solution. He was assigned to the sump pumps at the quarry, so he was outside, and he was due for parole at any time, which meant that he wouldn't chance offending prison officials by denying that his voice was the one heard singing. The officials named Chrysler as the source of the unexplained voice and they closed off the fields to trespassers for good.

The Joliet Singer had been given an official solution, but did the explanation really measure up to the facts in the case? Not everyone thought so in 1932 and not everyone does today. In the official version of the "facts," Chrysler was at the bottom of a quarry when he sang and his voice was transported to a hilltop about a quarter mile away. He had to have had a light with him in the bottom of the quarry, because it was otherwise pitch dark, and yet no one who searched the area reported seeing a light.

Another problem with the story is how Chrysler's voice could have been heard over such a distance. The "quarry as a sounding board" theory does make sense, but it is unlikely that the sound could carry anywhere other than inside the quarry and to a short distance around it. No one who searched the area ever reported hearing the singing coming from the quarry, which means that Chrysler would have had to have been purposely hoaxing the crowds by using ventriloquism. However, magicians and ventriloquists who were interviewed in 1932 stated that this would have been a very difficult, if not impossible, trick, especially for someone with none of the necessary skills. Chrysler readily admitted that he had never been trained in magic or in the art of throwing his voice.

And finally, strangest of all, why did no one ever report hearing the sump pumps at the quarry? According to the official story, Chrysler was out in the field because he was manning these pumps while singing to himself. If this was the case, then how could his voice be heard, but not the much louder sounds of the mechanical pumps?

Even with these lingering questions, it must be admitted that the singing voice was never heard again after Chrysler's "confession" and the closing of the field. Was the whole thing really a hoax? Or was it simply that the voice was no longer heard singing because people stopped coming to listen for it? One has to wonder what a visitor might hear today if he happened to be on that field some summer night near midnight.....?

After the Joliet Penitentiary closed in 2001, questions remained as to what would become of the old building. It sat empty for the next several years and then, interestingly, became the setting for the Fox television series *Prison Break*. Standing in as the fictional "Fox River Penitentiary," the Joliet Prison became the setting for the first season of this innovative television show. In the series, actor Wentworth Miller played Michael Scofield, a structural engineer who gets himself thrown into prison to try and save his brother, Lincoln Burrowes (played by Dominic Purcell), who was framed for murder and is scheduled for execution. Scofield has the blueprints for the prison cleverly disguised in the tattoos on his body and has created an elaborate plan to help his brother escape – which, of course, goes awry along the way. The highly rated series continued for additional several seasons, eventually leaving "Fox River Penitentiary" behind.

Shortly after the large cast arrived for filming at Joliet, they began to realize there was something not quite right about the old prison.

Lane Garrison, the actor who played "Tweener," a young convict, on the show, stated that standing in the shadow of the prison walls made it easier for him to get into his character. He recalled, "My first day here, I walked through those gates and a change happened. You see the walls and the razor wire, and you feel the history here. It's not a positive place. We do some stuff in Gacy's cell, which is really scary."

Rockmund Dunbar, who played the inmate called "C-Note," was usually the most creeped out of the

PART OF THE FIRST SEASON CAST OF "PRISON BREAK" (FOX TELEVISION)

cast and referred to the prison as "stagnant." He often refused to walk around in the cell blocks by himself. "You're expecting something to come around the corner and grab you. I don't go into the cells. I just don't want to get locked in there."

He was also the first cast member to admit that he believed the prison was haunted. "There were stories of neighbors who called, saying 'stop the prisoners from singing over there' – and the prison was closed!" he said.

Perhaps the one cast member to talk most openly about his strange experiences and haunted happenings at Joliet was Dominic Purcell, who played the ill-fated Lincoln Burrowes. Purcell's office on the set was John Wayne Gacy's former cell, which Purcell said was not a nice place, and "a little creepy." He added, "If I let my imagination run away with me, I can start to pick up on some stuff. I don't like to spend too much time in there, knowing that one of the world's most notorious serial killers was lying on the same bunk that I'm lying on. It ain't a comfortable feeling."

Purcell confessed that many members of the cast and crew believed that the spirits of former prisoners still lingered at Joliet. He described one weird incident that he personally experienced. "I had something touch me on the neck. I looked around and thought, 'It's weird', and blew it off and didn't think about it too much. Then, in the afternoon, one of the other actors came to me and said 'Did you just touch me on the shoulder?' No.... Then I went back to my little thing and said 'Hmmm', and the crew was starting to talk about the weird stuff that's going on. Some said the prison's known to have been haunted for a long time," he said.

Purcell, like Lane Garrison, admitted that it was easy to get into character after setting foot inside the prison's walls, but when the time came to wrap up filming for the day, he was always ready to leave. "I am always relieved to leave, always. You never want to hang out there by yourself. The corridors are long, so far, and you get creeped out exploring. There's a section in the yard where they used to do hangings, and you can see the foundations of what they used to use.

That place left a brutal impression on me. It ain't a place for the faint-hearted," he concluded.

Today, the Joliet Penitentiary still stands, slowly crumbling as the years pass by. What will become of this old place? Many locals consider it an eyesore and embarrassment, but still others see it as an important place in Illinois history. It's been a target for the wrecking ball, and been named as a possible historic site, but, for now, its future remains a mystery.

Do the ghosts of the past still linger in this place, trapped here in time as they were trapped in the cells that once held them? Many believe this to be the case, leading them to wonder what will happen to these mournful spirits if the prison that holds them is lost? Only time will tell....

THE GHOST OF MARY JANE REED OREGON, ILLINOIS

On a dark night in June 1948, a young girl named Mary Jane Reed went out on a date and never returned. Her death, along with that of her boyfriend, shocked the small town of Oregon, located on the Rock River about 100 miles west of Chicago. That night was the beginning of a curious, macabre series of events, which included a hushed conspiracy, a purported ghost and a crime that remains unsolved to this day.

MARY JANE REED

Mary Jane met her date for that fateful night, Stanley Skridla, through the DeKalb/Ogle Telephone Co., where the 17-year-old worked as a switchboard operator and Skridla, 28, was a lineman. Skridla was a Navy veteran who lived in Rockford, but was working in Oregon at the time. The two were attracted to one another despite their age difference, which was not really a concern for Mary Jane. The pretty young woman had dropped out of high school at fifteen to help take care of her mother, who suffered from severe arthritis.

The Reed family lived on Hastings Road, just east of the Rock River. The area was known as Sandtown since most of the residents worked at the town's silica plant. Sandtown was considered the wrong side of town but it didn't matter to Mary Jane, a headstrong and independent girl who was determined to never let her circumstances get in the way of what she hoped to accomplish in life.

141

Unfortunately, her dreams would never be fulfilled.

Mary Jane met Stan Skridla on June 24, 1948 for their first – and last – date. Various reports later had them at taverns on the east side and south side of Oregon that night. It's believed that their last stop was the Stenhouse (now known as the Roadhouse) and after that, they drove out to a popular lover's lane on County Farm Road in Skridla's Buick. They were never seen alive again.

The next morning, around 6:00 a.m., a state highway department employee named John Eckerd was driving to work on County Farm Road and noticed a shoe lying alongside the roadway. He stopped to take a look and discovered Stan Skridla's bullet-ridden body lying face down in a grassy ditch. Police later found five .32-caliber bullet casings at the scene. A pool of blood found on the edge of the road showed where the killer had dragged the young man's body into the grass. Skridla's Buick was found abandoned about an hour later, about one mile north of the lover's lane, where Illinois Route 2 and Pine Road intersected. Other than a lipstick-stained cigarette on the floorboard of the car, there was no sign of Mary Jane.

Back in Sandtown, Mary Jane's parents, Clifford and Ruth Reed, were already worried about their daughter by the time they got the news about Skridla's death. Before this, she had always called home if she was going to be late or spend the night at a friend's house. They feared that she had been kidnapped by Skridla's killer. Worried, two of the older children in the family went to see a psychic, who told them that their sister was still alive and was being held prisoner in a shack by an older man.

CRIME SCENE PHOTO OF MARY JANE REED'S BODY AS PUBLISHED IN THE 1948 ROCKFORD REGISTER-REPUBLIC NEWSPAPER.

Stan Skridla was buried at Calvary Cemetery in Rockford on June 28. The next day would bring terrible news for the Reeds. On June 29, two policemen came to the door and told them that they had news and it was not good. Mary Jane's brother, Warren Reed, was just five years old at the time but he still remembers that day. He recalled, "I was holding my mom's hand and I could feel the energy just drain out of her." The officers told Mrs. Reed that Mary Jane's body had been found in a patch of weeds along Silica Road.

She had been shot in the back of the head with what appeared to be the same caliber gun that had been used to kill Skridla. She was wearing brown loafers, a white blouse and her mother's wedding ring. Her brown slacks were folded neatly on her back. Ironically, the police had checked the area along Silica Road, now known as Devil's Backbone Road, several times after Mary Jane disappeared. Her father had even passed that way several times on his way to work at the silica plant. Her body ended up being found by Harold Sigler, a truck driver who was on his way to the plant. The height of the truck's cab allowed him to see over the weeds and catch a glimpse of the pale body that had been hidden among them. The police recovered a bullet casing at the scene.

The Reed family was devastated. Mary Jane's brother, Donald, was supposed to be married on June 26 and Mary Jane was to be one of the bridesmaids. The wedding was postponed until after the funeral, which was held on June 30. Mary Jane was laid to rest at Daysville Cemetery in Oregon but she would not rest there in peace.

With two murders on their hands, the Ogle County Sheriff's office enlisted the help of the state and local police. There were very few clues to go on but Chief Deputy Willard "Jiggs" Burright, the lead investigator, ruled out robbery as a motive. Skridla still had his wallet and Mary Jane was still wearing her mother's ring. Authorities began focusing on Mary Jane's previous relationships, surmising that jealousy may have been a motive for the killings. Detectives interviewed Skridla's family members and other men that Mary Jane had dated. The investigation extended to Dixon, Rockford, Freeport and Chicago. Police also looked for a couple that Skridla and Mary Jane had reportedly been seen arguing with before they went to Country Farm Road. A witness interviewed at the inquest said that he saw two suspicious men outside one of the taverns that the couple had visited. Most of the leads turned out to be dead ends.

As weeks, then months, passed, the slayings vanished from the front pages of local newspapers and eventually left the minds of everyone except for the friends and families of the victims. Ruth Reed was never the same after Mary Jane's murder and family members later sought psychiatric care for her. Warren Reed later reported that his mother would often hide him behind the couch in the living room, convinced that his sister's killer was coming after all of them.

The Skridla-Reed murder case was re-opened in the 1950s, but with no success. As the years went by, evidence disappeared from the original case files, including the bullet casings, photographs and investigation reports. Then, in 1970, Jerry Brooks became the Ogle County sheriff and he re-opened the case. He re-interviewed witnesses and wrote new reports from scratch because the case file was almost empty. Many of the original interviews could not be re-created because many of the witnesses had died or too much time had passed for them to remember specific details. His most intriguing lead was the report of the two men outside the tavern and he theorized that they might have followed the couple to the lover's lane. Brooks worked the case for almost two decades but was no closer to solving it than the detectives were back in 1948. Brooks left office in 1990 but he has never given up on the case; he still believes that a solution is possible.

And he's not the only one. Warren Reed thinks there is much more to the case than meets the eye. In 2005, he pressed for an exhumation order for his sister's body, wondering if clues might be found that were beyond the forensic skills of investigators at the time of the murder. In August of that year, an Ogle County judge approved guidelines for exhuming the body that would allow pathologists to examine Mary Jane's remains. Reed was thrilled with the outcome of the hearing. "I want to wake up the community. People just kind of hushed things up when they shouldn't have. This crime should have been solved. It probably took twenty years off my parents' life," he told reporters.

The grave was opened on August 23, 2005 and while it did not immediately point out her killer, the exhumation did manage to dispel some of the rumors that had circulated for decades, like those that claimed that her head was not buried with her body or that a gun had been placed in the casket. Officials were surprised to find that her corpse was mostly intact. She had been buried with all of her organs and skin still covered her body. Authorities kept the undergarments that she was wearing when she was buried and oddly, some additional clothing was found inside the vault. A dress and a slip were found wrapped in newspapers dated June 25, 1948, blaring headlines about her murder.

A few months after the exhumation, officials seemed optimistic when opening the grave yielded a few clues and pointed detectives in the direction of two "persons of interest" but that optimism soon faded. According to a 24-page report that was written by Captain Rick Wilkinson (with certain names and details blacked out) in February 2006, the sheriff's department faced too many obstacles when re-opening the case. "This investigation, in my opinion, was tainted and mishandled from the start, and nothing that I am aware of can possibly change those facts," Wilkinson said.

Wilkinson followed up on a number of original leads from 1948, as well as leads from the 1950s and the 1980s, when the case was opened again. No new evidence was provided by the exhumation, but, as Warren Reed wanted, it got people talking and witnesses came forward with information about two new "persons of interest." Unfortunately, both of them were deceased by 2006. "They're not here to defend themselves. They do have families that are still alive, and we can't definitely say they were the people who committed this crime," Ogle County Sheriff Mel Messer said.

After that, the case became cold again, but not everyone is willing to relegate it to the files of the unsolved. One of those who assisted Warren Reed in getting the exhumation and in his fight for answers was Mike Arians, a former insurance fraud investigator. Arians owned a restaurant in Oregon and was elected the town's mayor in April 1999. He was drawn to the mystery surrounding the murders because he became convinced, after some investigating of his own, that certain aspects of the case were covered up. He spoke at length about his investigation but was more uncomfortable about the other thing that led him to the case: namely Mary Jane's ghost.

Arians swore that Mary Jane and her mother maintained a "presence" at his restaurant, the Roadhouse, which in its former incarnation was the Stenhouse, possibly Mary Jane's last stop before she and Skridla drove to their doom. As proof of this, he claimed that the same haunting acoustic song, Sergio Mendes and Brasil '66's "After Sunrise," would play spontaneously and repeatedly on the jukebox; that employees had seen apparitions of Mary Jane and her mother; and that, without explanation, drafts of cold air or the overwhelming scent of flowers would permeate the surroundings. He admitted that spirits in the Roadhouse sounded "crazy," but added that he did not believe the ghosts would rest in peace "until this thing is resolved."

Arians' actual involvement in the case did not begin until shortly after he took office in 1999. People

THE ROADHOUSE RESTAURANT IN OREGON -- ALLEGEDLY HOME TO MARY JANE'S RESTLESS GHOST

soon began coming to him and telling him about the murders, eventually asking him if he would use his investigative skills to look into them. Arians agreed and soon after, the strange events began. In addition to the ghostly happenings at the Roadhouse, other ominous events began to occur, like the flower delivery that came to his restaurant for Mary Jane. No one could trace where the arrangement came from and the Roadhouse was closed that day. He later learned that it had been Mary Jane's birthday.

Will the case ever really be solved? No one can say but Warren Reed and Mike Arians aren't giving up hope. They have not given up on the idea that, eventually, some incontrovertible evidence will emerge that solves Mary Jane's murder once and for all. Until that time, these two men will continue their investigation and two lonesome ghosts will continue to walk at the last place that a beautiful young girl was seen alive.

SCREAMING LIZZIE, CHICAGO AVENUE MARY & OTHER ROADSIDE GHOSTS CHICAGOLAND AREA

The tale of the vanishing hitchhiker is a classic American ghost story. There is not a single part of the country that does not boast at least one tale about a pale young girl who accepts a ride with a stranger, only to vanish from the car before they reach their destination.

Stories like this have been a part of American lore for many years and tales of spectral passengers (usually young women) are often attached to bridges, dangerous hills and intersections and graveyards. Folklorist Jan Harold Brunvand calls the vanishing hitchhiker "the classic automobile legend" but stories of these spirits date back as far as the middle 1800s, when men told stories of ghostly women who appeared on the backs of their horses. These spectral riders always disappeared when they reached their destination and would often prove to be the deceased daughters of local farmers. Not much has changed in the stories that are still told today, outside of the preferred method of transportation.

Today, such tales are usually referred to as "urban legends." They are stories that have been told and re-told over the years and in most every case have been experienced by the proverbial "friend of a friend" and have no real basis in fact -- or do they?

Are all of these stories, as some would like us to believe, nothing more than folklore? Are they simply tales that have been made up and have been spread across the country over a long period of time? Perhaps this is the case...or perhaps not.

One has to wonder how such stories got started in the first place. Could any of them have a basis in truth? What if a strange incident --- perhaps an encounter with a vanishing hitchhiker --- actually happened somewhere and then was told, and re-told, to the point that it lost many of the elements of truth? As the story spread, it came to be embraced by people all over the country until it became a part of their local lore. It has long been believed that people willingly provide an explanation for something that they cannot understand. This is usually done by creating mythology that made sense at the time. Who knows if there may be a very small kernel of truth hidden inside some of the folk tales that sends shivers down your spine?

Tales of phantom hitchhikers can be found all over the world but in no area are they as prevalent as they are in and around the city of Chicago, which is home, of course, to America's most famous ghost,

Resurrection Mary. (For the complete story of Mary – and her true identity – see my book on the subject, aptly titled *Resurrection Mary*). There are a number of mysterious phantoms to be found in the Chicago area, from the typical vanishing hitchers of legend and lore to what some have dubbed "prophesying passengers" -- strange hitchhikers who are picked up and then pass along odd messages, usually involving the end of the world or something almost as dire.

A good example of such a passenger was reported during Chicago's Century of Progress Exposition in 1933, when a group of people in an automobile told of a strange encounter. They were traveling along Lake Shore Drive when a woman with a suitcase, standing by the roadside, hailed them. They invited her to ride along with them and she climbed in. They later said that they never really got a good look at her because it was dark outside.

As they drove along, they got into a conversation about the exposition and the mysterious woman solemnly told them, "The fair is going to slide off into Lake Michigan in September." She then gave them her address in Chicago and invited them to call on her anytime. When they turned around to speak to her again, they discovered that she had disappeared!

Unnerved, they decided to go to the address the woman gave them and when they did, a man answered the door. They explained to him why they had come to the house and he merely nodded his head. "Yes, that was my wife. She died four years ago," he said.

The mysterious passenger may have been a ghost but she was obviously not a well-informed one; despite her warning, the Exposition stubbornly refused to slide into the lake.

"SCREAMING LIZZIE"

A tragic murder occurred at streetcar stop at the intersection of Carmen and Lincoln avenues on November 18, 1905, when a young woman named Lizzie Kaussehull was killed by a crazed stalker named Edward Robhaut, who had been pursuing her for three months. During that time, Robhaut had tried unsuccessfully to win Lizzie's heart. He constantly bothered her, wrote her letters, sent her flowers, and simply refused to accept her rejection. Neighbors later recalled that he frequently waited around the corner of Lincoln and Carmen, waiting for the streetcar that would bring Lizzie home from her job at Moeller & Stange's grocery store, located farther south on Lincoln. Lizzie did her best to ignore him but he followed her home every night.

Lizzie became so fearful for her life that her family reported Robhaut's behavior to the police, including the fact that he told Lizzie that he would kill her if she would not marry him. Robhaut was arrested and a restraining order (called a "peace bond" in those days) was filed against him on November 11, but it had no effect on his actions. He continued to follow her home from the streetcar stop each afternoon, begging her to marry him and threatening to kill her if she did not.

On November 18, Lizzie finished her shift at Moeller & Stange's and, as always, rode the streetcar north on Lincoln. When she reached her stop, she stepped off with several girlfriends, all of them laughing and talking. Then, she saw Robhaut leaning against the wall of a nearby storefront. Lizzie's friends froze and Lizzie shakily put up a hand and stammered in his direction that the peace bond was still in place against him. Robhaut suddenly ran toward her and Lizzie began to scream.

Robhaut sprang upon her and plunged a knife into Lizzie's chest. She staggered away from him, but Robhaut attacked again, stabbing her three more times. Finally, her dress soaked with blood, she fell to the sidewalk. Robhaut looked down at the woman that he claimed to love so ardently that he had to kill her because he couldn't have her, drew a revolver, placed the barrel into his mouth, and pulled the trigger.

The back of Robhaut's skull blew out in a red spray of gore and his body collapsed on top of Lizzie's. They were finally together – in death.

But this was not the end of the story. According to legend, Lizzie's ghost has haunted the intersection at Lincoln and Carmen for more than a century now. The stories claim that, on nights of the full moon, Lizzie returns to the former streetcar stop and can be heard screaming – just as she did when she saw Edward Robhaut lurching toward her on the day that he ended her life.

THE FLAPPER GHOST

Another ghostly hitchhiker haunts the roadways between the site of the old Melody Mill Ballroom and Waldheim Cemetery, which is located at 1800 South Harlem Ave in Chicago.

The cemetery, once known as Jewish Waldheim, is one of the more peaceful and attractive graveyards in the area and is easily recognizable by the columns that are mounted at the front gates. They were once part of the old Cook County Building, which was demolished in 1908. This cemetery would most likely go quietly through its existence if not for the tales of the "Flapper Ghost," as the resident spirit has been dubbed.

The story of this beautiful spirit tells of her earthly existence as a young Jewish girl who attended

147

dances at the Melody Mill Ballroom, formerly on South Des Plaines Avenue in west suburban North Riverside. During its heyday, the ballroom was one of the city's favorite venues for dancing and played host to dozens of popular big bands from the 1920s to the middle 1980s. The brick building was topped with a miniature windmill, the ballroom's trademark.

This young woman was a very attractive brunette with bobbed hair and a penchant for dressing in the style of the Prohibition era. In later years, witnesses would claim that her ghost dressed like a "flapper" and this is how she earned her nickname. Legend has it that this lovely girl was a regular at the Melody Mill until she died of peritonitis, the result of a burst appendix.

The girl was buried at Jewish Waldheim and she likely would have been forgotten, to rest in peace, if strange things had not started to happen a few months later. The events began as staff members at the Melody Mill began to see a young woman who looked just like the deceased girl appearing at dances at the ballroom. A number of men actually claimed to meet the girl here and to have offered her a ride home. During the journey, the young woman always vanished. This fetching phantom was also known to hitch rides on Des Plaines Avenue, outside the ballroom, and was also sometimes seen near the gates to the cemetery. Some travelers who passed the graveyard also claimed to see her entering a mausoleum that was located off Harlem Avenue.

Although recent sightings have been few, the ghost was most active in 1933, during the Century of Progress Exhibition. She became active again forty years later, during the early 1970s, and stayed active for nearly a decade.

In the early 1930s, she was often reported at the ballroom, where she would dance with young men and ask for a ride home at the end of the evening. Every report was basically the same; a young man would agree to drive the girl home and she would give him directions to go east on Cermak Road, then north on Harlem Avenue. When they reached the cemetery, the girl always asked the driver to stop the car. The girl would explain to her escort that she lived in the caretaker's house (since demolished) and then get out of the car. One man stated that he watched the girl go towards the house but then duck around the side of it. Curious, he climbed out of the car to see where she was going and saw her run out into the cemetery and vanish among the tombstones.

Another young man, who was also told that the girl lived in the caretaker's house, decided to come back during the day and to ask about her at the house. He had become infatuated with her and hoped to take her dancing again on another evening. His questions to the occupants of the house were met with blank stares and bafflement. No such girl lived, or had ever lived, at the house.

More sightings took place in the early 1970s and one report even occurred during the daylight hours. A family was visiting the cemetery one day and was startled to see a young woman dressed like a flapper walking toward a crypt, where she suddenly disappeared. The family hurried over to the spot, only to find that the girl was not there and there was nowhere to which she could have vanished so quickly.

Since that time, sightings of the flapper have been few; this may be because the old Melody Mill is no more. The days of jazz and big bands were gone by the 1980s and attendance on weekend evenings continued to slip until the place was closed in 1985. It was later demolished and a new building was put up in its place two years later. Has the Flapper Ghost simply moved on to the other side since her favorite dance spot has disappeared? Perhaps -- and perhaps she is still kicking up her heels on a dance floor in another time and place, where it's 1933 every day!

CHICAGO AVENUE MARY

The town of Naperville, an affluent suburb located southwest of Chicago, is home to another of the region's roadside ghosts. In this case, the spirit in question doesn't hitch rides with passing motorists, she actually makes her spectral rounds on foot, which has created a romantic legend over the years that just may have a basis in truth.

The story of Chicago Avenue Mary, as she has come to be called, began more than a century and a half ago when a pale, devastated young women was seen crossing Chicago Avenue and vanishing into the gloom of the evening. Mary appeared from a home located on the corner of Chicago Avenue and Ellsworth Street in Naperville that once belonged to the E.E. Miller family. Some have surmised that Mary was their daughter but others believe that her true story is actually much older than that, largely based on the clothing that the phantom reportedly wears. It seems that every year, on what legend held was the anniversary of her death, Mary walked through the front door of the house, down to the sidewalk, turned right and walked to the corner. She crossed Chicago Avenue and walked down the hill, where she eventually disappeared.

In every report, Mary was described in exactly the same way. Every detail of her hair and clothing was alike, even though the sightings occurred throughout several generations to people who were strangers to one another. The stories claimed that she was wearing the same clothing she wore on the day of her death – a long blue skirt of a rough-spun material and a white blouse with puffy sleeves, similar to women's clothing styles in the middle 1800s. Mary was always described as a pretty young girl, possibly in her early to mid-twenties, with curly, brown hair pulled up in an old-fashioned style.

The other thing that witnesses always seem to remember about the young woman is the look of terrible pain, anguish and desperation on her face. Her eyes are filled with unbearable grief. She appears to be haunted, they say, for lack of a better term.

Mary has been seen on Chicago Avenue for many years but perhaps the most publicized sighting occurred in the late 1970s. Two college students were driving east on Chicago Avenue one night when a woman suddenly walked out in the street in front of their car. The driver slammed on his brakes but was unable to stop in time and he collided with the woman – or would have, if she had actually been there. The woman had mysteriously vanished. The couple searched the area, but there was no woman – injured or otherwise – to be found.

The legend of Chicago Avenue Mary tells of events that allegedly occurred in the middle 1800s, when a young Naperville couple fell in love. Mary and her boyfriend often met at a small, tree-shaded pool ringed with quarry limestone that was not far from where Mary lived. One day, after the two had become engaged, Mary's fiancée accidentally fell into the pool and struck his head on a rock. The blow knocked him unconscious and before Mary could summon help, he drowned in the cool water. Mary was unable to forgive herself for not being able to save her lover's life and she slipped into a terrible depression. She refused to leave the house except to walk to the pool where her fiancée had died --- leaving her front door, turning right down the sidewalk, crossing Chicago Avenue and walking down the hill to sit beside the water. She refused to eat or drink. She simply sat there, staring into the water, until her father or mother could come and lead her back home by the hand every evening.

Soon, Mary could stand no more and one night, she locked herself into her bedroom and committed suicide. Some say that she swallowed poison and others claim she hanged herself, but the end result was the same – she believed that she could be with her lover for eternity. Her grieving parents buried her next to him in the Naperville Cemetery.

But Mary's spirit was unable to find peace. On the first anniversary of her death, locals were stunned to see her leaving her house, walking to the corner of Chicago Avenue and Ellsworth Street and wandering down the hill toward the pool where she had mourned for her fiancée. She appeared year after year. Many brave souls attempted to communicate with her but she vanished when she was approached. After an iron fence was erected around the pool, Mary passed right through it since it did not exist in her place and time.

The romantic legend of Chicago Avenue Mary is often dismissed as a folk story – a tale of a woman with no last name, a fiancée whose name was never known and a series of events that likely never happened. Or did they? E.E. Miller, who once owned the house at the corner of Chicago Avenue and Ellsworth Street had a daughter named Mary, but she did not commit suicide, nor was she ever engaged to man who accidentally died.

So, if Mary is not this young woman, then perhaps she was another? Historical records show that the first house that was built on the corner belonged to Captain Morris Sleight and his wife, Hannah. The Miller House was later constructed by adding onto the home that already existed on the property. The Sleights had a daughter named Rosalie, who died on February 9, 1853, at the age of 23. Her cause of death was not listed, leading some to believe that she might have taken her own life. Her age at the time of her death, and the clothing of the period, leads us to believe that perhaps this is the "Mary" that haunted this particular roadside for so many years.

Whoever Mary might have been in life, she seemed doomed to repeat her annual journey over and over again through the 1960s. After that, Chicago Avenue Mary sightings became sporadic and finally tapered off in the middle 1980s. Many believe that Mary still walks today, but if she does it's unlikely that she recognizes the place that she once loved – then hated – for so long. The small spring has since been turned into a large pond by North Central College, with a fountain, landscaping and memorial plaques to designate donations from the families of college alumni. The old milk house that once stood at the site, along with the metal bench where Mary and her lover reportedly sat, is gone. The home from which the phantom girl emerged was destroyed in 2007 and was replaced by the Wentz Fine Arts Center, further erasing another remnant of Mary's past.

THE GIRL IN THE SNOW
THE HAUNTED CASE OF MARION LAMBERT
LAKE FOREST, ILLINOIS

The First World War was raging in Europe in the middle days of February 1916 but among Chicagoans and others across the country, one of the most riveting newspaper stories of the day was the mysterious case of Marion Lambert. The attractive daughter of the gardener at a North Shore estate was found dead in the woods near the Lake Forest interurban railroad station on the early morning of February 10. She had celebrated her eighteenth birthday just four days before and she had last been seen on February 9, when she had left for classes at Deerfield High School in Highland Park. She never arrived there, and was not seen again until her body was discovered the following day. She had been killed by a deadly dose of poison, although what exactly happened to her remains a lingering mystery to this day.

And because of this mystery, there are many who do not believe that Marion Lambert rests in peace. Like other restless young women in the Chicago area, her ghost is said to be seen along the area roadways, not far from where she died.

Marion Lambert was a beautiful young girl, as photographs that remain of her clearly show. She was a pretty and vivacious senior at Deerfield High School. Her light brown, wavy hair was cut stylishly short and her minister called her the liveliest girl at the Lake Forest Presbyterian Church. She lived a happy life, usually with a smile on her face. She was the beloved only child of Frank Lambert, the head gardener employed by clothing millionaire Jonas Kuppenheimer, on whose estate the family lived. The Lambert family did well for themselves and times were good in Lake Forest. Many of the local tycoons were becoming wealthier by equipping the warring armies in Europe and they paid their employees well. Marion was starting to dream of going off to college in the fall.

But perhaps the one thing that made her happiest was the young man in her life, Will Orpet, a college student three years older than she was. Orpet's father was also a caretaker; he worked on the estate of farm equipment tycoon Cyrus McCormick. The two families had known each other for years and were friendly with one another but the friendship between Will and Marion blossomed when he began sending her letters from Madison, where he was studying journalism at the University of Wisconsin. The letters were only flirtatious at first, but soon grew more serious. "I want to see you dearest, and want you badly," he wrote to Marion on April 8, 1915. "If only I could get my arm around you now, and get up close to you and kiss the life out of you, I would be happy."

It was later recalled that Will was not content with mere words.

MARION LAMBERT

151

WILL ORPET, MARION'S LOVER (RIGHT WITH SUITCASE)

When he came to see her, he sat scandalously close to her on the sofa, insisting on holding her hand and daring to kiss her. Marion did not approve at first but Will refused to give up and slowly, she started to give in to his advances. In September of that year, he came to her home in Lake Forest, took her for a drive and stopped at the edge of the woods just south of the Sacred Heart Convent. They went for a walk in the forest and then sat down together in a remote spot, carefully hidden among the trees. Marion gave herself to him there and they made love in the quiet of the forest.

Marion began dreaming of a wedding but Orpet, apparently bored after getting what he wanted out of the pretty young woman, began to lose interest. His letters became short and often he told her that he didn't have time to write. In November, when Marion confessed that she feared she might be pregnant, the letters grew even colder. Orpet was angry and stopped just short of calling her a liar. They had only been intimate once, he insisted, and he didn't believe that it could have happened.

In spite of his denials, he called on a pharmacist friend and sent Marion a potion that was meant to relieve her "delicate condition." Orpet was determined not to let his dalliance with Marion became a trap. She wasn't his only girlfriend – a college pal said that he had several others on the side -- and he wasn't serious about her. He was planning to marry another girl, a young chemistry teacher from DeKalb, and he wasn't going to let Marion trap him into a marriage that he didn't want.

By the time the holidays arrived, Marion undoubtedly knew that she wasn't pregnant but it's unknown whether or not she told Orpet about this. She wanted to hang onto him as long as she could, believing the two of them were meant to be together. On February 6, 1916, Marion celebrated her eighteenth birthday at a spirited party thrown by her best friend, Josephine Davis.

Two days later, while Josephine was visiting at her home, the telephone rang and Marion left her friend in the sitting room when she into the hallway went to answer it. The telephone call was from Will Orpet. Josephine later stated that Marion was uneasy when she returned to the sitting room, but later, at Orpet's trial, she said that Marion was "confused" and became "greatly distressed and depressed." She even testified that Marion confided in her that, "if Will throws me over and marries that other girl, I'll kill myself."

But was Josephine's testimony the truth? Marion's parents and several other of her friends claimed that the girl had been happy and untroubled in the days leading up to her death. This bit of testimony remains one of the lingering mysteries in the case.

On the morning of February 9, Marion, bundled up in a green coat, walked with Josephine to the Sacred Heart station, where they usually caught the train to Deerfield High School. But having arrived on the platform, Marion decided not to take the train. She told her friend that she had to go to the post office to mail a letter to her Sunday school teacher.

"Goodbye, old pal," she told Josephine, "I'll see you later."

But that turned out to be the last time her friend ever saw her alive.

Later that night, Frank Lambert waited for his daughter at the Sacred Heart station. Marion had told her parents that she was going to attend a party after school and would return on the 8:05 p.m. electric car from Highland Park. When the train arrived, though, Marion was not on board. She was not on the next train either. Lambert waited for over an hour before he drove into Highland Park. He was told that Marion was not at the party and in fact, her friends told him, she had not come to school at all that day.

Confused and worried, Lambert returned home and he and his wife spent a sleepless night waiting for and worrying about their daughter. Finally, before dawn, he couldn't wait any longer and he returned to the Sacred Heart station to search for any clues as to Marion's whereabouts. He stumbled about in the darkness, looking for footprints in the snow by the light of burning matches. It was too dark to see anything so he left to go get a friend. When they sun came up, they returned and found a line of footprints leading away from the station in the snow. One of the sets of prints was small, like a girl's, the other was larger. They formed a side-by-side trail that wandered out into the forest.

The two men followed the trail into a small clearing and there, beneath three winter bare oak trees, Lambert saw a bright patch of green in the snow. He let out a small cry and began to run toward it. He soon saw Marion lying there on her side, her school books tucked under her arm and the letter to her Sunday school teacher still in her pocket. Her right hand was ungloved and it stretched away from her body. In the palm of her ice-cold hand her father saw a smear of white, powdery crystals. Her lips were bloody and blistered as if they had been burned.

Marion's autopsy was performed at midnight, as soon as her body had thawed from the bitter cold. A few hours later, Ralph Dady, the state's attorney of Lake County, held a press conference for the horde of newspaper reporters that had gathered, seeking information about the tragedy. "We are confident Miss Lambert was poisoned," Dady told the reporters. We do not know if the poison was taken with suicidal intent or whether it was administered by someone else. We believe a man was with her when she died. We are bending our efforts toward locating that

THE SNOWY CLEARING IN THE WOODS WHERE MARION'S BODY WAS FOUND

153

MARION'S FATHER, FRANK LAMBERT, SITTING OUTSIDE OF THE
COURTROOM DURING WILL ORPET'S TRIAL

person, and when we do, we believe the motive of her act will be explained."

Although a search of the area by police detectives found no trace of a bottle, the coroner concluded that Marion had swallowed cyanide mixed into an acidic solution. That had caused the blistering on her mouth and had left behind the white residue on her hand.

Suspicion quickly fell on Will Orpet. A reporter for the *Chicago Tribune* was the first to track him down at his rooming house in Madison, Wisconsin. Orpet said that he was shocked by the news of Marion's death. He told the reporter that he and Marion had corresponded, but that they had not been involved in a "serious affair." In fact, he said he had just sent her a friendly letter wishing her good luck with some upcoming exams and expressing regret that he would not be able to come and visit her soon.

Orpet had indeed mailed the letter – but the rest of the story was a lie.

It was discovered that the affair had been serious and that Marion had thought she was pregnant after their rendezvous in the woods. He sent her drugs meant to cause a miscarriage, even though he claimed that he could not be responsible for her condition. The police searched the post office and found the innocent letter that Orpet had posted but at Marion's house, they found a different one. "Dear Marion," it read, "Jo has told me that you've been pretty sick. Just got word yesterday morning, hence the delay. I hope that everything is all right now and that you will soon be up and around. I'll try to get down to see you, probably the 9th of February, and will call you on the evening of the 8th. Remember the dates... If everything is not all right by the time I see you, it will be, leave it to me."

After this discovery, Orpet was arrested and subjected to serious questioning – first by a reporter who had arranged to have himself locked up so that he could share Will's cell, and then by a collection of police officers, prosecutors and private detectives. They interrogated him for a full night in Madison, then brought him to Lake Forest, where he was forced to walk for hours in the woods where Marion's body had been found. They even forced him to stand by the side of the road and watch as her funeral procession made its way to the cemetery.

Orpet's story changed several times but it came down to him admitting that he had kept company with Marion and may have loved her once, but his feelings had changed. He said he had been intimate with her only one time and while she told him that she thought she was pregnant, he didn't believe it. As it turned out, Marion's autopsy showed that she was not pregnant.

In early February, Marion had harassed him into coming to Lake Forest to see her, hinting that if he refused, she might kill herself. He eventually agreed but came in secret because, he said, he did not want his parents to know he was in town. He called her from the train station that evening, but Josephine Davis was at the house and Marion told him that he couldn't come over then. They agreed to meet the next morning in the woods near the Sacred Heart Convent. They walked in the woods for two hours before stopping near three oak trees. Marion pleaded with him to stay true to her, but Orpet refused. He planned to marry another woman, he told her, a chemistry teacher with whom he had fallen love.

Marion was crying when Will walked away. "Is there no hope?" she called after him.

Orpet didn't answer. He simply kept walking. After a few more steps, he heard the sound of a small cry. When he turned around, he saw that she had fallen into the snow and her body was violently shaking. In only a few moments, he could see that she was dead. Terrified of a scandal, he said he ran away and took the first train back to Madison.

Investigators doubted his story. Why had Orpet written that friendly letter to Marion that said he was unable to come to Lake Forest if he wasn't trying to establish an alibi? And why had he purchased an empty medicine bottle from a pharmacy clerk just before he left Madison? But the real evidence of his guilt came when the police searched the greenhouse at the McCormick estate, where Orpet's father worked as a caretaker. As they sifted through an ash heap in the basement, they found three large clumps of cyanide crystals. They were enough, State's Attorney Ralph Dady said, "to kill a whole high school of girls."

Will Orpet was arrested and locked up at the Waukegan, Illinois, jail. Three weeks later, a grand jury indicted him for Marion's murder and Ralph Dady vowed to send the killer to the gallows.

From jail, Orpet continued to proclaim his innocence, although it was hard for him to explain the letter he sent to Marion and the fact that he had rumpled his bed in Madison on the night before her death to make it appear that he slept there. He had actually, unbeknownst to his family, spent the night in the garage next to their Lake Forest home. He had not done this to create an alibi, he claimed, and he swore that he did not take the medicine bottle that he purchased to the meeting with Marion. The authorities could not link him to the purchase of any poison but they insisted that he could have easily obtained it from the cyanide in the greenhouse where his father worked. However, some of the newspapers pointed out that the poison could also have been found at the Lambert house and also in the laboratory of Deerfield High School.

The case finally went to trial at the Waukegan courthouse on May 15 with Judge Charles Donnelly presiding. The formidable prosecution included Ralph Dady, state's attorney of McHenry County, David R. Joselyn, who had been called in as a special prosecutor, and Eugene M. Runyard. They were opposed by a defense team that consisted of James H. Wilkerson, Ralph F. Potter and Leslie Hanna, who had been retained on Orpet's behalf by Cyrus McCormick.

That the people of Lake County heartily believed in Orpet's guilt was indicated by the fact that it took 23 days and more than 1,200 interviews to find a dozen men who said they could sit on the jury and review the evidence impartially.

In his opening statement, Ralph Dady stated that he would summon witnesses to prove that Orpet had murdered Marion Lambert because she was a threat to his future. He stressed that he would combat the suicide defense with testimony showing that the girl had left home on Wednesday morning in excellent spirits and happy with her life, not depressed or thinking of killing herself.

Then came setback after setback for the prosecution.

Dady's star witness, Josephine Davis, changed her story, telling the jury that Marion had threatened to kill herself if Orpet left her for another woman. Special prosecutor Joselyn had called her confidently to

THE COURTROOM IN WAUKEGAN DURING ORPET'S TRIAL

the stand and was stunned by the turn of events, asking the judge to be able to refer to Josephine's prior statements when interviewed by police. The young woman explained her change of heart by saying that he had originally been hostile and vindictive toward Orpet, blaming him for breaking her best friend's heart, but now she saw things in a different light. Marion had been depressed after speaking to Orpet on the telephone on the night before her death, she said, and claimed she would commit suicide if Orpet left her.

Although Joselyn managed to get Marion's parents and some of her other friends to refute this testimony, the damage had already been done. And there was more to come... A classmate testified that just before Marion's death, he had found her alone in the high school chemistry lab where cyanide was stored.

The prosecution bounced back with testimony from Dr. Ralph Webster, a toxicologist with Rush Medical College, who said that Marion must have taken the fatal dose in liquid form because the cyanide residue had been found in the palm of her hand. This went along with the theory that Orpet had mixed up a deadly concoction with poison from his father's greenhouse.

When Will Orpet took the stand, Dady was convinced that he could break the young man's story. He and his co-counsel were merciless, cross-examining him for nineteen hours over a four-day period. Orpet spoke in a subdued, monotone voice and admitted to terrible things. He had romanced, seduced and tossed away a fragile young woman and he was a liar, denying everything until the facts were thrown in his face. He was also a coward, he confessed, and had abandoned his one-time lover's body in the woods rather than seek help for her because he was worried about a possible scandal. But, he remained adamant, he was not a murderer. Marion had taken her own life when he told her that their relationship was over; he denied he had given her poison.

But for all of the drama that surrounded Orpet's testimony, the case really turned on the facts offered by three chemists that had been hired by the defense. Marion had been killed by potassium cyanide, the kind, it turned out, that could be found in her high school chemistry lab. But the poison that had the police had recovered from the greenhouse where Orpet's father worked was sodium cyanide. Sodium cyanide, it was brought out, had replaced potassium cyanide on the open market several years before but this had not been known to the general public – nor the state's expert, Dr. Webster. Recalled to the stand, Webster had to admit that he had not tested the Orpet poison for anything but its cyanide content. He had taken for granted that it was potassium cyanide, the type that had killed Marion.

This small fact clinched the case for the defense. The jury took three ballots, the third of which was unanimous, and on July 15, Orpet was declared not guilty. "I'm going to the country," he told reporters, "I've had a bad time but my nerve is still with me. I'm just going to start in where I left off and make good."

Will Orpet almost immediately vanished into obscurity. Within three months, he had left Lake Forest. Records show that he enlisted in the military and served as a sergeant in the U.S. Army Air Forces during World War I. Some stories claim that he later became an oil wildcatter and a cowboy in Wyoming. In 1920, under the assumed name of W.H. Dawson, he was briefly in trouble in San Francisco after he abandoned a nineteen-year-old bride whom he had lured from Detroit. After that, Orpet stayed out of the newspapers until he died in 1948. He was buried in a military cemetery in Los Angeles.

In spite of what the jury decided, the story of what really happened in the woods that day remained a popular subject for speculation. Many feel the case has never really been solved. Several pulp detective magazines recapped the story as an unsolved mystery. Chicago author Theodore Dreiser researched the Marion Lambert case when he wrote his 1925 book *An American Tragedy*, about a young man who murders his girlfriend when he fears that she will interfere with his dreams of a life with another woman. Ultimately, Dreiser's story is more closely linked to the murder of an upstate New York woman named Grace Brown, who was murdered by her boyfriend, Chester Gillette, in 1906. Gillette was found guilty and died in the electric chair in 1908. There is no denying, though, that the Marion Lambert case also figured into the novel.

The death of Marion Lambert left an unsettling mark on the annals of true crime in America – but it also left a mark on supernatural history as well.

Over the years, a strange story had circulated about a stretch of Sheridan Road in Lake Forest, near the site of what used to be Barat College. It was close to this spot in 1916 that Marion's frozen body was discovered by her heartbroken father. The story of the roadway involves a young woman who appears in the headlights of passing cars – and leaves a terrifying impression on the drivers who are unlucky enough to encounter her.

For instance, a woman was traveling along Sheridan Road one stormy night when she saw a rain-soaked, barefoot girl in a blue dress on the side of the road. As the driver approached, she started to telephone for help, believing the girl might have been in an accident, but before she could dial, she saw something truly out of the ordinary. The lights from her car seemed to pass right through the girl, as if she was not even real. When the car pulled up next to her and the driver slowed down to peer out of her water-streaked window, the girl smiled, displaying ruined teeth inside a blackened and burned mouth – almost as if she had swallowed a burning acidic poison.

The ghost stories have continued for years, often recounting such frightening details as the spectral girl's short brown hair or the terrifying burns around her mouth and lips. Is this chilling specter that of Marion Lambert, refusing to rest until her case has finally been solved? Or does her ghost still wander in search of redemption for taking her own life on that bitter February day?

We may never know.

GHOSTS OF THE GREAT NAPERVILLE TRAIN WRECK NAPERVILLE, ILLINOIS

Railroads provided the first means of mechanical transportation in American and ushered in an era of swift and relatively comfortable travel. For nearly two decades, the railroads were mostly free from serious mishaps, but by the 1850s, the primitive signals, unpredictable locomotives and hastily laid lines conspired to bring about accidents, disasters and deaths. As time passed, faster moving trains, faulty warnings and unreliable human nature claimed the lives of thousands of passengers and crew members on American trains.

Few times in American railroad history has such near-criminal negligence been demonstrated as in the horrendous crash that took the lives of 47 people, mostly passengers, in Naperville, Illinois, in April 1946. Not only does the true cause of the crash remain a mystery to this day, but it is also a disaster that has left lingering spirits behind.

Throughout the history of American railroading, collisions have been the leading cause of death for crewmen and passengers alike. In the early days, front-end collisions were common, mostly thanks to poor signal markers and confusing schedules, but after the Civil War, things began to change. In 1882, an editorial in *Scientific American* noted quite dramatically: "Collisions, in fact, like the assassin's stab, are now to be more dreaded from the rear than from the front."

After 1865, America's railroads changed from the early period of small, light trains into an era of long, heavy trains that were crowded with passengers. As traffic increased, it became necessary on heavily traveled roads to run many trains close together and with that, the threat of rear-end collisions greatly increased. If the number of passengers on a scheduled run exceeded the capacity of the train, the company would just put another train on the tracks behind the first one. This meant there would be two trains for the one that was actually scheduled. The second train would follow the first at a distance of about 100 yards and the trains were always in sight of one another, except when the first disappeared for a time around a curve.

The danger of rear-end collisions was slight as long as the speed of the two trains was slow – usually about 15 to 20 miles per hour. Later on, when train speeds began to increase, the very real danger of rear-end wrecks began to grow. Clearly, the practice of operating two trains together in such a manner was dangerous, as it was difficult to coordinate speeds and distances with the trains running one behind the other. Often collisions resulted when the first train stopped, slowed or broke down. Old-fashioned hand brakes were still in use on most lines until the 1890s and in those days, trains were hard to stop in an emergency. Because of frequent accidents, companies began running trains at intervals of five minutes between them, but this also had inherent problems. How was an engineer to know that he was precisely five minutes behind the train ahead of him when communications were questionable at best? Disastrous accidents occurred when the time intervals between the two trains failed and for five decades between 1870 and 1920, rear-end collisions were the single worst type of railroad accidents, according to *Scientific American.*

In the event of a breakdown or the unscheduled stop of a train, a flagman was sent out to protect the train and to warn any other train on the line that there was danger ahead. In the days before automatic signals, which came into use around 1880, "flagging" was essentially any kind of signal, including flags, lanterns or any kind of bright light. Any delay in protecting a stopped or disabled train could lead to a disaster.

But sometimes, even in the modern era of railroading, a flagman wasn't warning enough.

April 25, 1946 was a pleasant spring day in Naperville, Illinois. At 1:03 p.m., Northern Pacific train No. 11, called the Advance Flyer, was on its way from Chicago to Omaha. It pulled thirteen cars, all filled with passengers, many of whom were servicemen returning home after the end of their enlistments after World War II. The train was speeding westward when it was signaled to stop at Naperville by a brakeman who thought he saw a large object shoot from beneath the train as it traveled along the tracks. What this object might have been remains a mystery as nothing out of the ordinary was ever found.

The train made an unscheduled stop at Loomis Street to check for damage. While it was being inspected, the rear brakeman, James Tagney, jumped down from the train with a red flag in his hands and ran back along the tracks for a distance of about 800 feet. Although the track was level and straight and the afternoon was clear and sunny, Tagney waved the flag back and forth as a warning about the halted train on the tracks ahead. His efforts, though mandatory according to railroad regulations, were really supplementary since the entire route was marked by signal lights – all of which were red while the Advance Flyer was in the Naperville station.

Three minutes behind the Advance Flyer, and on the same track, was the Chicago, Burlington & Quincy train No. 39, the Exposition Flyer, which was racing toward San Francisco. Tagney could see the train coming in the distance but he assumed that it would stop in time. At the throttle of the train was M.A. Blaine, a 68 year-old engineer with many years of experience.

When he realized that the Exposition Flyer was not slowing down, Tagney began to panic. He jumped up and down and shouted, even though he knew his voice would be lost over the sound of the locomotive's engine. The Exposition Flyer kept coming and its speed was later estimated at between 80 and 86 miles per hour. All along its route, the approach signals were blinking red but Blaine either did not see them, or more inexplicably, chose to ignore them. Crew members on No. 39 later testified that they felt a slight decrease in speed, as if the service brakes had been applied, but it was not enough to slow down the speeding train.

With one last wave of the flag and a loud cry, Tagney jumped out of the path of the oncoming train. He saw its fireman jump down the stairs from the cab, swing outward for a moment while holding onto a safety bar and then, moments before No. 39 smashed into the stopped Advance Flyer, fall to the ground. His body was hurtled outward from the speeding engine and he was killed when he hit the ground.

Train No. 30 tore into the rear of the Advance Flyer at full speed. Its weighty diesel engine ripped into the last car, slicing through the middle of it with the sound of screaming metal. The locomotive refused to stop, ramming halfway into the next car and sending it hurtling with such force that it buckled the next car, a lighter weight dining car, into the shape of a U, killing almost everyone inside. The next car was thrown onto its side and the remaining cars all derailed.

A total of 47 people were killed in the disaster, most of them mangled so horribly that they were barely recognizable as human. Passengers had been crushed to death, ripped into pieces and heads and body parts were severed. Rescue workers were stunned by the horrific condition of the bodies as they began pulling them from the wreckage of the two trains. In addition to those killed, 125 people were severely injured.

Peter Kroehler, owner of the Kroehler Manufacturing Company, which was across from the railroad tracks on Fifth Avenue, closed down his factory for the day and allowed his workers to aid in the rescue

efforts. The factory floor was used as an emergency triage hospital for the wounded. Students from North Central College brought over the mattresses from their dorm rooms for the injured to be placed on. Throughout the day and into the night, ambulances ferried the victims to hospitals in Aurora and Wheaton.

The dead were laid out in long rows, placed side by side, on the lawns of homes along Fourth Avenue, parallel to the railroad tracks. The grim line of bodies stretched for almost a full block, from Loomis Street to the Naperville train station. Additions to the line were stopped at 3:00 p.m. when children were let out of nearby Ellsworth Elementary School and came running over to see the scene of horror. Rescue workers scrambled to move the corpses across the tracks to the Kroehler factory where they were laid out in a room on the west side of the large brick building.

To this day, the 1946 Naperville train wreck ranks as one of the worst railroad disasters in American history – one for which no one was ever really held to be responsible.

M.A. Blaine, the engineer of No. 39, had stayed in his cab at the moment of impact and had somehow survived. He was called before a board of inquiry but he could give no satisfactory answer as to why he had not stopped the Exposition Flyer in time. He was later charged with manslaughter, but a county grand jury did not indict him, due to insufficient evidence. With no real answers as to why the disaster took place, the cause of the Naperville crash remains unsolved to this day.

The cause of the crash is just one of the mysteries that lingers in regards to the disaster. Perhaps the most compelling question is whether or not the victims of the wreck are still wandering the streets of Naperville where the accident took place. Two of the blocks of Fourth Street, directly across from the old railroad line, are said to haunted by strange happenings, from eerie voices to ethereal figures, cold spots and touches by phantom hands. It was along this stretch of street where the

THE OLD KROEHLER MANUFACTURING COMPANY AS IT LOOKS TODAY

bodies of the accident victims were laid out in long rows before being taken to the Kroehler factory on the other side of the tracks. Did the spirits of the victims stay behind near their bodies, only to be left in limbo when the corpses were hurried away to another site? Many believe this to be the case, especially those who claim to have seen dark figures approach them in the twilight, only to vanish without a trace.

The old Kroehler factory building is also believed to be haunted. The building was first constructed in 1897 and was home to the Naperville Lounge Company, which made handcrafted furniture. The owner, James Nichols, hired one of his former college students, Peter Kroehler, to handle the business end of the company and by 1895, Kroehler had bought out the other shareholders and owned the company himself. After a devastating fire in 1913, Kroehler repaired the structure and painted its new name, Kroehler Manufacturing Company, across the factory's south wall. The business thrived, making leather sofas, divans, and daybeds for many years but cheap mass-production later replaced handmade furniture and the company was closed down in 1982. It stood empty for many years until developers turned the place into a shopping mall, restaurant complex and loft-style apartments. It re-opened as Fifth Street Station – home to upscale shopping and living and, according to some, a number of ghosts.

Business owners and tenants began telling eerie tales of resident spirits that were believed to be linked to the Naperville train crash due to the old factory being used as a temporary hospital and morgue. It was not hard to imagine that the weird goings-on could be linked to the macabre history of the building. Stories told of phantom footsteps, cold spots, whispers and voices, strange knocking sounds, unexplained locking of doors, slamming sounds and first-hand accounts of being touched and pushed by unseen hands. The former factory building was – and is – a very active place when it comes to the spirits of Naperville's haunted past.

GHOST OF THE "CAR BARN BANDIT"
THE OLD COOK COUNTY JAIL
CHICAGO, ILLINOIS

The first reports of ghosts at the old Cook County Jail reached the public in 1906. By that time, the old jail was a largely abandoned structure that had been built in the 1850s.

This was not Chicago's first jail. That structure, located just north of the Chicago River, was built in 1835 and was nothing more than a wooden stockade. By 1850, it was rendered obsolete and a larger court and jail facility was built at what is now 54 West Hubbard Street. Only offenders awaiting trial for serious crimes were held at the county's Hubbard Street jail. Their trials took place at the adjacent courthouse and those who were found guilty were sent into the state prison system to serve their sentences.

However, offenders who were arrested in Chicago for less serious crimes, like public drunkenness, fighting, and disturbing the peace, were not held at the county's jail. They were instead incarcerated at the city "Bridewell" (an old English word for a jail used to house inmates on a short-term basis). It was

OFFICERS AT THE ENTRANCE TO THE COOK COUNTY JAIL (CHICAGO DAILY NEWS)

162

built at Polk and Wells streets in 1852 and inmates were rarely held there for more than a few weeks. In the years that followed, the inmate count grew as quickly as Chicago's population. In 1871, just months before the Great Chicago Fire destroyed the Polk and Wells site, the Bridewell was moved to a new larger building at 26th and California, and officially renamed the Chicago House of Corrections.

Meanwhile, the old county jail on Hubbard Street was having its own problems with overcrowding. In order to make things safer, renovations were down and several small-scale additions were made to the jail. Most of the prisoners were moved out of the crumbling original sections of the jail in the early 1900s and placed in the newer cells. But soon, the jail was overcrowded again and some of the cells in the older part of the jail were put back into use again.

A return to the older part of the jail was the source of dismay for the prisoners and guards that were unlucky enough to be sent there. The old jail, they said, was haunted – plagued by the ghost of a young man named Peter Niedermeyer, one of the "Car Barn Bandits."

Depending on your point of view, the Car Barn Bandits, who wreaked havoc in Chicago in 1903, were either the first or the last of their kind. Some saw them as the first organized crime ring to operate in the city, making them a foreshadowing of things to come, while others saw their exploits as something out of a Wild West dime novel, hearkening back to an earlier generation. No matter what they were, they were undoubtedly one of the deadliest gangs to terrify Chicago in the early twentieth century.

The bandits, young men barely out of their teens, were Peter Niedermeyer, Gustav Marx, Harvey Van Dine, and Emil Roeski. They had grown up together on the northwest side of the city and they all came from respectable families that offered them love, support and good educations. Somewhere along the line, though, they simply went bad, creating a record of robbery and murder that shocked Chicago at the time of their capture.

The gang's criminal exploits began in the summer of 1903, when they committed a number of robberies, holdups and murders. On July 20, they robbed a bar on Milwaukee Avenue, wounding a saloonkeeper named Peter Gorski. On August 2, they struck again at a bar on West North Avenue and killed the owner, Benjamin La Grosse, and a 21-year-old customer. They committed their robbery and murder spree at Greenberg's Saloon, located at the southwest corner of Addison and Robey streets (now Damen Avenue), and followed up with another holdup in a tavern at Roscoe Street and Sheffield Avenue. By all accounts, the bandits were having more fun than they had ever had in their lives.

One August night, while wandering around the city, the gang noticed some men counting money inside a railroad car barn. This gave them an idea and they began planning another robbery. On the night of August 30, 1903, Niedermeyer, Marx, and Van Dine met on 63rd Street on Chicago's south side and walked two blocks to the City Railway Company car barn. Finding the door unlocked, they simply walked in and pulled their guns on the startled clerks. They immediately began searching for money. Van Dine smashed open a door with a sledgehammer and stormed into an office. According to Marx, he saw men whom he took for police officers outside, and to hurry things along, fired a few shots into the ceiling. A window was smashed and Niedermeyer began shooting out of it, aiming for the men that had been spotted outside. They weren't police officers but railroad workers and in the confusion, a railroad motorman was killed and two cashiers were wounded. Meanwhile, Van Dine had ransacked the office and came out with a bundle of cash under his arm. "I've got enough, boys!" he shouted at his friends and the bandits fled from the scene, running toward 60th Street.

The area seemed deserted and no one followed them as they strolled down the old midway into Jackson Park, the abandoned site of the World's Columbian Exposition of ten years before. They roamed the park and the ruins of the fair until daybreak, and then they divided their loot, which came to $2,250. They took a streetcar downtown and celebrated their success with cigars and a big breakfast. Afterward, they had a grand time reading about their "daring robbery" in the morning editions of the local newspapers. The stories noted that the police had no idea as to the identities of the young robbers.

The next day, the three boys, along with Emil Roeski, spent the afternoon in Humboldt Park, smoking cigars and reading more newspaper stories about the robbery. They began to dream of something even more adventurous – robbing trains. After a night at an expensive hotel, they used some of their ill-gotten gains to purchase train tickets to Denver, Colorado, believing that it would be easy to buy dynamite in one of the nearby mining towns. They enjoyed themselves for a few days in Denver and then went to Cripple Creek, where they purchased a bundle of dynamite in a mining supply store. They quickly returned to Chicago, still making big plans.

The robbery turned out to be a bust. They placed about fifty pounds of dynamite near the Northwestern tracks in Jefferson Park and made plans to stop the train. Roeski waved a red flag as it approached, but the engine never even slowed down. Angry, he pulled out his revolver and fired a shot at the train, which finally stopped. Unfortunately for their plans, it stopped too far away from the dynamite for them to rob it and the bandits ran away.

The failed robbery attempt frightened the young robbers and they became increasingly paranoid. Van Dine spent three days at his window with a rifle, waiting for the police to come. He finally calmed down but his paranoia, as it turned out, was not unjustified. The police were looking for them, not for the failed train robbery, but for their earlier robberies. The methods the young men had employed in various tavern hold-ups caused the police to suspect they were the Car Barn Bandits.

In spite of the fact that they knew the police were looking for them, the bandits boldly went out drinking, leaving big tips and brandishing their revolvers. The police tracked down Gustav Marx first, arresting him at Greenberg's Saloon, the same place he and his friends had robbed earlier that summer. Police Detective John Quinn came in the front door and Detective William Blaul slipped in through a side entrance. When Marx saw Blaul walk in, he quickly pulled his gun. Out of the corner of his eye, he saw Quinn come through the front door and he turned and shot and killed him. Blaul opened fire and wounded Marx in the arm then he grabbed the bandit, who tried to flee, and dragged him across the room to a telephone. He called the station house for backup as Marx begged him, "Kill me! Kill me now!"

But Detective Blaul didn't kill him. Instead, he took him to the police station and locked him up. Marx fumed in his cell for a while, and when his friends didn't show up to break him out, as they planned to do in the event that any of them were captured, he angrily decided to confess every detail of the Car Barn Bandits' crimes. He spilled his guts about twenty robberies and six murders – seven, counting the shooting of Detective Quinn.

The police began a massive manhunt for Niedermeyer, Van Dine and Roeski. Word came in that the owner of a general store had spotted them in the town of Clark Station and it was realized that they planned to make their escape into the wilds of the Indiana dunes. Eight detectives were dispatched on their trail but they quickly became lost in the tangle of unmarked roads, sand dunes and forests. They followed several leads but became lost over and over again. One of the wagons that they were traveling in overturned in the sand, injuring a few of the detectives. Eventually, late in the night, they found a dugout in the dunes that was located about two hundred feet from the Baltimore & Ohio Railroad tracks and three miles from the closest town. The hideout was empty but some leftover sausage links found inside showed that it had recently been in use. This meant the bandits were still somewhere nearby.

The detectives stayed the night in a barn near Edgemoor, Indiana. When daylight came, the farmer's

A NEWSPAPER PIECE ON THE CAR BARN BANDITS AND A MAP OF THE INDIANA DUNES TO WHICH THEY TRIED TO ESCAPE.

wife brought them coffee and they went out into the November snow. Later that morning, they found another railroad dugout, similar to the one they had discovered the night before. The dugout was the cellar of a railroad telegrapher's home that had burned down years before and it was surrounded by fresh footprints in the snow. However, the entrance to the dugout had been covered with boards and the detectives had trouble finding another way inside. After some time, they found an old staircase and the detectives took up position around it, revolvers in hand, and shouted for the bandits to come out.

A reply was heard from the darkness below. "We'll come out when you carry us out!" a voice cried, and the sound was followed by several gunshots.

The detectives fired their guns down the staircase and after a pause, Niedermeyer's face appeared at the bottom of the steps. The detectives assumed that he was surrendering, but instead, he pulled out two guns, fired manically at them and then ducked out of sight. The exchange of gunfire continued, with dire results for the policemen. Officer Joseph R. Driscoll was shot in the abdomen and Officer Matthew Zimmer was wounded in the arm. Harvey Van Dine came out of the dugout long enough to shoot Zimmer again, this time in the head.

As the police officers pulled back, the bandits made a daring escape from the dugout. They ran away, firing at the detectives as they hurried toward the woods. Niedermeyer was hit once in the neck as he ran down a hill into a ravine, but he managed to get back up and keep running with the others. The bandits escaped while the detectives wired for reinforcements and tried to tend to their wounded comrades. They were able to flag down a passing train and the wounded men were put on board and taken to a hospital. Officer Driscoll died a few days later.

Fifty police officers with repeating rifles were rushed to the scene on board a special train. They followed the tracks south, stopping to examine the deserted dugout where the bandits had been hiding. The room was well stocked with food and ammunition and outfitted with bunk beds.

The original detectives, now five in number, followed the bandit's trail through the snow, passing a brakemen's cottage that the outlaws had tried to break into and failed. As they followed the footprints and occasional spatters of blood, they were startled and opened fire on what turned out to be nothing but Niedermeyer's overcoat, which he had strung up in some tree branches as a decoy. One set of tracks, Roeski's, led into a cornfield and the others continued south. Roeski, who had been wounded badly in the

DETECTIVES INSPECT THE DUGOUTS IN INDIANA WHERE THE BANDITS HID OUT.

gun battle, was captured in the cornfield later that day.

Niedermeyer and Van Dine made it to the town of East Tolleston, four miles from the dugout. There, they found a Pennsylvania Railroad gravel train sitting on the tracks, preparing to leave. The engineer had gone to get dinner for the fireman, Albert Coffey, who was still in the cab. The bandits climbed into the cab and put a revolver to the fireman's head. A brakeman, L.J. Sovea, thought the bandits were rail yard drunks and he jumped up and grabbed Niedermeyer by the wrist. During a struggle, Sovea was shot in the face and his lifeless body was dumped on the side of the tracks.

The bandits forced Coffey to start the engine and he took them two miles to the town of Liverpool, where a locked switch prevented him from going any farther. Niedermeyer and Van Dine made him back up almost a half-mile and then they jumped out of the cab and ran across the prairie.

Meanwhile, posses made up of farmers and police officers formed in East Tolleston to pursue the men. Liverpool had been warned about them by telegraph and sent out a posse of their own. They tracked down the fleeing robbers as they ran toward a cornfield and opened fire on them with shoguns loaded with birdshot. Niedermeyer and Van Dine were both hit in the face but the wounds were far from fatal. Nevertheless, they surrendered. They were taken back to Liverpool and then sent back to Chicago. Indiana Governor Winfield Durbin promptly issued a statement: "I congratulate the authorities on the capture. Chicago can keep the prisoners – Indiana doesn't want them."

The six-month crime spree of the Car Barn Bandits had finally ended. The laughing young men were quick to admit to their robberies and murders, and all of them were soon charged with murder and put on trial. The bandits confessed to not only crimes in Chicago, but to other holdups around the country. They wanted to make sure that everyone knew just who had committed the crimes. Niedermeyer kept track of the crimes that offered rewards and demanded that his mother be given the money since he had provided the information. The confessions told of daring lives of crime that became the stuff of short-lived legend. It was revealed that they had robbed one hundred and fourteen people, and killed eight, in just sixty days. The case captured the attention of the public and newspapers around the country sent reporters to Chicago to cover the trial.

Nothing could be done to save the young bandits at their trials since they had already confessed to everything they had done. Niedermeyer and Van Dine, both 21 years old, and Marx, 22, were tried together. Roeski, 20, was given a separate trial since he wasn't present at the Car Barn robbery. Attempts

THE CROWDS OUTSIDE ON ILLINOIS STREET ON THE MORNING OF THE CAR BARN BANDITS' HANGINGS

GUSTAV MARX, THE ONLY ONE OF THE CAR BARN BANDITS WHO ALLOWED HIMSELF TO BE PHOTOGRAPHED BEFORE HIS EXECUTION.

were made to show that the boys were "victims of society" and also to show that insanity ran in Van Dine's family, but the jury wasn't fooled. The first three defendants were found guilty and sentenced to hang.

At Roeski's trial, Marx swore that he, not Roeski, had killed nineteen-year-old Otto Bauder on July 9 at Ernest Spire's tavern on North Ashland Avenue, a crime for which Roeski was accused. However, on April 20, 1904, Roeski was found guilty of murder, but the jury decided to spare his life since there was still some question as to whether or not he pulled the trigger during Bauder's murder. He was taken away to Joliet prison and his friends were scheduled to hang two days later.

The bandits were housed at the Cook County Jail before their executions. Niedermeyer attempted suicide by trying to cut his wrist with a lead pencil and by swallowing the sulfur tips of matches. On the day before the hangings, the three condemned man sat quietly talking and smoking with their jailers.

Outside the jail, a crowd of almost 1,000 people gathered to wait for news about what was happening inside. A detail of one hundred police officers surrounded the jail to keep the onlookers in line and to prevent them from loitering on Dearborn Street.

Niedermeyer was scheduled to be the first to die, insisting to anyone who would listen that he would "die game." But when the time actually came to go to the gallows, his bravado gave away and he nearly fainted. A contemporary report in the *New York Times* described him as being in a "surly" mood. Unlike his companions, who prayed fervently, the article described him as refusing to accept religious counseling.

Since he was unable to stand, the guards placed Niedermeyer on a gurney and wheeled him to the scaffold. Before he was hanged, he was asked if he had any last words and he sputtered, "You can't kill me, you scoundrels. I will come back and when I do, you will be sorry for what you have done."

Niedermeyer refused to stand up, so he was strapped to a chair and a hood was placed over his head. The trap was sprung and the bandit dropped to his death, still seated in the chair. The hood fell off and the assembled crowd was shocked by the gruesome sight of his face as he strangled to death. His neck was broken, but it took him nearly twenty minutes to die.

Marx was brought out next; like his fellow bandits, he wore a red rose in his lapel. He was praying and holding a crucifix as he walked to the gallows. He continued to pray as the shroud was placed over his face and the rope slipped around his neck. He died instantly.

Van Dine also prayed as the trap was opened and, like Marx, he died when his neck snapped.

For years, the Car Barn Bandits were hailed as the most famous criminal gang in Chicago history. On numerous occasions, gangs of amateur bandits who idolized them were captured, sometimes while lurking in the bandits' old hideouts. Eventually, though, they faded from the minds of the general public – but not from the minds of those who worked, or were locked up in, the older sections of the Cook County Jail.

Those who believed the jail was haunted were convinced that the ghost of Peter Niedermeyer was to blame. Rumors spread of his final words on the gallows and there were those who were convinced that he kept his promise to return. Soon after he was hanged, the haunting at the jail began terrifying those who were luckless enough to be stuck there.

Even the most skeptical admitted that the older section of the jail was the perfect setting for a haunting. The place had long since fallen into a state of decay and disrepair and was made up of four grim, brick walls without partitions of any kind. In the center, with corridors all around, were four tiers of cells that were eventually abandoned. Overcrowding in the newer sections put many of the cells back into use again and thanks to the number of men who died within the walls of the old edifice, it was no wonder that whispers began to circulate of ghosts. Many believed that Niedermeyer's ghost was not the only phantom that was present.

Before each hanging at the jail, strange manifestations began. Prior to one execution, prisoners and guards came to believe that the resident spirits carried out an execution of their own. The carpenters had put the scaffold in place and made all of the preparations for a hanging to be carried out the next night at midnight. The old jail corridor was dark, the workmen had departed, and the lights were turned down low. Then, there suddenly came a loud noise that startled every prisoner in the building and caused the jail guards to come running --- the drop of the scaffold had fallen on its own.

No effort was made to investigate the situation that night, but when Cook County Jailer John L. Whitman arrived the following morning, he sought to discover the reason for the accident. He found that the executioner's rope, the line that leads back to the small box where a deputy sheriff awaits the signal to use his knife when the noose has been drawn around the neck of the condemned man, had been cut cleanly.

Whitman was never able to explain the incident and, although he was not a believer in ghosts, he admitted there was something unaccountable about the affair.

In October 1906, an anonymous reporter went inside the old jail to speak with the guards and the prisoners and to try and get to the bottom of the rumored haunting. He described the walls of the old structure as being devoid of paint and plaster, leaving only bricks and the cement between them. The old building opened into the new jail, a large structure that faced onto Dearborn Street and hid the old jail, where the executions took place, from sight. A barred door and a second, steel door, separated the two jails, but at the time, only the barred door was being used because the old cells had been put back into service. Because of this, many of the strange sounds reported in the old building were being heard by inmates in the new part of the jail.

The reporter wrote, "Yet the prisoners in the new building have no fear, while in the cells of the squatty old structure the occupants are frightened and admit it frankly. They claim they are kept awake at night by poundings at their very heads. One of the prisoners said that almost every night a light was thrown over his eyes until he was awakened and that no sooner did he sleep than the demonstration was repeated. So many things have happened recently in the corridors of the old jail and down in the scaffold room of the basement that the belief has spread that the place is actually haunted. Along the 125 prisoners in the cells of the old structure this belief is supreme, and they assert the punishment by imprisonment is second to their punishment by fear."

According to the guards, prisoners were startled by weird happenings on a nightly basis. Screams were often heard and men were seen suddenly sitting up on their bunks, their faces frozen in stark terror. When asked what was wrong, most attempted to laugh it off, but they invariably admitted to be frightened by the ghosts. Even the guards allowed as to how they often felt frightened.

169

Chairs were unaccountably moved from place to place in the night and papers often disappeared, only to turn up later in unusual locations. One of the jail guards stated firmly, "I don't believe in ghosts but somehow I am getting creepy in this place. Last night, I sat here and heard someone pounding. I got up and the sound stopped. I went to the place I thought the sound had come from, but there was no one. I asked some of the prisoners and they said they had heard the pounding. So, what are you going to think about that? I wouldn't say the place is haunted, that would make me look foolish, but I want to tell you that I wouldn't stay in this place alone."

The prisoners that the reporter spoke with freely admitted to being frightened and most volunteered their encounters with the ghosts. One prisoner stated, "I know there are ghosts here. A few nights ago, I woke up and there was a dim light over my cot. I felt a hand placed on my head, and then the light went out. I jumped up, but the cell door was locked. No living man could have possibly been in my cell. You ask me if this place is haunted – I know it is haunted."

One prisoner, a young man, was so frightened by one night's stay in the old jail that Jailer Whitman, upon hearing his story, had him removed to the new section of the building.

Whitman himself was hard pressed to believe in ghosts, although sometimes he wondered about the strange incidents in the old jail. He was sometimes inclined to believe in the ghosts but he was usually able to attribute most of the mysterious happenings to natural causes.

He told the reporter, "I know of no way to determine whether or not the old jail is haunted. Certainly, it is a likely place for ghosts, if such things exist. Forty-five men have been hanged in those old corridors, and one, at least, vowed to come back and do us injury. I would keep no prisoners in the place if it were not absolutely necessary. The new jail is full and there are 125 prisoners being kept at present in the old jail. They are frightened at night, every sound disturbs them, and while I know that it is true that they have a creepy feeling the old place is haunted, I am unable to relieve them, except as vacancies are made by discharges from the new jail. When some person more superstitious than others is brought in, I seek to make a place for him that will not cause undue fear. And while I personally have no belief in ghosts, I must admit there are some strange happenings in the old jail."

BIBLIOGRAPHY

Adams, Len. *Phantoms in the Looking Glass;* 2008
Allen, John. *It Happened in Southern Illinois*; 1968
------------- *Legends and Lore of Southern Illinois*; 1963
Asbury, Herbert. *Gem of the Prairie*; 1940
Blane, Samuel S. *"Shickshack", Do You Know Menard County?*; 1989
Davis, James E. *Frontier Illinois*; 1998
Dickensen, Fred. *Album of Famous Mysteries*
Drury, John. *Old Illinois Houses*; 1948
Erickson, Gladys. *Warden Ragen of Joliet;* 1957
Fliege, Stu. *Tales and Trails of Illinois.*; 2002
Greene County Historical records and archives
Guiley, Rosemary Ellen. *Encyclopedia of Ghosts & Spirits*; 2000
Howard, Robert. *Illinois – A History of the Prairie State*; 1972
Huyser, Barb. *Small Town Ghosts*; 2003
Illinois Valley Cultural Heritage Association archives
Jung, Jim. *Weird Egypt;* 2006
Kleen, Michael. *Paranormal Illinois;* 2010
Ladley, Diane. *Haunted Naperville;* 2009
Lebanon Centennial Commission. *Lebanon, Illinois--History In A Nutshell* ; 1974
Lebanon Chamber of Commerce. *A Pictorial View of Lebanon*
Levins, Peter. *Album of Famous Mysteries*
Maruna, Scott. *Mysteries of Jacksonville;* 2006
Miller, Nancy. *History of William R. Duncan Family and Descendants*; 2008
Neely, Charles. *Tales and Songs of Southern Illinois*; 1938
Parrish, Randall. *Historic Illinois*; 1905
Quaife, Milo. *Chicago Highways Old and New*; 1923
Taylor, Troy. *Bloody Illinois*; 2008
------------ *Haunted Illinois;* 2004
------------ *Murder & Mayhem on Chicago's South Side;* 2009
------------ *Mysterious Illinois*; 2006
------------ *So, There I Was (with Len Adams)*; 2006

Personal Interviews & Correspondence

Magazines, Newspapers & Periodicals
Bloomington Pantagraph (Illinois)
Chicago American (Illinois)
Chicago Daily Herald (Illinois)
Chicago Daily News (Illinois)
Chicago Herald & Examiner (Illinois)
Chicago Sun (Illinois)
Chicago Sun-Times (Illinois)
Chicago Times (Illinois)
Chicago Daily Tribune (Illinois)
Daily Eastern News (Illinois)
Decatur Daily Review (Illinois)
Front Page Detective Magazine
Jacksonville Journal-Courier (Illinois)
New York Times (New York)
Springfield State Journal-Register (Illinois)
STL Today (Missouri)
St. Louis Post-Dispatch (Missouri)
True Magazine

Special Thanks To:
Jill Hand -- Editor
Mike Schwab -- Cover Design
Greg Olson
Rich Wagoner
Julie Warren
Steve Mangin
Sandy Guire
Adam White
Kim Adams
Bob Ringering
Rosanne Hamilton
Dan Davis
Haven & Helayna Taylor 🐢

THE WRITERS & ILLINOIS HAUNTINGS STAFF

TROY TAYLOR

Troy Taylor is an occultist, crime buff, supernatural historian and the author of nearly 80 books on ghosts, hauntings, history, crime and the unexplained in America. He is also the founder of the American Ghost Society and the owner of the American Hauntings Tour company.

Taylor shares a birthday with one of his favorite authors, F. Scott Fitzgerald, but instead of living in New York and Paris like Fitzgerald, Taylor grew up in Illinois. Raised on the prairies of the state, he developed an interest in "things that go bump in the night" at an early age and as a young man, began developing ghost tours and writing about hauntings and crime in Chicago and Central Illinois. His writings have now taken him all over the country and into some of the most far-flung corners of the world.

He began his first book in 1989, which delved into the history and hauntings of his hometown of Decatur, Illinois, and in 1994, it spawned the Haunted Decatur Tour -- and eventually led to the founding of his Illinois Hauntings Tours (with current tours in Alton, Chicago, Decatur, Lebanon, Springfield & Jacksonville) and the American Hauntings Tours, which travel all over the country in search of haunted places.

Along with writing about the unusual and hosting tours, Taylor has also presented on the subjects of ghosts, hauntings and crime for public and private groups. He has also appeared in scores of newspaper and magazine articles about these subjects and in hundreds of radio and television broadcasts about the supernatural. Taylor has appeared in a number of documentary films, several television series and in one feature film about the paranormal.

When not traveling to the far-flung reaches of the country, Troy resides back home in Illinois.

LEN ADAMS

Len Adams is the Vice President of The American Ghost Society and lead tour guide for Troy Taylors' Alton Hauntings Tours. Len is also the creator and guide of the Haunted Lebanon Tours in Lebanon, Illinois. An officer in the Lebanon Historical Society, Len was recently named Lebanon Town Historian, taking over the post from good friend and mentor, Dona Monroe. He was also the author of the book *Phantoms in the Looking Glass* about the ghosts of Lebanon, Illinois.

When not investigating or researching the paranormal, Len can be found donating his time and speaking at various charitable organizations, schools, and civic groups.

Through numerous magazine articles, television interviews(local & national), public speaking engagements and several books, Len has taken his humorous view of life and brought a common sense approach to studying and explaining the things that go bump in the night.

Born in St. Louis and raised in southern Illinois, Len resides in Belleville with his wife, Kim. His current home is "ghost free," but, as he says-----"there's always hope."

LUKE NALIBORSKI

Luke Naliborski is the investigations coordinator for the American Ghost Society. He's a paranormal investigator, speaker, author and tour guide for the Haunted Alton Ghost tours in Alton Illinois. Luke's first book, *The Lighter Side of Darkness* is a perfect display of his uncanny knack of presenting his ghostly adventures with a comedic twist that wins over all readers. As he states, "The Lighter Side of Darkness" is 'so funny you'll scream, and so scary you'll laugh, or vice versa'. Luke currently resides with his wife Heather and daughter Iris and son Jett in Mascoutah, Illinois.

JULIE RINGERING

Julie Ringering works as an R.N. and as a guide for the Alton Hauntings Tours. She became interested in the paranormal when she grew up in a haunted house. The story in this book, *A Haunting in Granite City*, is based on the experiences of she and her family. She is a paranormal investigator, researcher and lecturer. She lives in Bethalto, Illinois with her family.

KELLY DAVIS

Kelly Davis is the founder of the Macoupin County Ghost Hunters and a long-time rep for the American Ghost Society in downstate Illinois. She currently works as an Operating Engineer and has a background in law enforcement. Kelly is a musician, history buff and always on some sort of ATV or motorcycle. She is also the author of *The Paranormal Investigators Logbook*. She currently resides in Bunker Hill, Illinois with her husband and paranormal team co-founder, Dan, her step-son and step-daughter.

174

JOHN WINTERBAUER

John Winterbauer is an officer of the American Ghost Society & runs the Haunted Decatur Tours in Decatur, Illinois. His interest is ghosts, monsters & all things weird began at an early age and he has been conducting formal investigations into such subjects for more than a decade.

He is the father of three, a proud old rock 'n' roller and a diehard fan of the awesome destructive power of the Pittsburgh Steelers. John would like to thank Holly Henning, Stu Fliege, John Eden & George Whitney for instilling and encouraging his love of history and words. He'd also like to thank Stephen King, George Lucas, Ace Frehley & Warren Zevon because life would be dull without them.

John was born & raised in central Illinois and currently resides in Springfield.

LOREN HAMILTON

Loren Hamilton was already fascinated with the paranormal after visiting the Queen Mary in Long Beach, California, The Flamingo hotel in Las Vegas and the Birdcage Saloon in Tombstone (among others) before becoming the Western Illinois field representative for Troy Taylor's American Ghost society in 2005. In the fall of 2006 he became part of the staff of the American Hauntings tour company; hosting the Haunted Jacksonville tour and many of the companies public overnight investigations throughout the Midwest and the country.

Hamilton grew up in Jacksonville, Illinois and returned to the area in 1991. His career is in Law Enforcement; employed by the Jacksonville Police department as its Community Service Officer and Law Enforcement director for Crimestoppers of Morgan/Scott counties and is a sitting member of the Illinois State Crimestoppers board of directors. He and his wife, Rosanne, reside in Rural Morgan County where he serves as a trustee in the Village of Chapin.

Hamilton derives his greatest joy by assisting others with their interest in the Paranormal. He has taught classes on the Paranormal for LincolnLand Community College and hosts an internet paranormal radio show on BlogTalk radio with co-host Kelly Davis entitled "Bump in the Night." Hamilton has been interviewed on various radio shows and printed publications and is best noted for discovering the paranormal activity of the James J. Eldred house. Hamilton was one of ten investigators selected from across the country to be among the first to investigate the former Missouri State Penitentiary in 2011.

175

WHITECHAPEL PRESS

Whitechapel Productions Press is a division of Dark Haven Entertainment and a small press publisher, specializing in books about ghosts and hauntings. Since 1993, the company has been one of America's leading publishers of supernatural books and has produced such best-selling titles as *Haunted Illinois, The Ghost Hunter's Guidebook, Ghosts on Film, Confessions of a Ghost Hunter, The Haunting of America, Sex & the Supernatural* the *Dead Men Do Tell Tales* crime series and many others.

With more than a dozen different authors producing high quality books on all aspects of ghosts, hauntings and the paranormal, Whitechapel Press has made its mark with America's ghost enthusiasts.

You can visit Whitechapel Productions Press online and browse through our selection of ghostly titles, plus get information on ghosts and hauntings, haunted history, spirit photographs, information on ghost hunting and much more. by visiting the internet website at:

WWW.AMERICAN HAUNTINGS.ORG

AMERICAN HAUNTINGS

Founded in 1994 by author Troy Taylor, the American Hauntings Tour Company (which includes the Illinois Hauntings Tours) is America's oldest and most experienced tour company that takes ghost enthusiasts around the country for excursions and overnight stays at some of America's most haunted places.

In addition to our tours of America's haunted places, we also offer tours of Illinois' most haunted cities, including Chicago, Alton, Decatur, Lebanon, Springfield and Jacksonville. These award-winning ghost tours run all year around, with seasonal tours only in some cities.

Find out more about tours, and make reservations online, by visiting the internet website at:

WWW.AMERICAN HAUNTINGS.ORG

CPSIA information can be obtained at www.ICGtesting.com
Printed in the USA
LVOW051158221211

260692LV00004B/128/P

9 781892 523747